HARD LEATHER: A HISTORY OF CUBAN PROFESSIONAL BOXING

BY ENRIQUE ENCINOSA

Hard Leather: A History of Cuban Boxing
Authored by Enrique G Encinosa
Editorial Printed Fine Arts
ISBN-13: 978-0692779682 (Custom Universal)
ISBN-10: 069277968X Copyright Enrique Encinosa, 2016.

The content of this work may not be copied, reproduced, republished, downloaded, posted, broadcast or transmitted in any way without first obtaining publisher's written permission, unless being used for reviews of this work.

"BOXING IS HARD LEATHER"

CUBAN BOXING TRAINER CARON GONZALEZ, CIRCA 1985.

This book is dedicated to all members of the international boxing research organization –ibro- and the editors at boxrec.com- for their brilliant work and selfless dedication at rescuing boxing history from yellowed clippings and dusty archives and to the late Hank Kaplan, grand guru of boxing archives, outstanding historian, great friend and mentor.

INTRODUCTION

This is a book on the history of Cuban boxing, written to dispel myths, clear doubts, bring forth to light some key figures almost forgotten by history, and most importantly, to please the pugilistic historian and fan.

Some of the chapters have been previously published in trade magazines updated for this edition, while others are new, bringing forth fresh data produced by extensive research of original news clippings of the era and many interviews and conversations with old warriors, trainers and journalists.

As a child in pre-Castro Havana I remember watching Cuban boxing heroes Pupi Garcia, Florentino Fernandez and others on the screen of our home's black and white television set as adults commented on the weekly fights.

Other childhood memories include a brief chat with Luis Manuel Rodriguez and a beach outing where I crossed paths with heavyweight contender Nino Valdes, both men impressing me with their easy smiles and self confidence.

Boxing became an obsession not much later, as a twelve-year-old in Havana, when my school's physical education coach Fillo Echevarria –who had fought four world champions including Kid Chocolate- laced a pair of gloves on my hands and sent me forth to do battle against another twelve-year-old.

I won the fight and a deep love for pugilism was born in me, a love that has lasted through decades and will only disappear when I am no longer in this world.

I have boxed as an amateur –trained by Hall of Famer Johnny Coulon- winning more often than losing, learning lessons from both: I also worked as a trainer of amateurs and pros, managed and cornered prelim fighters and champions, was a matchmaker or press agent in over a hundred promotions including fourteen world title bouts and I have also been a ring announcer and color commentator for international broadcasts in both English and Spanish.

Above all I love historical boxing research; this book is a labor of love and I have enjoyed resurrecting historical figures from dusty clippings and faded films, interviewing old timers and newcomers, learning new facts about my boxing heritage every day.

Enjoy reading this book as much as I enjoyed writing it.

Enrique Encinosa
Miami 2016

PROLOGUE

Enrique Encinosa gets it. When Kaiser Bill decided to build a German High Seas Fleet that would challenge the naval supremacy of his cousin, the King of England, events were put into play that would give Jack Johnson his title shot against Tommy Burns. Enrique would run with that all the way Down Under. He knows, feels - has experienced - that boxing doesn't float like a balloon outside of the social milieu. From the time as a kid when he dove into the warm, deep waters of *boxeo,* Enrique got it.

Like Liebling's shoulder attached to the arm down to the fist - his first instructor had seen the business end of Kid Chocolate - Enrique drank the kool-aid of boxing's lineality. And what a sugar sweet kool-aid it is. Seven years after winning the title, an aging, dissipated Johnson defended his crown in Havana. Encinosa puts in the body blows, (capped in the penultimate round with Willard's straight right to the heart - the end was near for Johnson) in this all-important, boxing-in-Cuba, showcase.

Pierce Egan, in his sketches, biographies and ringside reports, showed the way. Encinosa adds warm links from the tropics to Egan's chain, from the father of Cuban boxing, Juan Budinich Taborga, through the Kids Chocolate and Gavilan, and beyond. Like Egan, Encinosa is generous with prizefighters up and down the line. Julian Echevarria is taken from his first fight in a San Sebastian arena, age 14, to Havana, and his destiny with Kid Chocolate. The Golden Age of English boxing is Egan's Regency Period; Encinosa's the 1950s. Castro's revolution would end prizefighting in Cuba, and subsequently shower South Florida in exiled talent.

The death of Paret, Pupi Garcia, the heavyweight Nino Valdez, Luis Sarria's magical hands, Sugar Ramos, Luis Rodriquez, Mantequilla Napoles, Florentino 'the Ox' Fernandez, the guileless Frankie Otero, and more, *mucho mas*. Nothing in Cuban boxing has Enrique Encinosa overlooked. Whatever he hasn't directly experienced he has grabbed, shaken and mastered in **Hard Leather**.

A movable feast.

DS Cogswell

CHAPTER ONE: IN THE BEGINNING

Boxing probably began in Ethiopia –about nine thousand years ago- as a form of hand to hand combat used by military units. As a sport it seems to have developed in Egypt, about six thousand years ago, eventually making its way to Greece, where it was featured in the first recorded Olympiad of 776 BC. Boxing also became a feature at the Roman arenas, where gladiators fought with the "*cestus*," a deadly weapon made of leather wrapping with spikes and stones, suitable for killing a man with a single blow.

Modern boxing was born in England in the 1600's as bare knuckle fighting, from which sprang its first stars: Jack Broughton, James Figg and a score of other lesser lights. Bare knuckle fighting was illegal yet somewhat allowed for there are abundant reports of bouts with thousands in attendance, including members of the royal family. The first set of uniform guidelines –the London Prize Ring Rules- came into being in 1743, during the peak years of British bare knuckle boxing.

In America, boxing was introduced during colonial times, in several different ways. Sons of the aristocracy sent to England to study returned with enthusiasm and some basic knowledge of pugilism. Slave owners matched their strongest slaves against each other in bare fists contests for wager money while the Royal Navy also had an influence in importing fist fighting to the thirteen colonies. Besides all this, by the first quarter of the 1800's, a number of British fighters had either toured the United States performing exhibitions with gloves or were –like William Fuller- residing in America, where they opened up boxing academies teaching the manly art of self defense with gloves, for bare knuckle boxing was an outlaw sport.

In time, boxing spread throughout the Caribbean as well as through Central and South America in much the same manner.

In Mexico, it crossed the border at the tail end of the nineteenth century as promoters skipped over Texas and Arizona borders to stay away from the law.

In Colombia in 1914, a Mexican circus with a boxing booth made boxing popular in Cartagena, while in Chile the sport was introduced by British merchant seamen in the port of Valparaiso.

In Cuba, U.S. occupation forces during the Spanish American war helped popularize pugilism.

Before the war between Spain and the US, Cuba had already begun to build a boxing tradition but it was sporadic, consisting of an occasional exhibition from travelling athletes passing through.

Curiously, the first two Cubans to have contact with pugilism were both historically prominent people.

Ramon Guiteras came from one of Cuba's most important families. The Guiteras clan has -in the last century and a half- produced a cluster of very eminent leaders, including a Cuban cabinet minister, several military heroes and outstanding businessmen. The Guiteras family had considerable wealth and commuted between Cuba and the United States, establishing residences in both nations.

Ramon Guiteras —son of Cubans- was born in New England and attended Harvard University, where he combined medical studies with amateur pugilism. Indeed, there are boxing record books that indicate that Guiteras fought a draw —sometime around 1878- against a promising amateur slugger named John L. Sullivan.

Some boxing experts dispute the bout, claiming that no primary evidence – such as a newspaper report of the match- has been found. Either way, it does not alter the fact that Ramon Guiteras was most likely the first man of Cuban heritage to lace on a boxing glove. There are clippings of the time that do describe Guiteras as the finest amateur boxer in the United States.

The amateur star graduated from Harvard and became internationally famous in the medical field, being the founding father of the American Urological Association, whose highest award is named after Guiteras. The well known doctor authored medical textbooks, was known for his charity work and continued to train and spar until well advanced into old age, being a firm believer that boxing was a sport that helped create discipline and self confidence.

The second Cuban to have contact with boxing was the nation's most prominent patriot, Havana born Jose Marti - a young lawyer and free lance journalist residing as an exile in New York- who was assigned the task of writing about the bare knuckle 1882 clash between Paddy Ryan and a young newcomer named John L. Sullivan.

Revered by his nation, Marti, a pioneer of modernist writing, was a master poet, playwright, diplomat and the leading rebel organizer in the Cuban struggle for independence from Spain, a passionate quest that would end with his death in battle in 1895.

In 1882, the twenty-nine-year-old Marti, already considered one of the brightest pens in journalism, authored a classic article on the Ryan-Sullivan clash, thus becoming the first Cuban boxing writer.

Marti captured the frenetic ambiance of the fight crowd as they gathered in New Orleans, preparing to travel to the secret fight site: "Everywhere one heard the clink of glasses, boisterous talking, heated discussions on stores and street corners of the respective merits of the fighters, and the rush of feet of people hurried to satisfy their hungry eyes with a glimpse of the broad back, sloping shoulders and whipcord thighs of the athletes… Ladies went to touch the gnarled fists of the heroes with their slender fingers… people slept in chairs, in sofas and elbow to elbow in balconies, fearful the train might leave without them…"

His report on the bare knuckle bout is vivid: "At the scene of the fight, which was the city of Mississippi, the approaches to the ring are already filled with people. Men are roosting from the trees, the curious peer from every balcony, and spectators stand embattled on the roof tops. The train unburdens itself of its human cargo. The ring is set up…. Sullivan enters the ring in short pants and a green jersey, and the handsome Ryan, the Giant of Troy, takes his place in the opposite corner, attired in spotless white…..In a moment one is down; he is dragged to his corner and feverishly sponged. They rush at each other again and deal each other mace-like blows; their skulls resound like anvils beneath the hammer. Ryan's jersey is crimson with gore, and he falls to his knees. The Strong Boy leaps back to his corner, laughing. The roar is deafening. Ryan rises shakily. Sullivan moves in for the kill with his lips twisted in a smile. They clinch and maul each other's faces; they stumble back against the ropes. Nine times the assault; nine times one goes reeling to the ground. Now the Giant is staggered, now his cleated shoes no longer can help him keep his footing, now he falls like a stone from a blow to the neck and on seeing him senseless, his second throws the sponge in the air in token of defeat…"

A decade after Marti reported on the Sullivan-Ryan bout, a young Cuban featherweight established a solid ring reputation in the New York area. Eugene Garcia was considered a very capable main event fighter as his incomplete record shows a draw with a well known battler of the time –Casper Leon- and a valiant loss in five by KO to Terry McGovern, a megastar of boxing in the last decade of the Nineteenth Century.

In the same decade, another transplanted Cuban named Emilio Sanchez fought main events as a lightweight, scoring a win over future champion Cyclone Thompson and fighting two draws with Mike Donovan, a very good headliner of the era.

Another Cuban fighter, known only as "Cuban Kid" was also active in Colorado rings in the first years of the twentieth century but little is known about the man.

During the last years of the Nineteenth Century, a black Philadelphia fighter named Frank McLean billed himself as the "Cuban Wonder," although he was not Cuban. It has been speculated that McLean passed himself off as a Cuban in order to be allowed to fight white men in states where interracial bouts were prohibited, but there is no evidence in his record to substantiate the speculations.

The Spanish American War became the first catalyst in the development of Cuban boxing.

Boxing in Cuba was up to then non-existent, although international fights were well covered by Havana newspapers and tabloids of the time, Many Cubans had been exposed to pugilism in their travels to the United States or Europe, the interest in boxing being wide enough that by the early 1900's boxing equipment imported into the island was assigned a tax tariff, as stated by historian David LaFavor.

American service men stationed at Guantanamo Naval Base often presented amateur cards but Cubans were not usually involved as participants although locals picked up knowledge from watching and sometimes sparring with the sailors.

In 1899, American soldiers boxed amateur bouts at the Sauto Theater in the city of Matanzas. The Sauto Theater bouts might have been influential in the creation of two boxing gyms which probably were Cuba's first boxing academies both located in the Matanzas region, east of Havana.

In 1901 an article in the "The Sun" titled "Cubans are Poor Boxers," proclaimed in its opening paragraph that: "The Cuban is not a natural fighter with his fists. If there is any scrapping going on when he's around it is generally done with a pistol or a knife."

The New York article stated that before the outbreak of the Spanish American War two instructors had attempted to start boxing seminars in Cuba but both had failed. Apparently, one –an Englishman- had abused his students in sparring and his classes had been boycotted while the second one had been trounced so badly in the first session by a student that no one had confidence in his teaching abilities.

The first Cuban boxing gym opened up in 1900 in the city of Matanzas, owned and managed by a man named Isidoro Bonelly.

A second gym opened by 1903, led by a young man named Teodoro Risquet, who in later years became a promoter. Risquet, from a middle class family, might have learned boxing while studying in the United States or picked up basic knowledge from the American military personnel in Cuba.

The American military bouts were held very often as documents of the era credit lightweight Sam Robideau as having fought thirteen military bouts in Cuba between 1911 and 1912. The American amateur bouts raised local interest in the sport and a few pioneers of Cuban boxing in Guantanamo, Santiago and Matanzas picked up basic skills from sparring with Yankee sailors and marines

By 1909 there were amateur boxing shows involving locals taking place at the city of Baracoa on Cuba's eastern tip. Boxing was slowly growing in Cuba.

The only consistent boxing instruction in Havana in the first decade of the century was at the Havana YMCA, where an American named Frank Fowler taught boxing since the association's establishment in Cuba in 1904, but his pugilism classes were small and competitive matches were not allowed until 1909. Risquet's boxing shows in Matanzas, the fight cards in Baracoa and Fowler's amateur shows of 1909 were probably the first regular running boxing promotions in Cuba involving locals competing at the amateur level.

Ramon Guiteras –the first Cuban boxer- was alleged to have fought a draw as an amateur against John L. Sullivan.

John Budinich –pioneer of Chilean and Cuban boxing- as a teenager.

Budinich at his peak as a middleweight.

Mike Febles was a Mexican who learned his craft in Cuba.

Victor Achan –a Budinich disciple- was Cuba's first flyweight champion.

CHAPTER TWO: THE CHARMING JOHN BUDINICH

Juan Budinich Taborga was born in Coquimbo, Chile, sometime in 1881, growing up of middle class background, the son of a merchant marine captain, a glamour career of the era. As a boy from a seafaring family he was groomed to be a naval officer.

An athletic teen, John Budinich was mesmerized by boxing and tales of the ring, yet the sport did not exist in Chile. There was interest in pugilism but the country –in fact all the Southern Hemisphere- lacked skilled coaches or experienced fighters. Without trainers or fighters, promoters could not exist.

It was logical that Chilean boxing would start in a seaport town like Valparaiso, where some of the very rough British or American merchant mariners passing through had knowledge of boxing basics, some willing to trade punches with a local for a little side bet.

The fight game in Valparaiso soon went from bare knuckle dock fighting to more organized smokers with a ring, gloves and Queensbury rules. By 1897 the Urriola Athletic Club in Valparaiso started to host frequent amateur smokers in which local brawlers fought with more zest than skills and bets were placed on every fight by a rough crowd.

Budinich was one of the pioneer boxers at the Urriola Club but unlike most of the warriors participating in the smokers, John had already received adequate professional boxing training.

As luck would have it, at the tender age of fifteen Budinich struck a friendship with a blacksmith named McDonald, who had acquired some ring experience in his younger days in Ireland.

The young teen asked McDonald to teach him to box and the old fighter – probably flattered by John's enthusiasm- obliged.

"He taught me the ABC of boxing," Budinich said in an interview, "How to hold your guard, how to cover up and the proper way to deliver punches."

Over the next few months, the strapping teenager learned footwork, jabbing, balance, honing his basic skills in sparring sessions with his teacher at the back yard of the veteran fighter's blacksmith shop.

Budinich's pugilistic training was soon enhanced as a naval cadet at the academy in Valparaiso. There, Budinich was delighted to find that the school was one of the few places in the country that provided boxing instructions to all future officers, the teachings of the Irish blacksmith being enhanced and polished by a military boxing instructor and sharpened by sparring sessions with fellow cadets.

In 1897, when the Colonel Urriola Athletic Club in Valparaiso hosted the first amateur smokers, sixteen-year-old naval cadet Budinich was significantly more experienced and ring educated than the rowdy, street fighting seamen and dockworkers he faced in the ring.

Budinich used his left jab to pop his rushing opponents as he sidestepped and inched his way out of the danger zone of wild swings. A well conditioned athlete –he never drank or smoked- John honed his boxing skills in dozens of amateur brawls facing tough full grown men with street fighting styles. In the years that followed his ring debut Budinich became the star attraction at the Urriola Club smokers and other new amateur venues, consistently winning.

By 1902 Budinich had become Chile's most experienced and well known amateur fighter. He had dropped out –or had been expelled for a fight with another cadet- from the naval academy and being an enterprising young man he opened up his own boxing school in the city of Santiago. Budinich's partner in the boxing gym was a transplanted American lightweight named Joe Daly, who claimed to have been the lightweight champion of the US Army before relocating to Chile. Daly did have solid skills as he had gained a local reputation in pro fights in which he had disposed of a black British merchant seaman named Frank Jones.

Besides making a living training fighters and promoting his first amateur cards, Budinich also earned a paycheck as an English translator and sports writer for the newspaper "La Union."

Encouraged by the fact that amateur boxing was developing in several cities in Chile, the enterprising Budinich decided to introduce professional boxing in his homeland, featuring himself in the main event. There had been some pro fighting in the country before but it did not involve Chileans, only foreign fighters, usually fighting in small saloon halls. Budinich —who was about to become the first Chilean pro boxer in history- wanted his debut to be a well promoted, well attended event.

The first pro boxing card promoted in Chile by Budinich and some financial backers was held at the Santiago Theater in 1902, where John made his pro debut by knocking out the same Frank Jones that Daly had twice beaten.

The first victory was followed by a knockout win over another transplanted foreigner. Tommy Wilson fell in six, victim of a well delivered hook to the liver.

Between his debut in 1902 and his first trip out of the country in 1905, Budinich had eight recorded fights, winning six by knockouts and two others on points over James Perry, a transplanted American fighter who resided for many years in Chile.

Twenty-four-year-old Budinich had achieved a measure of national fame in Chile, being its first amateur and pro star. Most young men would have enjoyed their local fame and never left the country, content to be headlining or promoting local club shows, running a gym and working as a sportswriter, but John Budinich liked to travel.

He left Chile in October 1905, working —or stowing away- on merchant boats until he reached the United States, surviving the San Francisco earthquake of 1906 before heading for New York.

The Chilean had a good knowledge of English and his fluency improved with practice. He enrolled at Columbia University where he studied physical education. As per his interviews in later years, Budinich claimed to have been the first Chilean to have attended Columbia University. He also claimed to have paid for his studies by working ring corners, boxing in prelim bouts and working as a sparring partner for the magnificent hall of famer Philadelphia Jack O'Brien as well as being one of his second for several bouts.

"The most pleasant moments of my boxing career," Budinich said in an interview years later, "were spent with that man. He was phenomenal in his ability…"

Indeed, the cultured former naval cadet and university student probably had the personality to mesh well with the light heavyweight champion, for Philadelphia Jack was also from a middle class background and was intellectually verbose and charming.

It has been written in several publications that Budinich was also a sparring partner for James J, Corbett but that seems unlikely as Gentleman Jim was well into retirement by the time the Chilean arrived in New York. It is possible however that Budinich might have sparred with Cobett after the champion's retirement, for Gentleman Jim continued to work out in a New York gym on a regular basis long after his ring career.

After his university studies, Budinich returned to Chile in 1907 and by 1908 landed in Colon, Panama, looking to fight a local hero named Sandy Odom.

Panama was a busy country, where thirty three thousand workers toiled building a historic canal across the isthmus. The many Americans and Europeans working on the project were starving for entertainment, therefore introducing boxing in Panama, where Odom was one of the early pioneers, having a reputation as a knockout banger.

Budinich –at twenty-seven years of age- was probably at his peak with more than a decade of ring experience under his belt; he was well conditioned and knew the fight game. The Chilean was not a topnotch fighter but he was a competent pro with a winning record, self managed and aware of his limitations.

In an interview in his old age he said frankly of his abilities as a pugilist: "I was never a shining star but I fought good rivals, strong men."

He saw Odom work out and figured the Panamanian fighter to be a strong, unschooled brawler, so Budinich set out to convince a group of local gamblers to partner with him to bet that he would defeat Odom. The Chilean bet every dollar he owned on himself and his enthusiasm and speaking skills convinced several heavy gamblers to back him with generous bets.

"In the very first round," Budinich said in an interview, years later, "I was dropped to the canvas by a well timed blow…at the beginning of the second round I was still groggy…I defended myself and suddenly, I landed a right and to the floor he went. From there on, I went full gallop."

The fight went the distance and the technically superior Chilean won on points.

A few weeks later they fought a rematch and the betting was not as heavy, for the first bout had been very closely contested and prudent gamblers did not want to take unnecessary risks.

Odom won the second match on points, a tough fight where both men were praised for their skill and grit. Both fights were profitable for Budinich claimed to have pocketed the large sum of five thousand dollars from purses, his own bet and a cut of the winning gamblers that backed him on the first bout.

In 1910, John Budinich headed for Cuba, where he found a virgin territory for his pugilistic ambitions. Although there were scattered amateur promotions in at least four cities in Cuba, Budinich became the key player in popularizing the sport in Havana and several other cities and towns in the island.

Boxing was almost nonexistent in Havana and John Budinich found a home. As in his native Chile, he became the city's boxing messiah. He rented living quarters at 72 Aguila Street –in a busy section of Havana- and proceeded to lease a modest locale, set up a ring and gym bags, followed by printing flyers to advertise the grand opening of the city's first professional boxing academy.

Within weeks his boxing school was packed with eager young men willing to pay for gym fees and private lessons. The group of hopefuls included longshoremen, construction workers, blacksmiths, soldiers and a considerable group of well-bred university students, the young sportsmen of Havana's society set. The best known among the local elite of boxing students included no other than 21 year old Miguel Mariano Gomez –son of Jose Miguel Gomez, president of Cuba- and a future president himself.

A cultured conversationalist, Budinich knew how to use his social skills, for within weeks of his arrival he was appointed boxing instructor at the exclusive "Vedado Tennis Club," teaching the aristocracy how to jab. With a prosperous gym and a salary at the country club, the enterprising fighter was ready for the next step in his career as a boxing impresario.

In order for boxing to progress, there had to be fights and paying audiences, so John Budinich became a promoter, becoming a partner with local businessmen doing small amateur boxing shows and exhibitions at the Actualidades Theater, as well as in dance halls or even in private homes with large courtyards, where he was also –very often- referee and sole judge. He picked up some more cash touring some Cuban cities, boxing exhibitions with his troupe of willing novices.

Budinich was involved in the promotion of several pro cards at the Molino Rojo Theater in Havana in 1910, featuring a friend he imported to Cuba, an American club fighter named Jack Ryan.

The Molino Rojo had promoted a number of Greco-Roman wrestling cards, featuring a group of grapplers from the Fuerte Athletic Club, an organization geared to body building and wrestling. The wrestlers were willing to lace on gloves to make a few extra bucks and Budinich helped promote Ryan in six round main events matching him against a few of the local pro grapplers, wisely building up interest for a good money match between himself and Ryan.

A week before facing Ryan, Budinich fought Cuban Jack Johnson –probably another grappler- in front of a packed house at the Payret Theater. The muscular Cuban Jack Johnson put on a spirited display but was outscored by the Chilean. The following night Budinich faced another brawler dubbed El Catalan, whom he stopped in five rounds.

At this time the Cuban press credited Budinich as having won 35 out of 41 professional bouts.

The Budinich vs. Ryan fight was not the first boxing card in Cuba but it was the first bout to receive a very high level of national attention. The match took place at the elegant Payret Theater in downtown Havana, a venue used for opera and concerts.

The Chilean –weighing 164 pounds- went into the ring with a bandage on one of his legs. A few days before the bout, Budinich claimed to have been gored by a deer while doing roadwork in a wooded area on the outskirts of Havana. This was very improbable but Budinich probably utilized a cut received in an accident to gain an extra headline in the local press leading up to the match with Ryan.

Fighting in front of a full house of over three thousand fans, Budinich won a six round decision but Ryan picked up an extra five hundred dollars for a contracted bet that he would last the distance against the Chilean.

A few weeks later Budinich travelled to Argentina where he disposed of Colombian welter Alfredo Culpin by knockout, before returning to Havana once again.

Budinich became a well known sports figure in Cuba, training, promoting and also touring several cities with a crew of young fighters –and his buddy Jack Ryan-, fighting exhibitions, picking up loose change while creating a growing interest in the sport throughout the whole island.

In 1912 Ryan and Budinich fought a rematch, the American winning by an impressive knockout in the second round. Both promotions were profitable with over three thousand fans and many local politicians and members of Cuban society in attendance.

One of Budinich's prospects –and public sparring partner in some of the exhibition tours- was a muscled laborer named Anastasio Penalver, proclaimed as the new "Heavyweight Champion of Cuba." Penalver was fairly green between the ropes, his claim of the Cuban title being based on a few prelim victories over other raw novices, several public exhibition bouts with Budinich and a twenty round win over Sebastian Coana, who was billed as being the "Heavyweight Champion of Mexico."

Top American heavyweight John Lester Johnson was matched to fight Penalver in a main event bout in Havana in 1915. The muscular but over matched Penalver was stopped in the second round, towel thrown in by Budinich as Johnson pummeled the Cuban.

Not content with one beating, Penalver faced Johnson in a rematch and was stopped even faster. The Cuban heavyweight was not gracious in defeat, causing an incident after the end of the fight card, when he threatened Johnson, using a rock as weapon.

Budinich decided to return to the ring to avenge Penalver's fistic demise.

At this time Budinich was in his mid-thirties and well past his peak. At his best, John Budinich had been a well conditioned good boxer of average ability who had ring experience and a winning record, but had never faced any of the top guns in the fight game. Self managed and smart, he knew his own limitations and had never attempted to break into the elite crust of the fight game, content to headline main events at his second tier level. That he decided to face the black body puncher with a dangerous reputation was a mistake but the veteran Chilean fighter knew that this was his last chance to enter the elite ranks of boxing.

John Lester Johnson was well on his way to becoming a heavyweight contender, one of a group of dangerous black fighters who often fought each other in what was called the "Chittling Circuit." Johnson had faced Joe Jeanette, Harry Wills, Sam Langford and Bill Tate, all of them high quality topnotch fighters.

At the time he fought Budinich, John Lester was a dangerous body puncher with solid skills, destined to fight a newspaper draw while breaking Jack Dempsey's ribs in a future bout. After a long career that would extend until 1929, John Lester Johnson found a second new trade as an actor. He appeared in almost three dozen films, working with Mae West, the Little Rascals, the Three Stooges and in Tarzan movies.

As it was bound to happen Johnson stopped Budinich in the very first round with a wicked body shot.

In five years –from 1910 to 1915- Budinich had successfully popularized and entrenched boxing in Havana and several other cities in Cuba. Although none of his students attained international acclaim or contender status, the Chilean did train a crop of good local fighters, creating a generation of pro battlers, future trainers and gym owners, including clever Victor Achan, tough Mike Febles, lightweight slugger Tomas Galiana and feather weight Chau Aranguren.

Victor Achan was quick to lace on gloves when Budinich opened Cuba's first private boxing academy. Achan was Cuban-Chinese and a fast learner, becoming one of the nation's early pros, recognized as the country's first national flyweight champion in 1913-1914. By 1916, as he ended his pro career, Achan became a partner in a boxing gym and trained dozens of pro fighters, including several headliners and national champions.

Mike Febles, another pioneer from the Budinich Academy, became a well known boxing figure in his native Mexico. Born in Veracruz, Febles spent some of his teen years in Cuba where he turned pro. Besides boxing, Febles practiced jiu-jitsu, beating a well known touring master named Mitsuyo Maeda in a 1916 Havana match.

Febles started his pro career as a lightweight in Cuba, but moved back to his native Mexico where he became a headliner and multiple national title holder, served as a cavalry captain under the orders of General Obregon during the Mexican Revolution and became a well known trainer, supervisor of boxing for the army and coach of the 1932 Mexican Olympic boxing team.

Achan and Febles were only two among dozens of amateurs and pros schooled by Budinich. A few became main event fighters for a short time but no great national heroes would emerge for several years; Cuban pros started out as fillers on cards featuring imported foreign fighters.

By 1915, although other gyms had opened and an American named Bradt was new competition in the promotional level, the Chilean was doing well. Budinich was not wealthy but his income was enough to pay the bills. There was some revenue from the gym, the private boxing lessons, local pros he managed, plus his country club salary and a small profit from promoting amateur and pro boxing shows at small venues. He married a Spanish woman and many believed that he would stay in Cuba, involved in the development of the sport, but the Chilean had a sense of adventure.

One day he left Cuba. Some claimed and newspapers even printed the story that the Chilean had decided to fight in the great epic in Europe, where men battled in bloody trenches and tiny planes engaged in aerial combat over a war torn land. It was announced that John Budinich was off to France, to wear the Kepi Blanc of the French Foreign Legion

John Budinich never returned to Cuba and for a time it was believed that he had perished in some forgotten barricade, like the poet Allan Seeger. Luckily, as with other myths about him, the reports of Budinich's death were highly exaggerated.

Many myths and falsehoods about Budinich have been repeated among historians and sports journalists for decades, contemporary sources quoting the originally wrong sources. Besides the repeated tale –not true- that Budinich had disappeared in the trench warfare of Europe, other false stories have claimed that he had been a bare-knuckle fighter or that he had lived and owned a gym in Mexico.

His ring career almost over, Budinich eventually returned to Chile with his wife, raising a family and opening his third boxing academy, a well run gym on the first block of Ahumada Street in Santiago. As a trainer he worked with South American Heavyweight Champion Heriberto Rojas and Calvin Respress, a former sparring partner of Jack Johnson who became a Chilean citizen. Budinich was also an occasional referee in pro boxing cards held in Santiago and it is likely that he worked closely with Chilean promoter Jack Martinez in bringing several American fighters –including Sam McVea and Dave Mills- to fight in Chile.

Budinich, pushing forty, attempted a final combat that ended in a KO loss for the old warrior at the hands of a transplanted American club fighter named William Daly.

Jon Budinich continued in boxing for the rest of his life. Besides owning the gym and working with pros, he became a boxing instructor at Juan Enrique Concha University and was in charge of the boxing program for the Carabineri, the Chilean national police.

In 1945, the National Boxing Federation of Chile awarded him a well deserved pension for his lifelong achievement in boxing. He died later that year at the age of sixty-five, a victim of pancreatic cancer. In his native city of Coquimbo a street bears his name, honoring the local fighter who pioneered boxing in three different nations.

About the same time that Budinich was ending his boxing career, American George Bradt -who owned a Havana newspaper-, became Cuba's top promoter. Bradt had deep pockets and imported top talent including former lightweight champion Battling Nelson, future welterweight king Ted Kid Lewis and established stars including heavyweights Sam McVea and Battling Jim Johnson, as well as middleweights Young Ahearn and veteran Willie Lewis.

Bradt did not make money in almost two dozen promotions. Although his cards had good attendance, his expenses were very high, paying considerable purses and travel and living expenses for the imported fighters while failing to build up local talent.

Battling Nelson fought three times on Cuban soil, all bouts in a two month period of 1915, stopping Stewart Donnelly and Dale Gardner and beating Jim Finley on points in twenty-five rounds. In that historic era where the world was at war, Nelson gained headlines in Havana by taping a photo of Germany's Kaiser Wilhelm on his heavy punching bag.

Most of the fight talk however, centered on the first world title fight to be held on Cuban soil, the upcoming scheduled forty five rounder between the brilliant and controversial Jack Johnson and the huge cowboy from Kansas named Jess Willard.

Attractive poster announcing the Johnson Vs Willard title fight.

Six-foot-six inches tall Jess Willard.

Willard set up a ring in the back courtyard of his hotel and trained under the broiling sun to become used to the tropical heat.

Johnson and Willard in the heat of battle, Havana 1915.

Willard beats Jack Johnson at Oriental Race Track in Havana, 1915
This rare photo shows the film crew on a platform.

The controversial photo of the knockout of Jack Johnson by Willard.

CHAPTER THREE: TITLE FIGHT IN HAVANA

The Johnson vs. Willard fight was a historical moment full of controversy as various versions of the events and the battle have been portrayed in Hollywood movies and Broadway plays, in serious non-fiction books as well as in various novels.

The eye of the storm centered around Jack Johnson, a powerful black man with great panache and a penchant for marrying white women –some of them working call girls- at a time when racial tolerance in America was scant, when lynching negroes still occurred, and the emotional scars of the bloody war between the states still affected many who had lived it as children, adults or slaves.

Although boxing was an integrated sport since the Nineteenth Century, with champions like "Little Chocolate" George Dixon and the boxing master lightweight Joe Gans, Johnson was the first black man to win the big prize: the heavyweight title.

It was not easy for the Galveston heavyweight to reach the top. During his early years in the ring, Johnson was part of a cast of talented black fighters that few wanted to fight so they fought each other over and over.

Besides Johnson, the "Chittling Crcuit" group consisted of Sam McVea, Joe Jeanette, Sam Langford, Klondike Haynes, Black Bill, Hank Griffin, George Cole, Denver Ed Martin and a dozen other dangerous heavyweights.

Many white fighters avoided facing the tough "Chittling Circuit" fighters for the low profit and the high risk of trading leather with the hungry blacks. One notable exception was Jim Barry, a fair skinned cowboy from Montana. Barry's name appears so often in the records of the best black fighters of the era that many boxing historians have mistaken his ethnicity.

Barry, who had an affinity for drugs and liquor and met his end in a bar brawl in Panama in 1917, fought Langford a dozen times and could boast of having decked the Boston fighter. Other black stars also traded punches with the

Montana cowboy, including Jeannette, McVea, George Cole and Jack Blackburn.

Jack Johnson established himself as the best of the dangerous black group; he fought Jeanette ten times -seven times in two years- he fought Langford once, Klondike and Hank Griffin three times each and twice with McVea and Denver Ed Martin on his way to an elusive title shot.

In 1908, Johnson cornered Tommy Burns in an Australian ring and became world champion, the first black man to achieve the coveted crown.

A fighter of immense talent, Johnson was an excellent defensive boxer who knew how to tie up his foes, punch or counterpunch with solid power, always dominating the flow of the action and his opponents as though he was effortlessly competing in a sparring contest. His high level of dominance made fights boring for he was vastly superior to all his opponents.

Johnson became one of the most controversial figures of the first two decades of the century. His boxing achievements were overshadowed by the headlines associated with his lifestyle, for the champion frequented bordellos, married white women –one of which committed suicide in his own restaurant- was often fined for speeding his fancy car or made headlines by his daring talk, sometimes sarcastic and often on target.

Most of white America hated Johnson. Other black champions had been accepted but Johnson stunned American society with unconventional moves, even angering many blacks who felt Johnson was not a good role model for his own people. To top it all, Johnson drew "the color line' and refused to defend his crown against Langford, claiming there was no gate money to be had in a title fight between two blacks.

Much has been written about how Johnson was persecuted by powerful enemies: how a law –The Mann Act- was enacted and used retroactively to entrap the champion who fled to Europe until the First World War started and a more suitable site was needed for a title fight to refill Johnson's empty coffers. So it came to be that Jack Johnson and his entourage headed for Havana to battle Jess Willard for a sizable purse of $30,000 plus expenses and a percentage of film revenues.

The racism unleashed against Johnson for his unconventional –and very shocking for the era- lifestyle had created a search for a "White Hope." Boxing people promoted local heroes and a cowboy from Kansas named Jess Willard emerged as the challenger for the Havana title fight.

Willard was a six foot six farm worker who weighed in around two hundred and forty hard pounds but the giant was not considered an exciting performer. Willard fought without anxiety and reacted to the fight strategy set by his opponent. The big cowboy was a solid hard puncher but was only aggressive when attacked by another fighter. Facing a non aggressive fighter, Willard would be content to coast at a steady pace, doing enough to win without hurting or being hurt.

Willard was not even considered the best of the fair skinned hopes –Gunboat Smith had beaten him- but big Jess was in spite of his easy going style, a force to be reckoned.

The cowboy was a man of great strength and excellent stamina, fast for his size as well as an adequate boxer with very good power, a reputation enhanced by the tragedy of having killed a man –Bull Young- in the ring. Although he had only fought 27 pro fights, not many when compared to more than ninety fights in Johnson's record, Willard's enormous size, weight and stamina made him a dangerous foe against any heavyweight of the time, including the aging champion.

The tale has been told –whether true or not- that Willard saw a black bird dying in the sand while doing roadwork on the Cuban shore and believed it to be an omen that he would win the title from Johnson. Feeling confident and hungry for fame, Willard set up camp in Havana and trained intensely, sparring in an outdoor ring under a broiling Cuban sun.

Sparring outdoors was part of the strategy, for the championship fight would be held outside and was scheduled for the very long stretch of forty five rounds, a tough proposition considering the heat of a harsh sun and the punishment doled out in such a prolonged battle. Willard understood that his key to victory hinged on top conditioning, in being able to win a long war of attrition against the high rolling, past his peak champion.

Willard trained to go forty-five rounds, building up stamina by running several miles daily, doing hard calisthenics workouts and sparring with four different fighters in an outdoor ring set up on the grounds of the hotel for his public workouts.

Johnson trained also, but at the age of thirty seven he was past his peak and it was beginning to show. He weighed in at 225, a full twenty pounds above his best weight, not looking fat but certainly bulkier and with less muscle definition than in previous fights. Writer Alexander Johnston described Johnson as "not hog fat, for even the fight pictures show that, but he did carry a layer of tallow into that tropical ring."

On April 5, 1915, the Oriental Park Racecourse was packed with sixteen thousand fans –including hundreds of women- attending Cuba's first world title fight. There were several hundred Americans in the audience, including sport writers, traveling fans and a number of yanks that resided in Havana.

The fight was filmed. Actually, besides the original crew that filmed the whole fight, a second crew filmed a few short highlights of the match. The Cuban promotional team of the Santos & Artigas Circus was given permission to film and show small clips of the fight in order to promote the full showing of the battle. The first showing of the promotional clip took place on June 19 at the Teatro Nacional in Havana.

It was a hot, bright day and Jack Johnson took an early lead, outscoring and out punching his tall foe who seemed content to box cautiously, using his weight in the clinches, occasionally landing solid body shots on the champion's midsection. Both men fought in spurts but Johnson held a clear edge in the first eleven rounds.

In the twelfth and thirteenth rounds Johnson went after the knockout, landing several hard shots flush on Willard's face but the Kansas cowboy did not fall and survived the onslaught.

The fight tempo then shifted. Feeling that Johnson had spent his guns in the previous two rounds, Willard asserted himself, moving in, pushing Johnson back, crowding him, jabbing, making the champion work; Willard became the aggressor and Johnson gradually faded, his black skin gleaming with perspiration, his reflexes slowing with every passing round. By the twentieth round the difference in the dynamics of the fight was evident; Willard, looking fit and strong, was methodically wearing down the thirty seven year old champion.

At the end of the twenty fifth round a Willard body shot shook Johnson who refused to go down. Big Jess opened up on Johnson in the following round, knocking him out with a pulverizing right hand that dropped the black man to the canvas where he seemed to shield his eyes from the sun as he lost his crown.

Years later, Jack Johnson wrote a confession that he sold to Nat Fleischer – the editor of Ring Magazine- where the former champion claimed that the fight had been fixed in exchange for leniency from the US government, but Fleischer never believed Johnson's story. Fleischer believed that Johnson would rather be shrouded in the controversy of a conspiracy than admit he had been outlasted by a big fighter of limited ring experience.

Historian Hank Kaplan agreed with Fleischer.

"Johnson had a tremendous ego," Kaplan said, "It would make sense considering his ego that he would rather claim to be the victim of a conspiracy than admitting he lost to an inferior white fighter. There's no doubt that Johnson was superior to Willard but Johnson was not in good shape for the Havana fight and he melted with the heat. Willard was not as good as Johnson but he was in terrific shape and had trained sparring in an outside ring so he did not melt….and Jess has been underrated also. He was very strong and could hit with power. I think the fight was on the level but it will remain a topic of conversation forever."

Based on such controversy a hit Broadway show and a movie portrayed the champion as victim of a conspiracy and several books have dissected different aspects of the event, but it is very likely that Nat Fleischer was right about Johnson's emotional justifications in seeking an excuse for a real defeat at the hands of a man he considered his ring inferior.

If Johnson was fighting a fixed bout why did he try to stop Willard in the first thirteen rounds of the fight? Why did he wait so long under the broiling sun before diving to the canvas? Indeed, if there was a deal with the US government why did Johnson wait five years before returning to the United States?

The conspiracy theorists point to a photo of Johnson shielding his eyes from the sun but emotional bias aside, there are logical explanations; Johnson might have been partially conscious and the bright sun shone directly on his face, bothering him, or the arms held at face level could have been caused by a defensive reflex

Promoter Jack Curley did use some of personal contacts to try to get leniency for Johnson but he always denied that those meetings had anything to do with a deal to throw the fight, emphatically stating that the match had been on the level. Curley met with U.S. government officials but had a clear answer –two months before the Havana title bout- that regardless the outcome, the government would not desist from prosecuting Johnson.

Johnson was neither foolish or naïve and would not have accepted a deal without proper legal representation, nor would he have believed that Curley had the political clout to swing a deal of such magnitude. Had the deal been consummated Johnson would have returned to the US, which he did not do for a half decade, living in Spain and Mexico while continuing to fight meaningless matches for small money.

In Cuba, the Johnson-Willard match helped boxing become a leading sport in the Island.

Boxing card in Holguin 1916.

Outstanding welter Enrique Ponce De Leon

Lalo Dominguez was lightweight and welterweight champion of Cuba.

Louis Smith and Mike Castro –two pioneers of Cuban boxing

CHAPTER FOUR: THE FIRST NATIONAL HEROES

The Willard-Johnson title bout had not only placed Cuba on the international boxing map but at the national level it served to create huge interest in pugilism. At least eight cities and towns in Cuba had professional cards in the months that followed the Willard-Johnson fight.

Some city majors prohibited boxing but the new promotional entities simply moved their shows to nearby towns and waited for the political storm to pass.

Teodoro Risquet promoted many amateur and some professional shows for a period of three decades in Matanzas. In Cienfuegos and Santiago de Cuba the gyms were busy and in Holguin, on Cuba's eastern end, the star attraction was the owner of a local pharmacy, a hefty fellow named Oscar Albanes. A photo of one of his 1916 bouts –at the Holguin Athletic Club- shows a ring made of wood boards without protecting canvas, the ringside seats placed on hard soil and a surprisingly large number of women in the audience.

In the five years following the Willard-Johnson match, Cuban boxing developed well, and four fighters stood out above the rest, becoming the first group of national stars, their exploits recounted often in the Cuban press.

The four were Louis Smith, flyweight Mike Castro, welter Enrique Ponce de Leon and lightweight Lalo Dominguez.

Louis Smith began his career while a teenager, debuting as a featherweight, but outgrowing several divisions with the help of a fork and knife. Photos of the era show a short, chunky man who was probably a welter, but did not mind overeating to gain a couple of dozen pounds to become the Cuban Light Heavyweight Champion in 1921, defeating Kid Cardenas by a fourth round knockout in a fight where the five hundred dollar purse was considered a large sum of money at the time. Smith was a gutsy fellow, described as an "elegant boxer" with a solid left hand in spite of his chunky physique. In 1921 a sportswriter described him as "short of body, loaded on the belly area, short of arm length and lacking length of legs but with awesome agility and above all, with a tremendous left hand…"

In 1916, Smith was scheduled to fight Chau Aranguren in a club card main event in a town in Matanzas Province when the card unraveled. To save the show Smith offered to fight a prelim bout in addition to the main event. The first opponent, one Luis Molinet, outweighed Smith by around fifty pounds but the young pro took him out in two rounds then went on to beat featherweight Aranguren over twelve stanzas.

Smith claimed to have fought over 100 fights in his career but barely a dozen bouts have made it to the record books. Upon retiring from competition, Smith partnered up with the clever flyweight Victor Achan, establishing a management-training team that guided many good pros, including several Cuban national champions.

Mike Castro was born in the town of Union de Reyes in Cuba, but spent most of his teenage years in Lancaster, Pennsylvania, where his father was involved in business. Mike grew to be a very tall –five ten- rawhide flyweight, boxing as an amateur while still in high school. He turned pro while attending Business College fighting at least nine bouts before returning to Cuba.

Setting up shop in Havana, Mike proceeded to win the Cuban flyweight title and also challenged for the national bantam crown. His polished boxing style, combined with an agreeable, courteous manner was loved by the press, but besides becoming one of the nation's first national idols, Mike Castro also opened up his own boxing academy, ran professional promotions with his brother and over the years managed or trained several very good fighters, including Louis Smith, Lalo Dominguez and future world flyweight contender Black Bill.

Mike Castro was a total boxing man. After hanging up the gloves in 1923, he continued in boxing as a trainer and manager for several years before switching to being the third man in the ring. After over a decade as one of Cuba's top refs, Mike Castro became the head of the Cuban National Boxing Commission, a position he held until his retirement.

Enrique Ponce de Leon was a native of the city of Cienfuegos, on Cuba's central southern coast. A good boxer with little power, Ponce de Leon held the Cuban welterweight title twice and globe trotted often, fighting beyond Cuban borders in the United States, France and Spain. His record shows a loss on points to future world champion Tommy Freeman and by TKO to the indestructible European middleweight champion Ignacio Ara, draws with the excellent Kid Charol and Olympic gold medalist Eddie Flynn as well as a win, loss and draw with the highly regarded Spaniard Juan Carlos Casala and a victory over fringe contender Larry Avera. He also surprisingly decked European champion Piet Hobin on his way to losing on points in a 15 rounder. His still incomplete record shows a 61-35-15 file with 24 KO wins.

The most popular of the four Cuban national heroes was Lalo Dominguez, a wiry blacksmith who turned pro at the late pugilistic age of twenty three without the benefit of an amateur background. "The Terrible Mulatto," as Dominguez was soon nicknamed, went pro in 1917, in a scheduled four rounder against an experienced lightweight prelim fighter named Frankie Torres. No one expected the novice to win but Dominguez proved all wrong, stretching Torres out in the third round and then beating him on points in a rematch.

The raw, unpolished Dominguez fought often, quickly developing into a tricky, smooth fighter. Lalo soon became Cuba's most popular local hero, boxing a draw with Louis Smith and defeating the best young local prospects as well as some imported U.S. club fighters. One of Lalo's epic early fights set a national record for knockdowns, when he dropped Jack Coullimber twenty six times in a 1919 Havana bout.

Dominguez fought from 1917 to 1928 –part of that time trained by Mike Castro- winning and losing the Cuban lightweight and welterweight titles.

Lalo Dominguez and Enrique Ponce de Leon fought at least eight times, Ponce winning one, Dominguez taking four and fighting three draws.
The high points of Lalo's career included wins over world rated Chilean lightweight Stanislaus –Tany- Loaysa in which Dominguez had the tough South American on the deck in the first bout.

Dominguez was also the best paid performer among the local heroes. For his 1925 bout against world class Spaniard Hilario Martinez, Dominguez was paid $1,550, a large sum in the first quarter of the century, enough to outright purchase a house. In his career, Dominguez earned several purses over $1,000 at a time when most local main event fighters seldom earned more than a couple of hundred pesos for a star bout.

After his career as a fighter ended, the "Terrible Mulatto," became a boxing commission staffer and also one of Cuba's top trainers, spending more than three decades teaching hundreds of youngsters how to box. He died in the 1960's of a heart attack at the Barrientos Gym in Havana, while working as a trainer in the sport that made him a national icon.

Smith, Castro, Ponce de Leon and Dominguez headlined many shows that created a boxing boom in the island by 1921.

The first decade of Cuban boxing (1910-1920) had been an era of development of a local boxing infrastructure, establishing gyms and frequent promotions in different towns and cities that allowed fighters to develop. The seed of knowledge planted by Budinich had blossomed into a productive crop. Although for a time boxing at the end of this decade was made illegal in Havana, fight cards were held in nearby cities and towns and public outcry forced the authorities to lift the ban.

In 1921, Havana had no less than eight private athletic clubs that taught boxing and sponsored amateur cards. The Cuban army and navy taught boxing at their bases, sponsored amateur contests and even hosted several pro shows at Columbia Military Camp in Havana with proceeds going to charity organizations. There were also several competing promotional enterprises, including the well known Santos & Artigas Circus.

Beyond Havana, young trainers were teaching the sport in several cities and towns, promoting club shows and building local talent. In 1921 dozens of pro boxing shows were held in Havana and Santiago de Cuba, as well as in Santa Clara, Holguin, Cienfuegos, Guantanamo, Matanzas and other cities in Cuba. In that year bureaucracy entered the boxing scene as a national boxing commission was formed to regulate the sport and a new crop of Cuban fighters produced the first contenders for world honors.

Cirilin Olano started his pro career in 1921 or 1922, going through the local lightweights in a blaze, knocking out national featherweight champion Jack Coullimber in five and winning the Cuban Lightweight Championship from Lalo Dominguez, stopping the tough fighter in six rounds. In 1925, Olano was one of a group of fighters selected for an elimination tournament to determine a successor for the world lightweight championship vacated by the retiring Benny Leonard.

In his first bout of the tournament Olano scored a TKO in five over Clonie Tait, Canadian lightweight titleholder.

Advancing to the semifinal round, Olano faced Chilean Stanislaus Loayza who stopped him in three, ending Cuba's hopes to crown its first world champion. Olano continued to fight for five more years but was no longer a world threat for the division, losing several fights he should have won.

The second Cuban to leap into the upper crust of the world ratings was a superb flyweight nicknamed Black Bill.

Black Bill was the first Cuban to challenge for a world title.

Black Bill and Kid Chocolate

CHAPTER FIVE: THE LEGENDARY BLACK BILL

Eladio Valdez –later known as Black Bill- was born in a blue collar neighborhood in Havana in May of 1905.

Eladio was a street urchin, a little fireball who fought other kids in street corners, survived on his wits and petty thefts and never weighed –even as an adult- more than a hundred and fifteen pounds.

At the age of thirteen or fourteen, the street urchin showed up at Mike Castro's gym, looking to expand his street fighter reputation. The Cuban champion took a look at the cocky runt and wasted no time in testing him, putting him in the ring with an experienced fighter to teach him humility.

"He weighed around 120 and I only weighed 102," Bill said in an interview, years later, "They gave the order to start sparring and the kid started dancing around me, hitting me with his left…I went crazy, rushed him and hit him on the tip of the chin. He dropped to the canvas and I piled down on him, keeping up my blows… I did not know…I figured boxing was like street fighting."

Castro, impressed with the little street urchin's panache, accepted him into the gym. Eladio however, did not have money to buy equipment, so he stole a pair of boxing shoes and trunks.

"I dyed them, changing the color," Bill confessed, "At the time we started training, those who had lost items were going crazy looking for them while I played the fool, off by myself learning to skip rope."

He did learn to skip rope, hit the bags and in the ring he learned balance, combinations, feints, pacing and a couple of dirty tricks. Before long the little hundred pound kid was handling bantams and feathers in the gym.

In those early months of learning how to box with Mike Castro, Eladio picked up the nickname Black Bill, which had been the moniker of a turn of the century U.S. heavyweight whose real name was Claude

Brooks. The original Black Bill had been a competent journeyman but his Cuban counterpart would be a first class contender.

Eladio turned pro at fifteen and Black Bill he became, winning his first paid encounter against Enrique Valdez, another young fighter.

Black Bill became one of Cuba's most popular fighters. The little flyweight was willing to give up pounds, height and reach to anyone and still beat them, overwhelming them with lightning quick combinations and blazing leg movement.

Promoters loved Bill not only for his skills and charisma but because the little fighter was always willing to help a promoter. Bill would fight a main event one week and a four round walkout bout two weeks later. It did not matter to him; he loved fighting and the paychecks were a bonus.

He fought every flyweight and several bantams who dared face him and seldom lost. When he ran out of opponents he fought rematches. Club fighter Modesto Morales tangled with Bill ten times, notching up a draw and nine losses. Young prospect Mike Rojo –who would later become one of Cuba's busiest referees, dropped two –one by KO- to the fiery Bill. Kid Guanajay lost four fights to Bill and Andres Urquia lost two.

Bill's most important fights early in his career were against Genaro Pino, a youngster from the city of Cienfuegos who was starting his own promising career that would see him win three Cuban titles and fight a draw and lose on points to future world champion Petey Sarron. The capable Pino beat Black Bill by disqualification but the victory was followed by three defeats to the speedy Bill on points.

By 1925, twenty year old Black Bill was a veteran of almost seventy pro fights of which he had lost less than a half dozen, becoming the toast of sport writers and a national celebrity.

Bill also had the best manager in Cuban boxing, a lean, mustachioed young man named Luis –nicknamed Pincho- Gutierrez. A businessman from a solid middle class background, Gutierrez was a student of boxing, attending fight cards, studying styles, learning the craft.

Trainer Caron Gonzalez said of Gutierrez: "Pincho knew his boxing. He could walk into a gym watch one round of sparring and give you a total analysis of both fighters. He could break down a match to comparing speed levels, techniques. He knew his stuff and he was nobody's fool."

Pincho took Bill to New York. The swift little fighter soon became a contender starting an eventual six bout series with future champion Corporal Izzy Schwartz, with Bill winning four out of six. The Cuban Ink Spot as he was soon nicknamed by sportswriters, tangled with the cream of the crop of the division including Ernie Jarvis, Marty Gold and Henry Catena before returning to Cuba in 1926.

Bill at twenty one was the toast of Havana and New York but he was still a wild man. He trained hard and played harder, dancing the Charleston at nightclubs, drinking and whoring with corpulent women. There were occasional scenes in public places, short brawls or heated arguments and misdemeanor arrests for disturbing the peace.

"There was this story told about Black Bill," Caron Gonzalez stated in an interview, "it took place in Cuba, Bill was sweeping rounds against a local prospect and one of the fans in the back row cheap seats started heckling Bill, who glanced up the stands and located his critic. After winning the fight on points, Bill skipped the dressing room and went straight for the stands, where he punched out the heckler."

By 1928 Pincho Gutierrez had an impressive squad of fighters that included flyweight contender Black Bill and an undefeated newcomer, a featherweight named Kid Chocolate.

The pair became good friends. After all, both were party animals and had the youthful energy that allowed them –for several years- to train diligently and also drink booze, smoke reefer and play with their female admirers.

When Pincho took the pair to New York, Gutierrez hired a young, very honest trainer and matchmaker named Sellout Moe Fleischer, who was also a solid handicapper with good connections in the New York fight trade.

"Black Bill was one good fighter," Moe said in an interview years later, "He could box, hit, fight inside or outside and he was slick, hard to hit. He had a lot of talent and he was in the top ten ratings for five years. I took him to Canada and he beat every one of those little guys over there. He also fought a lot in New York…. The trouble with Bill was his training methods. He was a hard worker at the gym but a harder worker with a woman, a bottle or a nightclub. People talk about Kid Chocolate and his partying…I tell you Bill was worse. He would get into street fights with bigger guys and get arrested. Bill drank, smoked, gambled and chased every skirt he could find even though he had just married a wife that was twice his size…she weighed over two hundred pounds."

"We had to hold his purse and give him money on a daily basis," Moe said, "if you gave him a thousand dollars it would be spent in a day….His whole weekly budget could be spent in a few hours and he would not have eating money for the rest of the week….On the train coming back from a fight he would say –Moe, give me money- but I would give it to Pincho and he would take care of Bill."

Pincho Gutierrez had established himself as a star manager. Bill was a rated flyweight contender and Chocolate also entered the top ten as a featherweight, turning in remarkable performances in the ring. Besides the two Cubans, Gutierrez was handling Ignacio Ara, a Spaniard who was destined to win the European middleweight champion and was never stopped in a 193 bout career and several other good fighters, including tough Relampago Saguero, who was Cuban welter weight champion, as well as top rated Canada Lee and Argentine heavyweight Victorio Campolo. .

Pincho was a good manager who advised his fighters well but the wild one did not listen. Bill contracted venereal diseases and neglected to treat them properly. Still, although somewhat dissipated by booze and skirt chasing, the tough flyweight had plenty of energy to out hustle the best men in his division.

Black Bill became the first Cuban to challenge for a world title when he fought Midget Wolgast in a New York ring, circa 1930, losing a tight decision.

"By the time Bill fought Wolgast." Moe said sadly "he was washed up. Bill had suffered venereal diseases and was going blind and he hid it from me. When Pincho and I found out about his bad eyes, we retired him, but it was a tragic ending. He had not saved a nickel and was too troublesome to hold down a steady job."

Bill was depressed. He had a few fights on his own, even managing to win his last one in Puerto Rico. His final record –probably incomplete- is 125-24-13 with 22 KO wins and three ND bouts. In 168 fights he was never stopped.

Bill returned to New York, where he lived in a tenement, the blindness increasing as well as the drinking.

One day he grasped a pistol, fired it at his wife but being unable to see, missed hitting her large body, then turned the gun on himself ending his life.

Black Bill was twenty-seven years old.

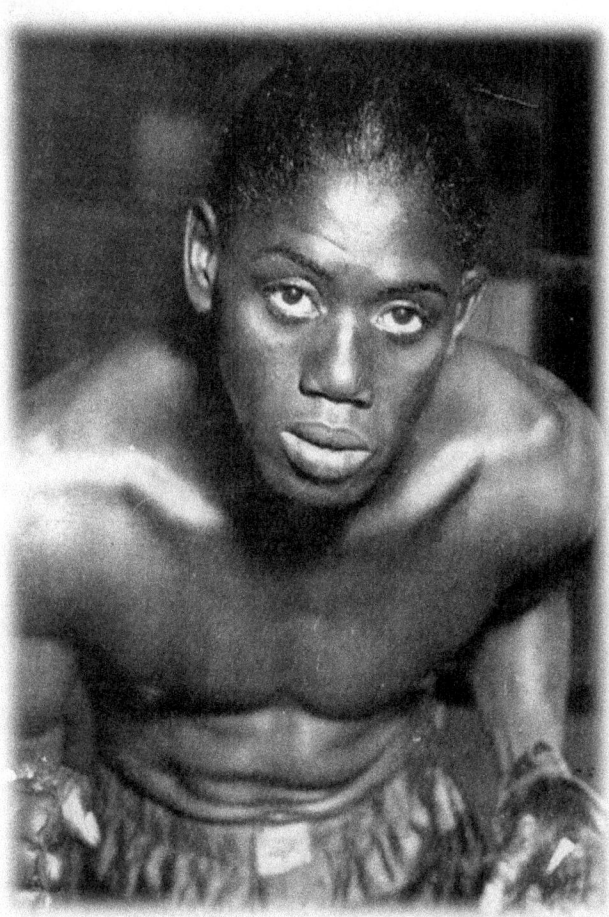

Kid Chocolate

Kid Chocolate and Pincho Gutierrez

Chocolate and one of his several vehicles

Chocolate in the ring at Arena Cristal in Havana

CHAPTER SIX: THE CHOCOLATE KID

Kid Chocolate –a child of destiny- was born Eligio Sardinas Montalvo on October 28, 1910, not January 1907 as it has been often reported.

The Kid grew up around boxing. His older brother Domingo was a prelim welterweight who fought pro under the name of Knockout Chocolate, so it was logical for the younger brother to become Kid Chocolate.

He was a happy child from a poor family who was imitating his brother's moves and hanging around gymnasiums at a time when other children were still playing with toy soldiers.

Many articles and books refer to Kid Chocolate as having been undefeated in 100 amateur fights, scoring 86 knockouts, but there is no truth to such numbers. The Cuban newspapers of the time, including "Diario de La Marina" and "La Noche" –a sponsor of amateur tournaments- covered the Cuban boxing scene very well with detailed results of every card at both the pro and amateur smoker level. The publications and other research account for twenty two amateur fights for the undefeated fighter, including one against Mario Kid Sanchez that was described as "controversial." Sanchez, from the city of Holguin, would also turn pro, becoming national bantamweight champion.

Some record books also state that Chocolate scored 21 straight knockouts when he entered the pro ranks in Cuba. Again, these numbers are really only press copy material, figments of a press agents imagination.

Kid Chocolate became a semi-pro fighter at the age of seventeen. The semi-pro category used in Cuba at the time was real professional competition but only among newcomers to the pro ranks. It was a similar concept as the novice division for amateurs, which allowed the new pros to fight for a time at an equal level of competition that would avoid overmatching them against very experienced fighters early in their careers.

The new rising star of the semi-pros was Johnny Cruz, a clever featherweight who had won amateur tournaments in New York and had scored a good win in his first semi-pro bout. Kid Chocolate was paid $40 to face Cruz, dancing and jabbing his way to a point victory over six rounds then stopping Johnny in five for a $100 rematch. Cruz would in later years become a good journeyman main event fighter, an excellent trainer and a well known referee. The one hundred dollar purse was unusually high pay at the semi-pro level but Chocolate and Cruz were considered the two best amateurs in the island and their semi-pro clashes received wide attention in the Havana press.

The Kid had another seven wins in the pro and semi-pro ranks in Havana. Instead of twenty one knockouts, Chocolate's early Cuban record is verified as nine fights with six of the victories by knockout. By then he had also signed up with the man who managed Johnny Cruz, the well dressed, amicable Pincho Gutierrez.

Another press agent fib involved Pincho and Chocolate, stating that when they started out together both were so naïve about boxing that they learned the technique by watching fight films. While it is true that both studied fight films, they were far from being greenhorns at the fight game. At the time they met, the Kid had an undefeated amateur career, while Pincho had managed several fighters including the idol of Cuba, Black Bill, who already was a world class flyweight.

Not yet eighteen –in the summer of 1928- the Kid headed for New York with Bill, Pincho and several fighters. Trained by Moe Fleischer, the Kid's American debut was against a club fighter named Eddie Enos at Mitchell's Field, Mineola, New York. Pincho and Chocolate had altered a birth certificate to make the Kid a couple of years older so he could be legally allowed to fight main events.

Enos was a veteran of over forty pro fights, winning some and losing others but always putting out an honest effort. His ring experience did not help him as Chocolate moved out of his corner assuming total command of the fight, striking the Brooklyn fighter at will, peppering him with quick combinations. The brave journeyman tried his best but could only land glancing blows on the lightning quick Chocolate. Soon after the third round started the referee stepped in, his arms holding up a battered, dazed Eddie Enos.

The fight crowd was impressed with the lightning moves, machine gun combinations and elegant style of boxing. Offers came and Pincho accepted them all, sixteen fights in five months to the end of 1928. Chocolate won fifteen -nine by KO- and drew with Joey Scalfaro in front of a crowd of nineteen thousand fans at Madison Square Garden. In a matter of months,

Chocolate established a reputation as the hottest new star in the boxing horizon and earned thousands of dollars a fight.

"He was some fighter," trainer Moe Fleischer said years later, "I think he was the greatest fighter I've ever seen, and I've seen them all. He could do everything and I saw him make some moves I've never seen other fighters make. He was so fast, that he would hit you three times in a row with the left jab before you realized he had thrown the first one…"

"Once," Moe Fleischer recalled, "we were fighting up in Pennsylvania and I left the dressing room for a few minutes. When I returned, I smelled gas. Someone wanted the local boy to win badly and they could have killed Chocolate with that open gas line. By fight time the Kid was woozy and I wanted to cancel the fight but the Kid insisted he could beat the local boy even drugged up. I beat him Moe-he said-I beat him. I was worried but Chocolate won every round. It was all instinct. He was a natural, the best fighter I've ever seen."

The Chocolate that returned to Havana in 1929 was still a teenager but very different from the undernourished fighter in hand me down clothes and little sophistication; the Kid was now a sharp dresser, wearing tailor made elegant suits and silk shirts. He wore diamond rings and a gold watch but for all his freewheeling spending, he took care of his mother, buying her a large house, gave gifts to all members of his family and spent a few hundred bucks buying toys for the neighborhood kids,

He had earned thousands of dollars on his New York tour but it all went fast. It did not matter for the Kid was willing to fight anyone to line up his pockets once again. He turned up in Havana, beating import Chick Suggs for something billed as the "Colored Featherweight Championship of the World," before returning to New York.

In May of 1929 the eighteen year old Cuban outscored -by a narrow disputed margin- former flyweight king Fidel LaBarba, whom he would fight three times in his career, winning twice.

The important victory over LaBarba was followed by seven more triumphs in ten weeks, setting up a fight against future world lightweight champion Al Singer that drew a huge gate of fifty thousand fans paying $225,000 to see the two men trade leather at the Polo Grounds. The Kid was paid fifty thousand dollars which was a lot of money for the era, when a single dollar could fill a man's belly with a very good meal.

It should be noted that Chocolate was one of the rare black fighters of his era that was very popular with all ethnic and racial groups and his purses –even before he was champion- were very large.

The Singer bout was a very attractive match for Chocolate was unbeaten in forty two pro fights and Al, the idol of the New York Jewish community, boasted wins over Bud Taylor and Carl Duane and a draw with the mighty Tony Canzoneri.

The fans were not disappointed. Singer tried to force the fight inside and Chocolate, moved, slipped and threw dozens of combinations, clusters of hooks and jabs, remaining undefeated at the end of the night. The elated Cuban wired home a descriptive message: "The Chocolate is hot; just ask Al Singer."

The day after his victory, the dapper Kid went shopping. He bought a Packard and ordered it freighted to Havana, to be parked on his mother's driveway. He visited a top tailor and ordered a dozen suits, went shopping for a few pair of shoes and spent some more money later that night, drinking with his date-du-jour at a nightclub.

Happy go lucky Kid Chocolate continued his party lifestyle but also kept on winning. On March 21, 1930 at Madison Square Garden, Chocolate shared billing with his buddy Black Bill. The little Havana flyweight lost his title bid against tough Midget Wolgast and the Kid faced a tough New Jersey fighter named Allie Ridgeway who had recently defeated top British featherweight Nel Tarleton.

In one of his peak performances, Chocolate dispatched Ridgeway in two rounds, knocking him down for four counts of nine.

"I fought good fighters in my time," Allie Ridgeway said years later, "and I beat some very good fighters like Nel Tarleton, Buster Brown, Harry Sankey and others, but everyone always remembers how I was stopped by Kid Chocolate, but there's no shame on that because I fought him close to his peak…. He was so fast you could not see the punch coming and besides hitting hard he was right on target….you could not hit him with a load of buckshot. He slipped punches very well…"

Five months after beating Ridgeway, Chocolate –with a record of fifty five wins and one draw- faced a tough little Englishman named Jackie Kid Berg, a knockout artist who had only lost four out of ninety fights. Berg had won the NBA Light welterweight title and outweighed the Kid by almost ten pounds. The Kid was paid $38,000 at the time when the U.S. had already entered the Great Depression, an era when a family could cover all basic expenses with less than a hundred dollars a month but many were unemployed, homeless and hungry.

Berg and Chocolate put up a sensational scrap. Berg started with a savage, relentless attack and by the third round the Kid was admitting to his corner that his legs were not responding well. The savvy Moe Fleischer advised Chocolate to avoid the clinches and stop fighting the Englishman on the inside, where Berg could use his weight advantage. The Kid boxed brilliantly, often resting on the ropes, slipping and countering his opponent but Berg kept coming, throwing hooks and uppercuts. At the end of ten rounds, Berg was declared the winner of a hard fought bout, ending Chocolate's win streak.

The Kid cried when he lost and drowned his sorrows with champagne, a couple of girls and buying a dozen tailored suits with matching footwear.

Two months later the Chocolate man came back to the ring stopping a fair lightweight named Benny Nabors in the first round, but before 1930 ended the Kid lost two more, to old foe Fidel LaBarba and to Bat Battalino, for a New York version of the featherweight title.

"Chocolate got a string of knockouts from here to China," Battalino told boxing writer Peter Heller in an interview years later, "The first round, the first punch, he dropped me. Caught me cold, down I went….I punched the shit right out of his belly…. I just walked in, bing, bing….He's hitting me in the face, I'm hitting him the belly. Finally, I beat him the whole fifteen round fight."

After the Battalino fight, Chocolate returned to Cuba for a few months, where he drew admiring crowds every time he went on the town, dressed in impeccable suits and elegant jewelry.

In May and June of 1931, Chocolate returned to New York rings, winning four fights in two months before facing Benny Bass for the New York version of the World Junior Lightweight Title. Bass was a very rugged ring warrior. In over 150 fights he had built a reputation as a hard puncher with a solid chin and a dirty style of fighting having lost seven bouts by disqualification.

Twenty year old Kid Chocolate stopped partying, went into training –even doing hated roadwork- and Pincho brought the Kid's mother from Cuba to New York. Her presence motivated him to behave and achieve optimum condition, although the four wins in two months had already kept him in good fighting trim.

"The night I fought Bass," Chocolate said, "I was as sharp as a barber's razor. I hit Bass with everything… hooks, uppercuts…. In one round I hit him twelve straight jabs before he even countered…..He hit me a loud punch in the chest in the second round but it did not bother me…..I cut his face, lips….He was bleeding bad and I could hear people screaming to stop it…."

Bass landed a few solid shots but the Kid had him against the ropes in the fourth, cut his face in the fifth, opened a gash on his mouth in the sixth and stopped him in the seventh, the third man stepping in to save a battered champion.

The Cuban nation celebrated when Kid Chocolate became the first of its fighters to win a world crown. Chocolate had not only become a national idol in Cuba, he had become a household name to the world and the Kid feasted on the banquet.

Besides his boxing income, Chocolate made endorsement money and even posed nude for an art book, an event that in its time was very daring, for it was unusual that a professional athlete would pose in the buff. The Kid grabbed headlines for the nude posing, which art critics described as the unveiling of a "perfectly symmetric" body.

The Chocolate man was an impeccable dresser. He did not dress gaudily but elegant in satin, summer linen and silk. His shoes were patent leather two toned, always well shined; his ties were held in place by a gold clip with a diamond.

Three months after beating Bass, the Kid defended his title against old foe Joey Scalfaro, who was known as the "Fighting Chemist," for he had used his ring earnings to pay for his pharmaceutical studies. The first fight with Scalfaro had been a draw but the second was a blowout, Chocolate stopping Joey in the first round.

This was Chocolate's prime for although still very young, the Kid had worked hard at ruining his health and conditioning and his skills would begin to erode soon, early in his career.

The Kid scored four more wins, one of them over a top gun named Lew Feldman before moving up to the lightweights to challenge the mighty Tony Canzoneri for the world crown.

Little Tony was a master among the ring ropes. At the time he faced Chocolate, Tony was a twenty three year old ring idol with over 100 pro fights and only nine defeats on his ledger. Canzoneri had knockouts over Jackie Kid Berg and Al Singer and wins over Benny Bass, Bud Taylor and dozens of good fighters.

The fight was described by the New York Times as "one of the greatest lightweight championship battles in local ring annals." Canzoneri and Chocolate set a blistering pace in a match that changed at times from a boxing chess match, each man maneuvering, feinting seeking an opening, to a slugging brawl in which both men traded vicious hooks and uppercuts. In the seventh round the Kid hit Canzoneri with lightning combinations, cutting his lip and eyebrow. In the eighth the tenacious lightweight came back, slamming hard body shots to Chocolate's rib cage. The fight was close; Canzoneri was battered but ended the fight stronger than the Cuban.

Canzoneri won a split decision but some sports writers –including the boxing reporter for The New York Times- felt Chocolate should have been declared the winner.

The Kid felt he was robbed but he was too busy buying a sixteen cylinder, silver Cadillac and a few more suits and trinkets, to dwell on the loss. He returned to Havana on a first class cruise cabin, taking with him a sizable cargo that included eighty suits, fifty pairs of shoes and the new car.

He fought twice in Havana, the second fight being a defense of his junior lightweight title to Davey Abad, a well known Panamanian fighter who had a win over Tony Canzoneri. Abad was a good fighter but not in the same league with Chocolate, who won with ease, coasting to an easy victory.

In the two months following his title defense, Chocolate returned to the United States where he won six fights in eight weeks, winning them all and beating Lew Feldman and Roger Bernard, two solid performers of the era.

In good condition, Chocolate faced Jackie Kid Berg once more, but his skills were already eroding. His lightning speed was still there but in spurts rather than every second of every minute. His punches still came in clusters but he sometimes missed, something inconceivable only a couple of years in the past. Still, like the Canzoneri fight, the second loss to Berg was a close fought affair that some sportswriters felt should have resulted with Chocolate as the winner.

The Kid fought eleven times in the last five months of 1932, winning them all, defending his junior lightweight title twice and also winning the featherweight crown from his old foe Fidel LaBarba, in another close fight where the sportswriters were split on their judgment, many disagreeing with Chocolate winning the title belt.

After a five month layoff sampling the restaurants and nightclubs of Havana, Chocolate defended his titles in the same month beating Johnny Farr and Seaman Watson before booking a first class statcroom on a ship to Europe.

He won fights in Madrid, Barcelona and Paris, where he hung out with Carlos Gardel, the most famous Tango singer in the world, caught the shows at the Follies-Bergere, sampled French prostitutes and drank magnums of champagne while dazzling the crowds as he walked –impeccably dressed- on the streets of the City of Lights.

He fought a rematch with Canzoneri at the end of 1933, in a bout that would mark the end of his peak years and his decline. Tony was still a well conditioned battler and Chocolate was no longer the burning comet. Canzoneri stopped the Kid in two swift rounds.

A month after losing to Canzoneri, Chocolate lost his title to Frankie Klick by a seventh round TKO, looking worn and sluggish. Klick was a competent pro, but his quality was far from greatness, having lost three in a row before facing

Chocolate, making his win over the Cuban Bon Bon the biggest upset of the year, an outcome totally unexpected in the fight game.

Pincho Gutierrez was a good manager who loved boxing and cared for his fighters; he understood that Chocolate was on the downslide and would not retire at the age of twenty three, so adjustments had to be made.

Gutierrez lowered the bar, matching Chocolate with care. Staying away from the heavy punchers that would damage the Kid, Pincho featured the former champion in main events in Havana against imported journeymen club fighters.

Chocolate also fought in the United States, packing venues like Ridgewood Grove and the Broadway Arena against modest opposition. The Kid was half of what he had been but half of Chocolate was much more than most fighters could handle; of the last fifty fights of his career, Chocolate lost only three and drew five.

His last great ring performance came in 1938, when in front of a packed arena in Havana he outscored Fillo Echevarria, a very tough Spanish featherweight who held wins over Baby Arizmendi and Corporal Izzy Schwartz. At twenty seven a washed up shell of his former self, Chocolate trained diligently and recaptured some flashes of his youth, pulling off a hard fought win.

His next bout after beating Fillo was his last fight, a merciful draw against Nick Jerome, a tough Brooklyn club brawler. Jerome had a 28-20-4 record when he faced Chocolate; he made the great fighter look like an old man.

Kid Chocolate's final ledger included 136 wins -51 of them by KO- 10 defeats -2 by KO- 6 draws and one ND, totaling 152 pro fights with a 34% knockout average.

All he had left was his house in Havana. The Kid survived after retirement doing endorsements for a dairy company, a restaurant and a sporting goods store; he trained several fighters of little consequence and was a partner in a Havana boxing gym. He was occasionally arrested for being intoxicated in public or smoking reefer but friends always paid the fines.

The Kid never complained. Sports journalist Sarvelio Del Valle remembers interviewing a middle-aged Kid -his black slicked hair turning the color of cotton- and the topic of misspent fortunes came into the conversation.

"I felt sad to see him flat broke," Del Valle said, "Neatly dressed but flat broke. I was young and I made a dumb comment I should have avoided had I been older and wiser. I said something like – Wow, Kid, you really made and spent a fortune or two- and the Kid looked at me and smiled."

"I spent a lot of money on booze, reefer, women, nightclubs, gambling and parties," Chocolate answered smiling, "and I wasted the rest."

Chapter Seven: the Legend of the Cuban Baron

Our story begins in Santiago de Cuba.

Santiago is located in the southeastern tip of Cuba, where a green valley of mountains and flowing creeks meet a deep bay of tropical waters. For almost five centuries, since 1514, the city has survived plunder by pirate attacks, wars against the French and the British, hurricanes and revolutions.

By 1907, Santiago de Cuba was a bustling seaport center, a city of cobbled streets, colonial stone, and stucco homes protected by iron-grilled gates and horse-drawn carts. Only nine years earlier, Santiago had been the center stage of a world conflict, as United States Navy iron ships had pounded Admiral Cervera's wooden fleet into oblivion, bringing defeat to the Iberians and wiping out the last remains of the once powerful Spanish empire.

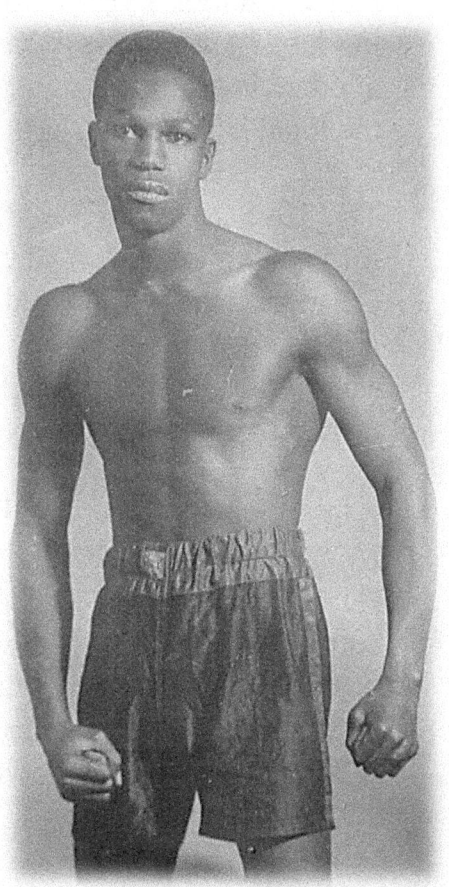

On Wednesday, April 5, 1907, a premature baby was born in Santiago de Cuba, baptized with the melodic name of Ramon Cathcart Grenot, being the sixth child of a Jamaican couple who had settled in Cuba sometime after the Spanish-American War.

Thomas Cathcart was a mechanic who worked hard to provide for his family but lived in an age before antibiotics and laser surgeries, dying of a ruptured appendix when Ramon was only 5. Ramon's mother, Clemencia Grenot, returned to Jamaica with five of her children, inexplicably leaving Ramon behind to be cared by an aunt.

Ramon grew up in Santiago de Cuba in blue-collar poverty. He worked from early childhood, selling mangoes to travelers at the train station. He was a self-sufficient boy who earned his keep from an early age and managed to study all the way through the seventh grade, a considerable feat for a boy growing up in an impoverished environment during a time when making a wage to earn a meal was more important than an education.

During Ramon's years growing up, boxing was developing into a major sport in Cuba. American sailors from nearby Guantanamo Naval Base fought one another in smokers, contributing greatly to create interest in boxing among the local islanders.

The 1915 Johnson-Willard heavyweight title fight consecrated Cuba as an international center in the pugilistic world. Young boys in every town and village in Cuba dreamed of fame between the ropes and big purses for important fights. Ramon was one of those boys inspired by press reports of ring heroes. While living in Las Tunas, he hung a sugarcane bag full of rags from a tree and practiced his first boxing moves.

Ramon began boxing while still underage, borrowing a birth certificate of an older friend named Ramon Castillo. Not much is known of his amateur career. He probably started in Cuba, fighting in cock-fighting arenas or dance halls converted into fight smokers where amateurs were paid off with a few quarters, enough for a couple of square meals at cheap eating houses. An old newspaper clipping states that Castillo won an AAU championship in the U.S., but nothing is known about this trip abroad, perhaps his first of many globe-trotting adventures.

By 1924 young Ramon Castillo was a good friend of Kid Charol, a sensational Cuban national middleweight champion who worked with Castillo in the gym, helping him perfect the left hook and suggesting that he turn pro, which Ramon did, scoring a first-round knockout over a willing club fighter named Dativo Fuentes. Thus, Ramon Castillo started a career that would extend for over two decades and take him to several nations and continents.

Castillo was a very intelligent young man. Although his education only ranged as far as the seventh grade, by his teen years he was well read, being fluent in Spanish and English, and with a working knowledge of Hebrew, which he'd learned from a neighbor. Ramon was a handsome youth with an engaging smile, a Swiss-chocolate complexion and an elegant personal style.

Nature had gifted him with a hard, lean body and hollow bones, for although he was a featherweight, Ramon was an inch short of 6 feet, giving him a marked height advantage over anyone in his division. Weight, however, seemed to matter little to him, for throughout his career he often fought lightweights, welterweights and the occasional middleweight. Castillo was tall, fast, could hit with power and had an iron chin.

Ramon Castillo was part of a small crop of very tough Cuban road warriors that were active in the 1920s and early '30s. The group included heavyweight Goyito Rico, middleweights Peter Sung and Eliseo Quintana, and welterweights Serafin Centeno and Baby La Paz. The traveling fighters were active throughout South and Central America as well as the small islands of the Caribbean, fighting in numerous venues against other tough locals with bold names, such as Trinidad's Diablo Rojo and Jamaica's popular Kid Silver.

Ramon Castillo would become the most traveled of the group. After a few bouts in Cuba, including a draw in a rematch with Dativo Fuentes, Castillo - now billed as Champion of Oriente Province -- went on the road, leaving Cuba for almost a decade, seeking his fortune and living a very interesting life.

First stop was the U.S., living in New York and later in Chicago, scoring a string of wins that included knockouts over Harry Kid Brown and KO Brennan - good fighters -- and draws with some prominent leather slingers, including Baby Joe Gans, southpaw Harry Wallach, and a tough lightweight named Benny Nabors. The young Cuban was soon billed as the Colored Lightweight Champion of the World. A newspaper clipping of the time indicates that Castillo did not lose a single newspaper decision in his American tour.

Afterward, Ramon Castillo headed for Europe, where he became a boxing star in France, Spain, and Hungary, where Castillo, now dubbed the Cuban Baron, was more than just a good pug making money fighting the best in Europe.

Parallel to his fighting career, Ramon became a journalist and author of pocket novels, writing newspaper articles and dime novels under his real name, Ramon C. Grenot. His writing style in Spanish was fluid, showing excellent command of journalistic structure. He became a well-known figure among the European intellectuals of his time, becoming fluent in French and picking up a working knowledge of other languages.

A university in Spain granted him an honorary degree, the city of Budapest proclaimed him an "adopted son," and a playwright in Holland wrote a play based on the adventures of the Cuban featherweight. The play *Waar De*

Rumba Lokt featured actor Robert Sobels in the role of Ramon Castillo.

As an entertainer, Ramon was a first-rate tap dancer. A French article of the time commented that Castillo was good enough to be considered a partner for Josephine Baker. He did share stages with the legendary Nicholas Brothers of Cotton Club fame and formed his own nightclub act, providing another source of income for his expensive lifestyle.

For Castillo was a man who dressed sharp and was often photographed at social functions dressed in formal wear or an elegant suit; for a time, he even had his own chauffeur, yet he was not an irresponsible cad, for he even provided a pension to the mother that had abandoned him in his infancy.

Ramon Castillo's life encompassed the artist world of Paris in the '20s, where the Cuban became a good friend of the legendary tango star Carlos Gardel. It has been said there are two kinds of tango singers: Gardel and everyone else.

The famous singer and Castillo were good friends, talking music and boxing at the famous Mont Matre Club. It was there where, according to Kid Chocolate biographers, Castillo introduced the famous singer to his fellow Cuban, the world champion on tour of Europe. Gardel, Chocolate, and Castillo partied together, enjoying the champagne and showgirls of the Parisian clubs.

Artistic ventures aside, Ramon Castillo was above all a very good fighter, scoring a knockout over German lightweight champion Fritz Reppel and a wins on points over Spanish welterweight titleholder Ricardo Alis. In a bout with a Spanish middleweight brawler named Pere Antonio, Castillo was dropped in the second round by a hard right cross. Surviving the round, he proceeded to give the bigger man a boxing lesson, winning easily on points.

The Cuban Baron fought like he danced, smooth and slick, long arms jabbing and crossing, hook flowing from the straight left, footwork gliding without effort. Ramon Castillo was a craftsman at his game. A possible clash with Tony Canzoneri fell through when Castillo lost on a foul to French featherweight champion Gustave Humery.

As political changes came to Europe with the rise of fascism and Spain spiraled towards a civil war, Cuban newspapers speculated that their globe-trotting featherweight had been killed in a cross fire in the early fighting. Ramon had been near enough to the roaring guns to understand the brutality being unleashed in the Spanish conflict; he packed his expensive leather luggage and headed back to Cuba.

Ramon continued to dance, write, and fight, scoring a win over a future Spanish welterweight champion -- then based in Havana -- Jose Garcia Alvarez. By 1938 Castillo was an English professor at a private school, Academia Superacion, in Havana and still dabbling in his intellectual pursuits.

The Second World War interrupted Castillo's ring career and nightclub performances. He joined the merchant marine and later the U.S. Coast Guard, spending most of the war crossing U-boat-infested waters, carrying weapons and supplies to Allied Forces fighting Nazis.

After his tour of duty, the Cuban Baron returned to the stage and ring, but his career was winding down with age and loss of reflexes. He retired after fighting a four round ND in 1948, ending a career that had probably encompassed over 150 pro fights and dozens of exhibitions.

The wandering former fighter settled in New York, where he became a boson in the Merchant Marine, a job that fed his wanderlust. He married for the second time (little is known about the first marriage) in 1957. Three children would be born out of the second marriage, and all would graduate from college, an accomplishment that made the old fighter proud.

The old warrior was pushing 70 when he was pensioned by the National Maritime Union. He died at the age of 88, in the Bronx, New York.

Somewhere in time he's still with us, in yellowed clippings that praise his ring performances, in lines of record books, in history footnotes of Carlos Gardel and Kid Chocolate, and most of all in the memories of his friends and family, who knew him as an artist, a writer, an entertainer, and a ring warrior who fought with professional pride and a touch of class.

Always a touch of class.

Armando Santiago decked the mighty Tony Canzoneri for a nine count and scored knockouts over Joey Sangor and Dick Finnegan.

Santiago Esparraguera was a good boxer-puncher and champion of Cuba.

Kid Tunero holds five victories over world champions.

Cirilin Olano was one of the fighters in the tournament to determine who would earn Benny Leonard's crown.

 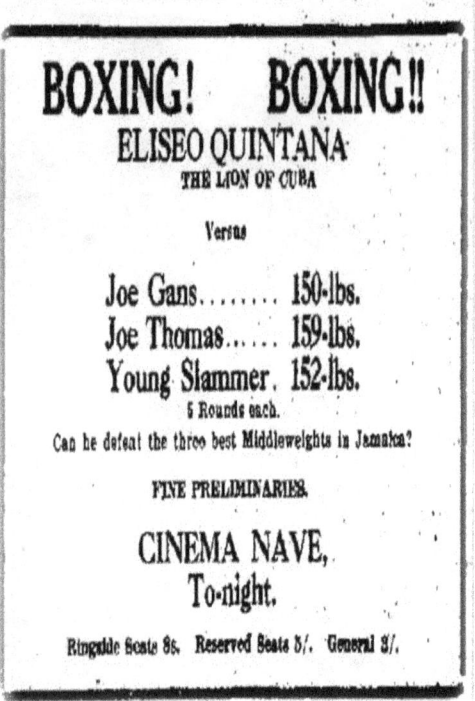

Eliseo Quintana –The Lion of Cuba– defeated three top Jamaican fighters in a Kingston boxing card.

Relampago Saguero was national champion of Cuba and a top welterweight internationally.

CHINO ALVAREZ
Southern Lightweight Champion

Chino Alvarez was a top featherweight and lightweight who won and lost to Hall of Famer Lew Jenkins.

CHAPTER EIGHT: THE TWENTIES AND THIRTIES

Kid Chocolate and Black Bill were the international stars of Cuban boxing during their time but the two decades from 1920 to the end of the thirties era produced some additional first rate talent.

The best Cuban heavyweight of this time was Goyito Rico, a hard hitting dirty fighter who had power and strength but lacked speed and finesse. Rico had a fair career at the journeyman level as he scored wins over Ted Sandwina, Clayton Petersen, Tiny Jim Herman and Argentine champion Raul Bianchi but was defeated three times by heavyweight contender Isidoro Gastanaga, a fourth bout ending in a no contest.

The outstanding Cuban light heavyweights of the era were Corporal Santiago Esparraguera, Roleaux Saguero and Clemente Sanchez.

The Cuban soldier held national titles at light heavyweight and heavyweight. An excellent boxer with a crisp jab and solid power, Corporal Esparraguera scored a first round knockout of Frank Hoche, a Frenchman who had fought draws with Dixie Kid. The Corporal also scored wins over American journeymen Homer Smith and Chief Metoquah, as well as a couple of knockouts over Nero Chink, a tough and tricky Puerto Rican fighter, while losing to world rated Jack Renault and Leo Houck.

The Corporal's nemesis was Roleaux Saguero, also a good boxer with power in his hands but a soft chin as a handicap. Esparraguera fought Saguero ten times as they took turns holding the Cuban light heavyweight and heavyweight crowns and all ten bouts ended in knockouts, the Corporal winning four and Roleaux winning six.

Light heavyweight Clemente Sanchez "The Panther of Camajuani," was a top main event fighter and road warrior who was very popular in both Cuba and Jamaica but tragically died from ring injuries after a 1929 bout in Uruguay.

THE MIDDLEWEIGHTS

The middleweights produced Kid Tunero, one of the greatest fighters never to hold a world title. Tunero stands out in this era head and shoulders above the middleweight talent produced in Cuba during this time period. A handsome, well mannered and soft spoken mulatto from the town of Las Tunas, he was a leading middleweight contender for over a decade, losing on points to Marcel Thil in his only bid for a world crown.

Kid Tunero holds five victories over world champions. He beat Marcel Thil one out of three; defeated Anton Chrisotforides twice and drew once, defeated Ken Overlin on points and won a split decision over a young and dangerous Ezzard Charles. Besides the impressive victories over four champions, Tunero also had wins and losses with Holman Williams, a triumph over Jose Basora a draw with European champion Ignacio Ara and a string of victories over the best European fighters of the era.

The classy Tunero was a good friend of Ernest Hemingway with whom he occasionally sparred.

Trainer Jose Caron Gonzalez was a sparring partner for Tunero in Havana during the forties and held the middleweight in high regard.

"He was a textbook fighter," Caron said, "He did not make mistakes. Tunero took his time, looked for openings and was a good thinker at strategy. He was so good he was boring to watch. There was no anger or desperation and he took his time and did everything perfect and was a master at his craft…"

Tunero had a 96-32-16 record with 34 KO wins and only 2 KO defeats. After his fighting career ended he became a top manager and trainer in Barcelona, Spain, managing fellow Cuban Jose Legra to world titles and several Spaniards to European crowns.

Former lightweight contender Frankie Otero visited Tunero at his Barcelona gym in the seventies and was impressed with the venerable old man.

"He spoke in a very correct manner," Otero said, "with good diction and without cursing. He was a class act, a real gentleman."

Other top Cuban middleweights of the time included Kid Charol, Eliseo Quintana and Antonio Dominguez.

Charol –real name Esteban Gallard- came from the city of Sagua in central Cuba. An excellent boxer with a crisp punch, he was a dominant figure in Cuban and international boxing, beating Panama Joe Gans and Larry Estridge as well as fighting a draw with Dave Shade. Tragically, he died of tuberculosis when he was only 28 years old.

Eliseo Quintana was tough as nails. He did not reach the status of world class that Tunero or Charol achieved, but he was a star performer in Cuba and Jamaica, highly regarded as one of the toughest main event fighters in the Caribbean. On the 28th of June, 1924, Quintana –dubbed the Lion of Cuba- fought three Jamaican middleweights in one night at the Cinema Nave in Kingston, Jamaica. He beat all three, two of them by knockouts. Quintana liked Jamaica, where he married a local girl and lived until his death in 1945.

Antonio Dominguez –from Camaguey- was a good boxer and fair puncher who faced some top guns of his era including Tommy Freeman, Baby Joe Gans and Ignacio Ara. He was popular in both Cuba and Florida rings.

THE WELTERWEIGHTS

The welterweights produced Relampago Saguero and Baby La Paz.

Relampago Saguero –real name Reemberto Duo- was a rugged performer who was the dominant figure in the welterweight division in Cuba during the late twenties and early thirties. A national champion, Saguero won four out of four against Spaniard Hilario Martinez, a world class fighter who had wins over Jack Britton, Johnny Dundee and Sid Terris.

The tough Cuban also showed his skills in rings in Puerto Rico, Mexico and the United States. Saguero claimed over 150 pro fights. His still incomplete record shows a creditable 89-32-9 with 43 KO wins and only one loss by stoppage. After his ring career, Relampago stayed in boxing as third man in the ring, working many shows in Cuba and the United States. He died in the United States in 1996, at the ripe old age of 88.

Baby La Paz –from the town of Fomento- was a likeable seaman in the Cuban Navy who boxed well and did not mind traveling to fight in foreign lands. Besides Cuba -where he held the national welterweight title- La Paz fought in Peru, Panama and Jamaica. His brother Jose La Paz was middleweight champion of Cuba.

THE LIGHTWEIGHTS

The 1920 decade started with Cuba's first boxing idol, Lalo Dominguez, followed by the capable Cirilin Olano who fought in an international lightweight elimination tournament to determine a successor for Benny Leonard.

One star of the late twenties, often forgotten in the present day era was Armando "Jack" Santiago. A hard hitting lightweight who fought out of two cities -Havana and Chicago- Santiago was a product of the early Cuban amateur program where he won a national title. Turning pro, he won the national lightweight championship in 1927 by scoring a sensational knockout over a slick young fighter named Anisio Orbeta. Both men fought on even terms until Santiago landed a crushing body blow, stopping Orbeta.

Santiago was a good boxer and a solid puncher; at one time he was written about as a possible contender for a world title after he scored impressive knockouts over Joey Sangor and Dick Finnegan, both well regarded, competent fighters.

Hard hitting Santiago is best known for having decked the great Tony Canzoneri for a seven count in the first round of a 1929 confrontation eventually won by Tony on a fifth round TKO. Santiago also twice tangled with world champion Benny Bass.

The top Cuban lightweight of the thirties was Oscar –Chino- Alvarez. Born in the seaport town of Mariel, near Havana, his Cuban-Chinese parents migrated to Tampa when Chino was three years old. He became an idol in both Tampa and Havana. Turning pro as a 98 pound flyweight at the tender age of fifteen, Alvarez logged a pro career ledger of 126-40-17 with 76 knockout victories and two ND, growing from a flyweight to a junior welterweight, facing top men in three different weight classes. Alvarez was a good boxer and a hard puncher whose career spawned from 1928-1946.

Chino won and lost to the hard hitting lightweight Lew Jenkins, both victory and defeat coming by the way of knockouts. Both men were considered among the best punchers pound per pound at any weight and it was safe money that the fights would not go the distance. Both times they clashed in Dallas, in 1938 and 1940.

In their first bout Chino was a young veteran with over 150 pro bouts and Jenkins was a hard punching prospect with a win over veteran Lew Feldman. The Chinese Cuban slugger and the motorcycling wild man from Texas fought a hard brawl and Chino won by a TKO in eight rounds, the most significant win of his career. By the time they battled the second time, Alvarez was a top pro near the end of his career and the hard drinking Jenkins was on a hot streak, only four months away from winning the lightweight title. Jenkins surprised Alvarez, knocking him out in the first round with a two punch opening salvo.

Another highlight victory in Alvarez career was over fellow Tampa resident Manuel Quintero. As the opening bell rang, Quintero had been praying, but as he turned he was surprised by Alvarez who had rushed from his corner as the bell rang, unloading his bombs, dropping Manuel on his own corner, scoring a KO in the first round.

Alvarez lost to the fabulous Cocoa Kid and to Eddie Cool but also scored wins over Cool, over Cuban national welterweight champions Relampago Saguero and Baby La Paz, Cuban lightweight king Sixto Morales, as well as over Charlie Gommer, Enrique Santos and many tough main event fighters active in his era.

After retiring, Alvarez remained in Tampa where he died in 1996, less than a week away from his 83th birthday.

Aramis del Pino was an outstanding boxer who won Cuban national amateur titles in two weight classes. Del Pino turned pro as a main event fighter and after a fair ring career earned a living as a boxing promoter, physical education teacher and sportswriter.

Enrique Santos –El Baturrito Holguinero- from the city of Holguin was a tough main event fighter who also fought in Jamaica and the United States.

Sixto Morales was a prolific road warrior who fought a large part of his career in Florida rings.

Joe Coego was a charismatic fighter who fought pro during the whole decade of the thirties, twice holding the Cuban lightweight championship and also challenging for the national welterweight crown. Coego –who worked as a lineman for the Cuban Electric Company- was a busy fighter with considerable heart and ordinary power. The popular Coego traded leather with the best lightweights and several of the finest welters active in Cuba and the Caribbean.

Other top lightweights of the era included knockout artist Juan Cepero and the slick and crafty Anisio Orbeta, who later became a promoter, manager and trainer of fighters.

THE SMALLER GUNS

The smaller weights also had some talent with international experience in the 1920-1930 time periods.

National featherweight champion Gilbert Castillo had a busy career where he beat Tony Leto and Chino Alvarez and lost on points to Petey Sarron.

Anthony Santana was a knockout artist from the city of Ciego de Avila who was trained in New York by master teacher Jimmy De Forest. Santana had over sixty pro fights in Cuba and the United States, but quit the ring while in his early twenties to work as a lineman for the Cuban Telephone Company. Santana became one of Cuba's top referees, working fights involving several champions, including Sugar Ray Robinson.

Santana's bantamweight nemesis was Divino Rueda from the city of Cienfuegos. The tough scrappers fought at least three times, Santana winning two on points and Rueda scoring a knockout in the third bout. Rueda had a good career fighting in both Cuba and Panama before retiring to become a trainer and gym owner in the city of Cienfuegos.

Flyweight Genaro Pino was a top gun among the little men. He was Cuban flyweight and bantamweight champion, holding a win and a draw with world champion Petey Sarron. Pino was a world class fighter but was overshadowed by Black Bill, who beat him three out of four times.

Rafael Valdez, who held the national flyweight title, did well in Cuba but lost often on trips to Europe.

FIGHTERS FROM OTHER LANDS

Many top fighters of the age fought in Cuba and some – like Spanish featherweight Julian Fillo Echevarria- stayed in the island, raising families, being adopted as locals.

Among the top Spanish fighters displaying their skills in Havana rings one must mention European Middleweight Champion Ignacio Ara, a magnificent craftsman who was never stopped in a 193 bout career. The iron chinned Ara had an impressive ledger having faced the best in his class, including Joe Dundee, Marcel Thil, Kid Tunero, Izzy Groves, Canada Lee, Relampago Saguero, Eddie Ran and Sergeant Sammy Baker.

Two very good heavyweights from Spain travelled to Cuba. The best known was European titleholder Paulino Uzcudun and the other one was Isidoro Gastanaga, a very hard puncher who liked to drink and party, dying young in a violent brawl in an Argentine tavern. World class lightweight Hilario Martinez and Spanish welterweight champion Ricardo Alis were also often featured in Cuban boxing cards.

A middleweight from Spanish Morocco named Abd El Kebir resided and fought some bouts in Cuba. Record historians have stated that El Kebir was really an American fighter from New England named Billy Edwards, based on a comment made in a Ring Magazine of the era.

Abd El Kebir, however, was not an American.

Cuba's "Diario de La Marina" stated on several occasions that El Kebir was from Spanish Morocco. His interviews on Cuban press were done in Spanish and the newspapers did not make any references as to the fighter having an American accent.

Spain's newspapers -La Vanguardia and Mundo Deportivo- referred to him also as being a black Moroccan, interviewed him often and reported of his fights in Egypt.

El Kebir was a stablemate of Spanish Welter Champion Ricardo Alis and his chief sparring partner in Barcelona. Both traveled together from Europe to Cuba and on to the United States and on at least one occasion fought each other to save the card. There are no mentions of El Kebir being American in any of the numerous reports in Cuban and Spanish publications of the era.

Other well known fighters that traded leather on Cuban rings included handsome heavyweight contender Young Stribling, Luis Firpo, Arturo Godoy, top middleweight Panama Joe Gans, welterweight Tommy White, lightweights Fast Black and Joe Dundee, Belgians Armand and Arthur Schaeckels and a most interesting character named Nubby Joe Gans.

Nubby Joe –real named James Cleary- was an American fighter nicknamed "Nubby" because he was missing one hand. In the ring a glove was attached to the nub, but in spite of his handicap, Cleary was a solid main event fighter who scored wins over Lalo Dominguez and hard punching Agustin Lillo.

Julian Fillo Echevarria, a world class pro who won and lost to champions.

Fillo Echevarria
Vs Kid
Chocolate

CHAPTER NINE: THE LIFE AND TIMES OF AN OLD WARRIOR

The year is 1927 and the boy is not yet fifteen years of age, weighing in at a hundred and ten pounds after a solid meal.

The boy is worried, but does not show it. He is minutes away from his first pro fight, the virgin walk to ringside, the strange feeling that one is now the center of attention that this is no sparring session but the real thing, the first pro fight that one will never forget, regardless of outcome.

It has been a short ride. A few months before, wishing to learn self-defense, he signs up for boxing lessons at the gym in San Sebastian, his hometown in the Basque region of Spain, near the French border.

The gym is crowded with hungry fighters and little attention is paid to the boy, who trains himself, picking up knowledge from listening to trainers give advice, watching others, from imitating moves, After a few months of training and sparring with other green boys and after a short amateur career, a promoter offers him a pro fight and the boy agrees, eagerly wishing to prove himself.

The day before the bout the fourteen-year old boy learns that the match is a main event ten rounder against Martinez Segundo, a veteran of eighteen pro fights.

I'm being set up -the boy thinks- I'm expected to be another notch on Martinez' record, an easy knockout to pad his ledger. I have fought very little as an amateur and my first pro fight ever is going to be a ten-rounder. It's not fair, but I am not going to back down. I gave my word and I will do my best tonight.

The boy's name is Julian Echevarria, but in the Basque region they call him Fillo -which means child or boy- because of his small size in a land that is producing big men of the ring, like Paolino Uzcudun and Isidoro Gastañaga.

The arena in San Sebastian is packed with men wearing berets and smoking brown cigars. Martinez Segundo -a grown man with a five o'clock shadow and battle scars on his face- is several pounds heavier than the boy.

Martinez comes out confidently, looking to end the fight quickly with a swift blow well delivered against the chin of the inexperienced child. The first hook lands and the boy does not flinch, but counters with awkward punches thrown with wild abandon. Martinez Segundo lands a second hard shot followed by a quick combination and the scrawny kid answers with a volley of his own, rocking the experienced fighter with a wild roundhouse punch.

The pattern is set in the first round. Martinez is the better boxer but his power does not make a dent on the hard little boy from San Sebastian. Fillo, the raw novice, is tough, hits hard enough to hurt Martinez and is also endowed with an abundance of heart.

Martinez boxes, throws combinations and attempts to side step and confuse the boy. Echevarria attacks, misses two, three, two more, but also connects, raising angry welts on his opponent's flesh. Martinez Segundo backs up, attempts to counter punch. Fillo does not offer the pause, constantly swinging, hooking, swarming, chopping down the seasoned fighter with desperate energy.

Martinez Segundo collapses in the second round, the first victim of the boy's raw power and iron will. Fillo Echevarria has won the first pro fight of his life, becoming a prospect in Spanish boxing circles.

The knockout over Martinez Segundo impresses the Spanish fight crowd so much that flyweights and bantamweights go into hiding. Fillo only fights five more fights over the next couple of years, scoring a draw, two wins and two losses, one of them a ten rounder to a good bantamweight prospect named Mariano Arilla.

At seventeen -with just a few pro fights and almost three years of gym work- he has evolved into a real pro fighter, with proper balance, a sense of timing and a style of his own. Although some sportswriters will refer to him in the future as a slugger, Echevarria is more counter puncher than brawler. He attacks in spurts, counterpunches effectively when attacked, fights well inside, punches without fear and is blessed with a granite chin and the stamina of youth.

Enter Manolo Braña, a Cuban promoter with good contacts in Spain. The Iberian promoters book their top talent in Havana rings including Hilario Martinez -who defeated Jack Britton and Johnny Dundee- welter Ricardo Alis and heavyweights Isidoro Gastañaga and Paolino Uzcudun.

Cuba has become a hot bed of boxing activity. Between 1925-1930, the active talent includes future world champion Kid Chocolate, flyweight contender Black Bill, middleweight Kid Charol -who fought a draw with Dave Shade- top welterweight Relampago Saguero, lightweights Cirilin Olano and Armando Santiago, as well as dozens of main event performers and good club fighters.

Braña is looking for a heavyweight but his first choice is the boy from San Sebastian. An offer is made for a trip to Cuba and the chance to fight top talent. Echeverria does not hesitate, being a hungry young fighter with a sense of adventure. How could a boy say no to an opportunity to leave his hometown of San Sebastian in the cold Iberian Peninsula and cross the sea, expenses paid to a tropical land of sun baked beaches?

The promoter does not waste time. Echeverria shadowboxes and works out on the deck of the passenger ship headed for Havana. The young pro does not mind working hard. At seventeen he is disciplined, clean living and mature beyond his years.

In 1930, the Cuban economy is hurting but fairly stable in comparison to their neighbor to the north, crunched by a stock market crash and a time of soup kitchens and farm foreclosures.

Fillo falls in love with Cuba's tropical beaches, sun bleached avenues, musical tempo and loud, boisterous culture. The Island, in turn, adopts the little Basque fighter. Within months, Echevarria becomes a local hero with a cheering audience of transplanted Spaniards and local Cuban fans that appreciate his hard counterpunching style.

Fillo beats every Cuban bantamweight that dares to face him. In 1932, the nineteen-year old fighter faces the biggest test of his career, a ten rounder against former flyweight champion Corporal Izzy Schwartz, a veteran with over 120 pro fights on his record.

The Corporal is ready for retirement and Fillo is the messenger. Echevarria's persistent slugging wears down the old soldier. The fight is stopped in the fifth round. Havana fight fans mill around Fillo at ringside, shaking his bandaged hands, slapping his sweat drenched back, congratulating him on scoring a crisp win over a former world champion.

The local celebrity status does not overwhelm Fillo. He works in restaurant management while living an athlete's life, fighting often, defeating Baby Malpica, Divino Rueda and knockout artist Anthony Santana.

Santana is a tough little scrapper who won dozens of fights in various Cuban venues, New York City -where Jimmy De Forrest trained him- as well as in Panama. Fillo and Santana fight three times. Echevarria wins two on points and scores a TKO victory in the other bout, counterpunching effectively against the Cuban prospect.

In 1934, Fillo returns to San Sebastian to visit relatives. In the Basque country he is also a celebrity, as the local papers have been reporting his Cuban victories. He accepts offers from local promoters and stays home for over a year fighting seventeen times, winning a ten rounder over Spanish lightweight champion Segundo Bartos, defeating former Olympian Lorenzo Vitria and fighting a draw with Carlos Flix in a challenge for the Spanish bantamweight crown.

At the age of twenty-two, in 1935, after fighting briefly in the United States, Fillo —now a featherweight- faces Baby Arizmendi, another former world champion -partial recognition- with a sixty fight record in his young twenty-one years.

It's a war of attrition, an honest brawl where Fillo's raw courage, good counterpunching and top condition earn him a victory in ten stanzas. It is a significant victory for the young featherweight who can now boast of an impressive record with two wins over former titleholders. There is serious talk after the Arizmendi victory of Fillo being in line for a non-title ten rounder with titleholder Freddie Miller.

Waiting for an opportunity to tangle with Miller, Echeverria stays busy winning club fights against tough Conrado Conde, Baby Face Matheson and other journeymen opponents.

Freddie Miller, a 24-year-old from Ohio, is a slick southpaw with almost 200 fights on his ledger, including almost a decade as a contender or champion. A supreme globetrotter, he has fought in dozens of American and English fight venues as well as in France, Belgium, Spain, Canada and Mexico.

The Miller-Echeverria fight takes place in Havana in 1936. Fillo fights in top form but his best is not good enough. Miller is faster, too fast for Fillo to counterpunch effectively, too fast to chase. The champion's right jab snaps constantly at Echevarria. Miller moves out of harm's way, winning the ten rounder with ease, but Fillo remains a hometown hero in his adopted Havana.

"Miller is one of the greatest featherweights of all time," Fillo says after the match, "Fighting him is an honor. He anticipated all my moves and he was hard to corner. Miller is a tricky fighter who has very good aim. He knows how to place his punches."

Less than three weeks after losing to Miller, Fillo returns to the ring, stopping journeyman George Dixon in two. Before 1936 ends he scores a significant win over a tough Filipino fighter -Paul Dano-, who had beaten him in Los Angeles in 1935.

Echevarria's most important fight takes place in 1938. Kid Chocolate is at the tail end of a brilliant career, his amazing ability dulled by years of whoring, drinking and smoking reefer. Chocolate is only twenty-seven, a couple of years older than Fillo, but the Cuban Bon Bon is a fighter whose talent has eroded.

Although Chocolate is clearly past his peak, he is still a topnotch fighter who has not been defeated in his last thirty-some outings. The Kid is no longer a meteor in the fistic world but he is still a formidable foe. His lightning speed has withered down but he is still quite fast, fighting in quick spurts; the smooth combinations are still thrown, with less frequency but with pinpoint accuracy. In a recent bout with Young Chappie, the Cuban won easily but looked bored and sluggish, generating speculation that the former champion was ready to hang up the gloves forever.

The Chocolate-Echevarria match is a Cuban promoter's dream, matching the top ticket sellers in the island: a fading superstar with a younger contender, a master boxer against a good counter puncher, an adopted Spaniard against a homegrown legend.

"Chocolate was my hero," Fillo says years later in an interview, "When I arrived in Cuba as an unknown fighter he was already a star in New York. I admired his skills. Chocolate was a complete fighter and I was in awe of his ability. It's tough to fight your idol."

Fillo and Chocolate are friends. The San Sebastian fighter admires the chocolate man but knows the fight game and understands that pros must fight each other and idols can be dethroned.

Fillo has the confidence of a topnotch fighter. He is an experienced pro with wins over two former champions; he has never been stopped and has done his share of decking other tough guys to the canvas.

Echevarria is offered three thousand dollars to fight Chocolate. It is a large sum of money in 1938, enough to buy a modest house or pay for a year's worth of room and board. Fillo signs the contract and the fight is set.

Echeverria's fans argue that the fight will go the distance, for both men have iron chins, but Fillo's excellent conditioning will wear down the fading former champion.

Chocolate fans point out that their fighter, even at the downhill end of his amazing career, is still an excellent performer, unbeatable at times. If his skills have eroded in half, the other half is still good enough to beat most top featherweights and lightweights. Chocolate -his fans proclaim- has not lost a fight in over two years and Echevarria will not be fast enough to overtake the Kid.

Havana newspapers write reams of copy on the upcoming event, comparing styles, quoting trainers and former fighters, taking polls among fight fans.

Chocolate has never lost on Cuban soil, as an amateur or pro. The Kid realizes that Fillo -the adopted hero- will be a hard foe to beat. The Basque is a good fighter with great condition, abundant heart and a chin made to go the full distance.

Chocolate speaks confidently but is worried, for he is well aware of his vanishing reflexes. The former champion knows that Echevarria is not just another journeyman fighter content with coasting to a sparring rhythm but a very tough pro that will fight hard all ten rounds without toppling to the canvas.

The former champion, motivated by pride, decides to train hard once more, to recapture the magic one final night.

Chocolate puts the bottles of champagne aside and trains hard for weeks, sparring dozens of rounds with four different fighters, running uphill for roadwork, abstaining from the night life to try to recapture -for a few fleeting rounds- the lightning moves of his younger days when he packed Madison Square Garden to the rafters.

Fillo works hard as always, doing miles of roadwork, sparring, aiming to be at 124 for the weigh in, ready for battle. Echevarria knows the fight game, understands strategy. The Basque fighter knows he will not win against Chocolate by counterpunching, for the flashy Cuban -even past his peak- is still a fighter with the moves of a master.

No, Fillo thinks, if I try to counter he will rip me apart with combinations, set the tempo of the fight and make me eat a lot of leather. I must beat him like Battalino and Bernstein did, by attacking him; I have to wear him down with body shots, draining him of stamina, making him fade in the late rounds. I will have to set a fast pace in order to win.

Fillo is no longer the little Basque boy from San Sebastian, but a full-grown featherweight with a fighter's face, cracked nose and thin lines of scar tissue over his eyebrows. He's twenty-four and has over ten years of fighting under his belt; he has confidence in his own ability to adapt, to switch from puncher to counter puncher, to accept or inflict pain, to dig inside for more when there's nothing left to give. He knows it all and so does Chocolate and they pack the Polar Stadium in Havana on a March afternoon.

Chocolate enters the ring wearing his trademark cocoa brown robe with gold letters. Echevarria and the former champion strip off their robes, each glancing towards the opposing corner, inspecting the physical condition of the foe to be faced, measuring the strength and power in the other man's body language.

It is four in the afternoon when the fight begins as both men move to center ring, setting the pattern of the fistic journey. Fillo moves forward, cuts the ring, attempts to corner his foe but the Cuban glides and jabs, fights in spurts, the flash combinations impressing the crowd.

Chocolate is in shape, the best he's been in at least two years. His legs are responding well and his speed is still considerable; he times his pace, saving energy for the final stretch as Echevarria chases the cocoa ghost, landing some good shots but always against a moving, slippery target.

Chocolate piles up points, wins some rounds big -with quick moves and flashy combos- and others on strategy. The Kid is a craftsman who measures distance, moves, sidesteps Fillo, jabs once, twice and opens the scar tissue over the Basque's eyebrows.

Fillo bleeds but does not complain, trying hard to slow down Chocolate. Echevarria lands a few good body shots and Chocolate gasps for air in the clinches, then moves out of range once more.

Chocolate knows how to measure distance. As he fights, his inner radar makes him aware of his body's position in relation to his foe. At times, the Kid seems to be within range of Echevarria while actually being an inch outside the danger zone; at other times Chocolate inches forward and strikes, moving towards the target with an undetected slide.

By the end of eight rounds Chocolate is assured a points victory. It is a good fight but the former champion has won most rounds, with a solid performance that flash images of his championship years. Fillo has small cuts over each eyebrow and his nose is bleeding. He knows he is behind but he is aware that Chocolate is tired.

The magnificent one is fading, Fillo thinks, I can feel him weaker in the clinches. I heard him grunt as I hit him a body shot but he has surprised me with his speed and condition. He is even faster than he looks and he knows every trick. Now I have two rounds left and if I win it will have to be by knockout.

Echevarria lands a hard shot in the ninth round, the punch landing flush on the Kid's countenance. Chocolate is hurt but he moves back out of range as Fillo unleashes a barrage of leather.

Chocolate is hit again. His eyes cloud briefly. The Kid's legs feel stiff but his body responds to reflex as he maneuvers for position and is hit once more by the tough Basque fighter. The punches have placed Chocolate in the danger zone of being separated from his senses for a ten count, but the Cuban Bon Bon jabs, clinches, jabs again, slips punches and is still on his feet at the end of the round.

"I know I hurt him," Fillo said years later, "but he was so skilled that it was very difficult to follow up. Chocolate would slip, clinch, move at angles to make himself a more difficult target and it was very difficult to nail him with two good shots in a row. When I fought him he was at the end of his career but he still had good reflexes, not as fast, but still plenty fast. And he had about 150 fights and knew a lot of tricks. He was amazing. He was Kid Chocolate."

The final round is packed with drama. Echevarria seeks a knockout and Chocolate, inspired by the loud Havana fight crowd, decides to spend all his energy reserves on the final three minutes of the match.

The Kid lets it all go. He hits Fillo with quick combinations but the Basque responds with valor. They trade punches and both land but the Kid has the edge on the numbers. At the end the crowd gives both men a standing ovation.

Chocolate wins in what is his last great performance. Nine months later he fights again, barely obtaining a draw in an uninspired performance against a slugging club fighter named Nick Jerome. It is the final curtain for Chocolate, who retires before the year ends.

For Fillo there are other fights down the road but he is also aware that retirement looms near. The wear and tear of over a hundred pro fights is taking a toll. His mind is not damaged and his speech pattern is clear but he is beginning to decline, the reflexes a little slower to respond, the timing a fraction off the usual tempo. Echevarria sees the signs and knows he can still go fifty or sixty more fights but it would be a downhill slide that his self- pride will not allow. Besides, Fillo is in love and his fiancé does not want him bruised and cut; he owns real estate and has money in the bank.

He fights for a little while. After Chocolate he faces Lou Salica, another world champion. Salica is a seasoned fighter with a light wallop who accomplishes the feat of stopping Fillo for the first time in a career that started in a San Sebastian ring and ended in a Havana fight arena.

After the loss to Salica, Fillo winds down his career, retiring after losing by TKO –due to a fractured jaw- to Pedro Pablo Medina in Havana. His probably incomplete record is verified so far to be 74-19-7 with 25 KO wins and only two losses via KO.

The story does not end yet. Married, with a daughter, Fillo works as a clerk for the Claims Court administration in Havana but boxing is in his blood so he stays in the fight game managing a boxing gym and training fighters. For over two decades he handles dozens of amateurs and pros, including world rated flyweight Hiram Bacallao. During this period Fillo also becomes a part-time sportswriter for small newspapers and trade journals and a physical education coach at a private school in Havana.

With the triumph of the Cuban revolution in the sixties, Fillo worries for his safety and the future of his family. Castro bans pro boxing but the pugilistic ban is nothing compared to the turmoil of a country where several thousand Cubans are executed by firing squads in the first four years of the new system.

Fillo heads for exile in Mexico with his family. He lives there for several years, writing a sports column for a Monterrey newspaper before moving once more, to Miami, where he works for the administration department of a hospital.

The little featherweight retires to enjoy his sunset years. He often attends the Cuban old-timers boxing dinners where he mingles with other gray haired ring veterans who talk of the times when Fillo and Chocolate traded leather at the Polar Stadium in Havana.

Julian Echevarria dies in a Miami hospital -surrounded by his loved ones- on December 31, 1997. In Cuban Miami, where exiles revere the traditions and culture of another era, the local radio stations pay homage to the little warrior who has taken the final count.

So it ends, except for the lines in record books and old clippings of another era and the memories of those who knew him and remember the little old man with a broken nose, a wide smile and a deep love for the fight game.

The Sparrow Hawk –Gavilan– was a world champion with flashy moves and an iron chin.

Publicity photo of Gavilan and Bobo Olson.

Gavilan and Carmen Basilio trade punches.

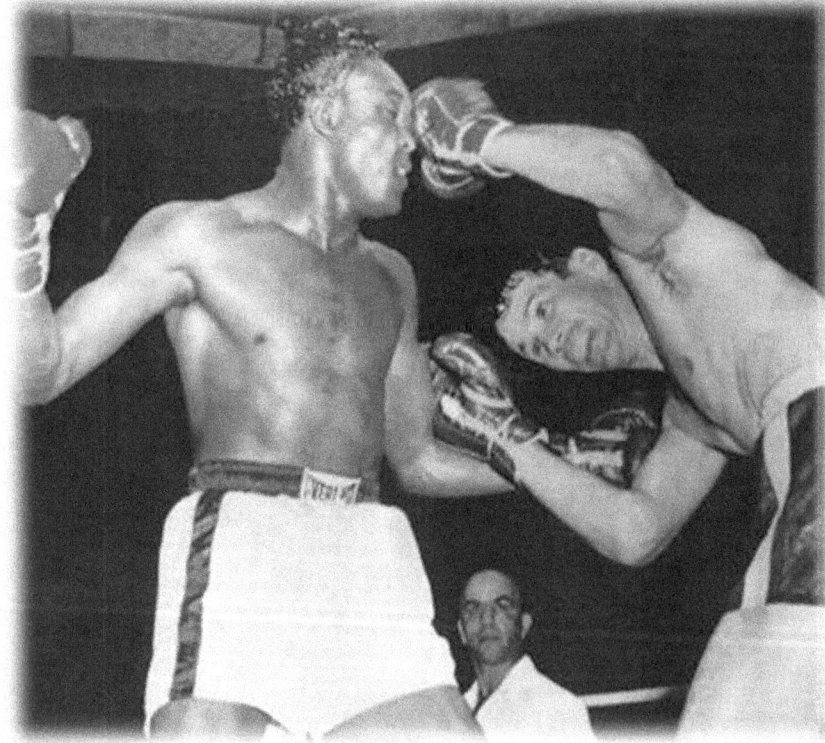

Kid Gavilan defeats Bobby Dykes.

CHAPTER TEN: GAVILAN, THE SPARROW HAWK

Icons and legends are human beings born common and unknown, but molded into greatness by time and historical events.

The legend of whom I write was born in Camaguey -the cattle province of Cuba- on the 6th day of January 1926, being baptized with the name of Gerardo Gonzalez.

As a boy he had little schooling, working since he was very young, shining shoes at a street stand, peddling newspapers on street corners and working at an ice factory. Yet, those were jobs to pay for room and board while learning his craft, for the boy was born to box.

His amateur career began as a ninety-pound flyweight in a cock-fighting ring in the hamlet of Palo Seco, where young Gerardo swarmed over his surprised foe. He won his first one and was back the following week, scoring another win.

By the age of fifteen, Gerardo was one of the most recognized amateur stars in Cuba. He turned pro at seventeen, under the guidance of Fernando Balido, the proprietor of a fruit stand called "El Gavilan" -The Sparrow Hawk- a name soon borrowed to market Gerardo as Kid Gavilan.

Cuban boxing had a distinguished history before the Sparrow Hawk turned pro. The previous decades had produced world champion Kid Chocolate and top contenders in several weight classes, including Black Bill and Kid Tunero. This history had a price, for Cuban contenders were forged in the heat of battle. Promoters did not offer easy fights and the crowd did not accept them; good young pros were moved quickly against quality fighters in a fast game of survival of the fittest.

Gavilan made a name for himself very quickly. He won four prelims and scored a knockout in his first main event. His sixth fight was against Bombon Oriental, a good headline fighter with years of ring experience and dozens of pro fights. The Kid won with ease and repeated the win in a rematch.

Kid Gavilan was a prodigy inside the ring, an athlete of destiny, a natural at the fight game. He had an iron chin, fast hands, quick legs, good heart, a sense of flash and daring, all wrapped up in an exciting style of fighting in spurts, jabs, hooks and uppercuts swarming around his opponent's guard in blitzkrieg assault.

The Sparrow Hawk also possessed that quality that is described in Spanish speaking pugilism as "to have angel," the charisma that attracted crowds that responded to his showmanship, as he performed for them wearing his trademark snow-white boxing boots and white trunks with black trim.

Gavilan won 29 of 31 battles fought between 1943 and 1946, scoring wins over quality fighters, men such as Santiago Sosa, Hankin Barrows and Miguel Acevedo. He lost and won to tough Mexican brawler Carlos Malacara, who became the first fighter to ever deck the Kid, a rare event, for the Cuban was never stopped in his fifteen- year career.

In 1947, Gavilan was rated seventh among the welter elite; in 1948 he was the top contender for a title shot. It was also the year Gavilan lost a close one to the magnificent Sugar Ray Robinson. The Sugar man and the Hawk tangled twice, the second time for the title, and both were close fights in which Robinson emerged the winner, yet Ray would always claim that the two toughest fights of his career were against the Cuban fighter.

"We were both very fast," Gavilan said in an interview, years later, "and we both took turns attacking and countering. Sugar Ray liked to set his tempo to the fight and I gave him trouble when I attacked in spurts. It broke his rhythm."

In New York, Gavilan hooked up with Angel Lopez, a restaurant impresario who had managed some fair talent and the Sparrow Hawk piled up wins and captivated audiences with his trademark "bolo punch," a flashy, wide punch with more charisma than power.

The diamond had serious flaws. The talented fighter was also somewhat wild. One of the Beau Jack fights was canceled when Gavilan was hurt in a street fight; although married, the Hawk liked to party with the ladies.

"He trained very hard," boxing trainer Luis Sarria once said of the Kid, "and he partied very hard also."

Gavilan also performed to the level of his opposition. When facing a topnotch fighter the Kid performer at his best, but with lower caliber boxers facing him his interest waned, causing him to sometimes lose to journeymen like Danny Womber and Sugar Costner.

Gavilan became champion on May 18, 1951, in New York, scoring a disputed victory in fifteen over Johnny Bratton. Although only 25 years old, Gavilan entered the ring against Bratton as a veteran of 87 professional battles, with 72 victories, 12 defeats and 3 draws. His win resume included the prestigious names of Ike Williams, Beau Jack, Billy Graham, Joe Miceli, Gene Hairston and Tony Janiro, all top guns in the fight game.

Gavilan was a very active champion. From May of 1951 to the end of 1953, the bolo- punching Kid defended his title on seven occasions and participated in eighteen non-title bouts. His seven defenses were against Johnny Bratton, Carmen Basilio, Chuck Davey, Gil Turner, Bobby Dykes, and two against Billy Graham. Basilio -one of the toughest men ever to lace on a glove- decked Gavilan, but the Kid managed to survive the round and rally to win. Southpaw Chuck Davey was handed a drubbing, the Hawk winning by TKO in ten.

"Gavilan was a hard guy to fight." Basilio stated in an interview, "He did not hit hard but he was fast and would throw punches in clusters. He took a very good punch but I timed him and clocked him good, dropped him clean. It was a tough fight but I thought I won. That disputed loss and the knockdown got a lot of ink."

At least one of Gavilan's defenses -against Billy Graham- was fixed by the mob. It was a sad moment in the sport when Graham, a good boxer and a decent man, was robbed and denied the crown that he deserved for its effort.

Gavilan was a paradox. He moved his father out of poverty and paid the family bills, but on another occasion left his wife and three children in New York -to depend on public charity- while he partied in other corners of the globe.

The Kid worked hard at squandering his fortune. Restaurant and nightclubs benefited from his patronage, as did chorus girls, bartenders and lawyers. Gavilan accumulated a debt of 68 thousand dollars with the IRS while boasting of having racks of tailor made suits and dozens of expensive shoes.

The Kid also had some splendid moments. He supported relatives, donated to charities, sponsored an amateur baseball team and bought an ambulance for a village clinic that needed a vehicle.

The decline of his career began in 1954, a year in which he fought only four times. After scoring two wins in tune up fights, Gavilan tried to capture the middleweight title held by Bobo Olson.

Olson, native of Honolulu, was a hard man that had entered the pro ranks at the early age of fifteen, tattooing his arms to pretend being older. Bobo was a good boxer, a decent puncher and experienced in ring warfare. A solid middleweight, he was too strong for Gavilan, who had already begun to lose the marvelous reflexes that carried him to fame in the ring.

After the Olson defeat, Gavilan returned to the welters, losing his crown to Johnny Saxton, a hungry contender with 44 victories in 48 encounters. Gavilan -with 28 years of hard living and almost 120 fights- was a champion on the decline.

After Saxton, the Kid became an opponent. The chin was still there, but the lightning speed was gone and the timing was no longer razor sharp. From 1955 to 1958 he fought 26 times, winning ten, losing fifteen with a draw, announcing his retirement after being defeated on points by Yama Bahama, a good middleweight boxer from Bimini.

The record book reads 108-30-5, with 28 KO wins and the claim to fame of not having been stopped in 143 pro fights. The men Gavilan faced included Sugar Ray Robinson, Carmen Basilio, Bobo Olson, Johnny Bratton, Johnny Saxton, Miguel Acevedo. Santiago Sosa, Ike Williams, Beau Jack, Rocky Castellani, Gil Turner, Tony Janiro, Paddy Young, Eduardo Lausse, Tony De Marco and Ralph Jones.

Retirement was not easy. Of the almost two million dollars earned, all that remained was a small farm in Bejucal, Cuba, and a closet full of clothes that soon were no longer fashionable.

He tried acting —starring in a boxing flick- and did some nightclub shows dancing and joking with the audience, but audiences only paid big bucks to see him perform inside the ring. His acting and dancing career ended in dismal failure.

Sometime in the late fifties or early sixties, the Kid turned to religion, becoming a Jehovah Witness. His timing was poor, for the new power in Cuba -Fidel Castro- did not believe in human or religious rights. The Kid was arrested a few times, interrogated and harassed. His farm was taken over by the revolutionary regime and by 1968 Gavilan arrived in Miami, joining hundreds of thousands of his exiled countrymen in South Florida.

He was broke and almost blind from cataracts in his eyes. The Cuban exile community passed the hat and paid for the operation to restore the former champ's eyesight.

Gavilan was offered several jobs and accepted to become part of Muhammad Ali's staff, but the job did not last long, ending with Gavilan threatening a lawsuit. The Ali camp settled for forty thousand dollars and the Kid spent the money as fast as it was paid.

Again insolvent, Gavilan continued his life of indiscipline, being arrested in 1974 for illegal possession of a firearm and causing a disturbance in a dance hall. Friends vouched for him and for a while he trained amateurs for promoter Julio Martinez, but that line of employment ended because of the Kid's excessive drinking.

Gavilan was blessed with a guardian angel named Hank Kaplan, a former boxer and grand guru of boxing historians. Hank took care of Gavilan, being instrumental in setting up personal appearances for the Kid at different banquets and events throughout the United States.

The Kid -by then residing in a nursing home- not only made some pocket change at these events, but also enjoyed the applause, the warmth of the fans and once again being the center of attention. Hank took the Kid on the yearly pilgrimage to the International Boxing Hall of Fame in Canastota, where Gavilan happily signed hundreds of autographs and spent many happy hours chatting with boxing fans.

Gerardo Gonzalez -better known as Kid Gavilan- died on February 13, 2003, of a heart attack at the Miami nursing home where he resided. It was a grand wake, not of mourning but a final salute to a legend, a great athlete with great flaws, a historical figure beloved by his nation and by fans from all corners of the planet.

Florentino Fernandez, the left hook artist and former middleweight contender attended the wake, as did Pupi Garcia, the crowd-pleasing featherweight of the fifties, former NABF Junior Lightweight Champion Frankie Otero, former headliner Johnny Sarduy, as well as ex welterweight Marcelino Gonzalez, former flyweight scrapper Kiki Casanova and ex pro Dwayne Simpson.

Boxing historian Hank Kaplan arrived accompanied by Jack Kearns Jr. Boxing trainer Dave Clark, boxing promoter and former mayor of Hialeah Julio Martinez and several young amateurs came to pay their respects to the fallen icon.

The Kid rested in his coffin, dressed in a blue pin stripe suit, a white boxing robe neatly folded across his stomach. The flower arrangements that filled the room included Cuban flag designs and a large arrangement that featured boxing gloves made from red roses.

Reporters and camera crews from three local television channels showed up, interviewing friends and relatives of the Kid. As I watched the TV crews at work, a fellow radio journalist nudged me.

"No one ever stopped him," he said, "that's incredible."

I nodded as I looked at the metal casket where the Kid rested remembering a phrase said by the clever Wilson Mizner when told that middleweight champion Stanley Ketchel had been shot to death.

"Start counting to ten," I said to my fellow journalist, "he'll get up."

Two world rated fighters: lightweight Orlando Zulueta and heavyweight Nino Valdes

Omelio Agramonte went ten rounds –twice- with Joe Louis.

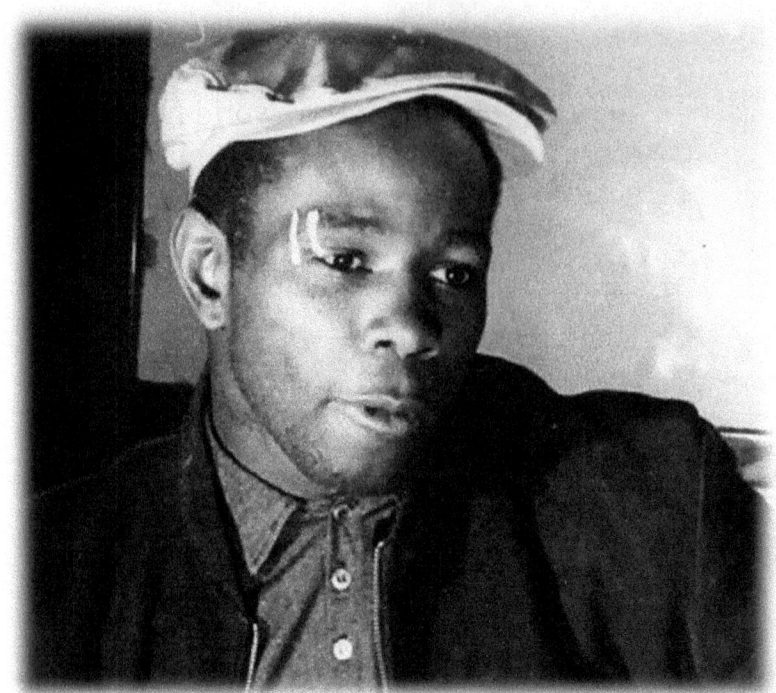

Isaac Logart fought for the world title losing to Virgil Akins.

Joe Legon fought Cocoa Kid and beat Kid Azteca.

CHAPTER ELEVEN: THE 1940-1950 DECADES

In the heavyweight division Nino Valdes was a dominant figure from his pro debut in 1941 until his last bout in 1959. A good boxer and a hard puncher, the easy going fighter compiled a 48-18-3 record with one no contest and 36 KO wins. He fought four world champions and scored a victory over Ezzard Charles.

Omelio Agramonte was another outstanding Cuban heavyweight. In his up and down career Agramonte had the distinction of being able to boast that he went the ten round distance twice in losing efforts with the great Joe Louis. Agramonte (50-21 with 32 KO) was a tough spoiler, holding wins over two well known fighters of the decade, Joe Lindsay and Johnny Holman.

Julio Mederos (21-19-3 with 14 KO) was a national amateur champion who started as a light heavyweight and grew into a solid 200 pounder. Mederos, coached by a clever young trainer named Luis Sarria, knocked out Roland La Starsa, won and lost to Bob Satterfield and at the end of his career lost to George Chuvalo and was stopped by Sonny Liston.

A heavyweight who started his career in the thirties and stretched it well into the forties was a muscular, handsome black man named Young John Herrera (42-22-3 with 28 KO). He held the Cuban light heavyweight and heavyweight titles, went the distance in a losing effort with contender Arturo Godoy but will be best remembered as Teofilo Stevenson's first boxing coach in the nineteen sixties.

THE MIDDLEWEIGHTS AND WELTERWEIGHTS

Kid Tunero was still around for most of the decade, his amazing career winding down towards retirement, but the old master still had enough to beat Ezzard Charles and win the national middleweight title from Mario Raul Ochoa (37-22-4 with 25 KO).

Ochoa –from the city of Holguin- was a very good fighter. He won national titles at middleweight and heavyweight, even though he never weighed over

170 pounds. In 1943, the "New York Times" placed Ochoa number fifteen among the middleweight ranks. The tough Ochoa beat Nino Valdes, Omelio Agramonte, Wildcat Henry and lost to Cocoa Kid.

The dominant Cuban welter of the forties was Joe Legon (59-15-8 with 30 KO), a gutsy Havana bus driver who was murdered in a street argument over a dice game in 1947. Legon won and lost with Mexican icon Kid Azteca, dropped one to Holman Williams, won, lost and drew with Hankin Barrows and twice held the national welterweight title.

In his fifth fight with Hankin Barrows –a very capable fighter from Belize- both men went all out. Legon was staggered badly in the late rounds, returning to his corner on wobbly feet; the quick thinking, tricky bus driver sat on his stool and told his corner man to remove one shoe and one sock.

"What?"

"Just do what I tell you," Legon answered.

As the round was about to start, a stunned referee walked over to Legon, who was standing, resting against the corner post; the third man inquired why a shoe and sock had been removed.

"I get a better grip when I punch," Legon answered.

"You can't do that. You have to put your sock and shoe back on."

"No. There's nothing in the rule book against me doing this…"

An argument ensued that interrupted the fight for a couple of minutes, enough time for the cobwebs to clear and for Legon to regain his wind. The fight resumed and the barefoot Cuban stopped Barrows in the tenth round.

A world rated Cuban welter whose career extended from 1949-1966, Isaac Logart (69-32-10 with 25 KO) lost to Virgil Akins in his only title shot but did well in a long career where he faced ring men of top caliber.

Logart's distinguished career include encounters with men of high caliber, including Emile Griffith, Joe Brown, Gaspar Ortega, Don Jordan, Luis

Manuel Rodriguez, Nino Benvenuti, Rip Randall, Federico Thompson, Joe Miceli, Yama Bahama and Bobby Cassidy.

Former contender Bobby Cassidy said of Logart:"I had a tremendous amount of respect for Isaac Logart. He had already had over 100 fights when I fought him at the Garden. A few years earlier he was rated number one in the world. So I knew this would be a good test for me. He had complete command in the ring. Everything was second nature to him. The way he moved, he was very relaxed. He was very smooth. Logart was also very smart in the ring. In terms of fighting, his mind was sharp. He just didn't have the speed any more to beat a younger fighter. You could see that his mind still knew what to do, but his body couldn't execute it. Once I was able to hurt him, there was nothing he could do to keep me off of him. In that sense, beating him was a little bit sad. But I wouldn't say he was completely shot. A few fights later he drew with Blair Richardson, who was a pretty good fighter. And they fought in Richardson's hometown, so that means Logart probably won the fight."

"Logart had a pretty close fight with Emile Griffith. He beat Gaspar Ortega and he beat Joe Miceli a few times and Joe was a good friend of mine, so I knew how good he was. Years later when I fought Luis Rodriguez we were at a press conference and Rodriguez looked at my record and said he knew I was a good fighter because I had beaten Isaac Logart. That was meant to compliment me but that was a good compliment for Isaac Logart too."

LIGHTWEIGHTS AND FEATHERWEIGHTS

Kid Bururu –real name Juan Sierra- was a very slick lightweight from Santiago de Cuba whose career began in the early thirties and extended into the fifties. Bururu (39-21-7 with 9 KO) was a national champion, lost twice on points to Kid Gavilan and became a boxing trainer in the fifties, teaching –in a Santiago gym- the basic moves to a young boy named Jose Napoles.

Orlando Zulueta (69-45-14 with 7 KO) was a boy wonder. He turned pro at eighteen, was fighting main events after only six months and faced the legendary Sandy Saddler at the age of nineteen, going ten rounds with the great champion. In a career that extended from 1946-1962, Zulueta was a top a rated fighter, losing a heartbreak title bid against Old Bones Joe Brown.

In 128 recorded fights the light hitting Zulueta only scored seven knockouts, but with his clever boxing he held wins over Wallace Bud Smith, Paddy De Marco, Jimmy Carter, Don Jordan, Arthur Persley, Glenn Flanagan and Ludwig Lightburn. After retiring from the ring, the well mannered Zulueta worked as a full time bartender and part time professional photographer until 1971, when he was murdered by two drunken bikers in San Francisco.

The creation of the Cuban Golden Gloves tournament in 1938 produced an excellent annual crop of amateur fighters, several becoming world rated fighters in the forties and fifties.

The cream of the crop in this decade included world class talent including Ciro Morasen, Miguel Acevedo, Humberto Sierra, Santiago Sosa, Diego Sosa, Pupi Garcia and Luis Galvani.

Ciro Morasen (77-14-10 with 23 KO) is considered one of the greatest Cuban fighters of all time. In a career that extended from 1943 to 1958, the master boxer was world rated as high as third among the world featherweights, holding wins over Cecil Schoonmaker, Bill Bossio, Sonny Leon as well as over every good Cuban featherweight of the forties and fifties, including the charismatic Pupi Garcia.

Miguel Acevedo (52-20-6 with 20 KO) beat Orlando Zulueta, Pat Brady, Lulu Constantino –twice- and drew with Phil Terranova. Acevedo was a world rated, tough, crowd pleasing fighter.

Humberto Sierra (47-23-5 with 11 KO) was brave and although he lacked power, he did deck the great Sandy Saddler on his way to an upset win. Besides winning and losing to Saddler, Sierra beat Pat Brady, Jackie Callura and lost twice to Willie Pep but sadly ended his career with dementia pugilistica.

Santiago Sosa (36-17-5 with 14 KO) was Cuban champion as a featherweight and lightweight. He was twice defeated by Kid Gavilan and won twice in bouts against Clarence "Cotton" King.

The very active "Tiger of el Cerro" Diego Sosa (94-35-10 with 50 KO) fought anyone and often fought them four or five times. He drew twice and lost one to Zulueta, won once and lost three to Sierra, knocked out and lost to Jackie

Graves, beat Harold Dade and went three and three in six clashes with the magnificent Ciro Morasen. Diego Sosa fought for the Junior Lightweight title in 1951 in Havana, being stopped by Sandy Saddler in two rounds. He went on to become a highly regarded amateur trainer.

Pupi Garcia (36-8-4 with 17 KO) was the biggest ticket seller of his era, filling arenas while building up a large fan base that was thrilled by his aggressive warrior style. Pupi, younger brother of Lino Garcia –a competent main event fighter- was world rated. During his career the little slugger held wins over Pappy Gault and Luis Galvani but was never able to beat Morasen.

Luis Galvani (47-8-9 with 26 KO) seemed destined for a world crown but a playboy lifestyle was his downfall. Galvani was undefeated in his first 36 outings, but by the early fifties his star faded, destroyed by an abusive lifestyle.

Kid Rapidez was a flashy featherweight with little power who dazzled with his clever moves but was not in the same level as the very good Cuban featherweights of the era. His name will be remembered not for his boxing record but for his training skills. Rapidez became a first rate trainer who worked with such ring legends as Sugar Ramos, Jose Napoles and George Foreman.

Other popular fighters of the forties included lightweights Rene and Chile Cantero, Chico Morales and featherweights Orlando Castillo –The Rooster of the Ring- and tough and clever Johnny Sarduy.

THE FLYWEIGHTS

The flyweight division had two outstanding little men in Oscar Suarez and Black Pico.

Little Oscar Suarez (55-13-3 with 21 KO), whose career stretched from 1946-1959, fought and lost in his only bid for the world title, being out pointed by champion Pascual Perez.

The five foot tall Suarez turned pro at the age of twelve and did not outgrow the flyweight division for eleven years, towards the end of his career. Suarez fought club fighter Orlando Rodriguez ten times, winning eight and losing twice. By 1954 Oscar Suarez was national flyweight champion. In 1955 he scored a sensational three round knockout over world class fighter Fernando Gagnon, a hard hitting Canadian who was only stopped three times in a 143 bout career.

National flyweight champion Black Pico (48-21-9 with 13 KO), whose real name was Ramon Gonzalez Rojas -from the city of Sagua- was a very good boxer who often fought bantamweights. Pico had a memorable series of fights with bantam Armando Puentes Pi, but was unable to beat the bigger fighter. Three fights were draws and Puentes Pi won the other four.

FIGHTERS FROM OTHER LANDS

Among the boxing talent imported to Cuba in the forties, one must mention the legendary champion Sandy Saddler, the two magnificent globe trotters Holman Williams and Cocoa Kid, Mexican battlers Carlos Malacara and Luis Castillo, welter Hankin Barrows from Belize, the North African Ben Buker and Spanish welter champion Jose Garcia Alvarez.

Nino Valdes, dressed elegantly.

Valdes advertising a soft drink.

CHAPTER TWELVE: THE GREAT HEAVYWEIGHT

The first time I saw Nino Valdes was in the mid-fifties, when as a child I spent summers with my family at a beach cottage in Guanabo, a few miles from Havana, snorkeling in the emerald green Cuban waters and watching grown-ups play dominoes.

I saw Nino leaning against the counter of an open-air beach café. From my perspective -all four-feet-something and some seventy pounds- the man standing in front of me looked as big as a boulder, with hands like ham hocks and arms the length of telephone poles. In reality, he was a muscular man, six feet three and 215 pounds with a gentle face and a warm smile. He spoke slowly, with a thick voice that was misleading, sometimes giving the impression that Valdes was slow witted, yet although he had an obvious lack of schooling, the big Cuban was a street smart man child, possessed an abundance of warmth, a fine sense of humor and an engaging personality.

As a boy he learned his craft in a Havana gym while working an assortment of jobs that included pin setting in a bowling alley, delivering blocks of ice to cafeterias, shining shoes and working in construction, digging ditches and hauling concrete bags on his young shoulders. Nino was a hungry teenager with big dreams when he turned pro in Havana at the tail end of 1941, knocking out Basilio Ayestaran in three rounds. Cuba was a boxing hotbed, but only for featherweights, lightweights and welters. Heavyweights were few and even fewer ones wanted to fight the young black slugger with solid power in either hand.

So Nino Valdes worked as a longshoreman and construction laborer while fighting only a dozen fights in four years, winning ten of them by knockout. In 1945 Valdes was matched with the only other Cuban heavyweight everyone avoided, a muscular veteran named Federico Malibran.

The two men went at each other with gusto. Malibran was a quality journeyman fighter, who held the national heavyweight championship. He was a crafty veteran with over fifty pro fights and a decade and half experience in Cuban and European rings. Malibran used a bag of tricks on his opponent, stopping the still inexperienced Valdes in the fourth round, chopping him down with combinations. Instead of moping around, Valdes asked for a rematch and stopped Malibran in eight.

"The fights with Malibran were wars," he told me, years later. "He was strong and fast and so was I. The first fight I was nervous and he was a very seasoned fighter and I lost. I wore him down in the second fight, pounding him and he took a good shot. Those fights made me feel good. People knew who I was and I became aware that I could go far in boxing, trade with the best."

Five more years went by and not much happened. Valdes fought a few fights in Cuba and some in the United States. He fought only nine times in those five years, losing only to Archie McBride, a likeable, talented fighter managed by best-selling author Budd Schulberg.

One of the big thrills of Nino's life was having boxed three exhibitions with Joe Louis in 1949 and 1950. Valdes always spoke about the Brown Bomber with reverence.

"It was solemn," he said, "like being with royalty."

In spite of the three glorious exhibitions with Louis and a string of wins over club fighters, Nino grew discouraged. He was by then a fully matured fighter in his twenties with a 17-4-2 record with 15 knockouts and empty pockets. He quit boxing for a year, working at the docks.

Nino launched a comeback, which started with a trip to New York and a management contract with Bobby Gleason, a well connected, picturesque gym owner and booking agent. Gleason loved Valdes, for the big Cuban was by then a seasoned, experienced fighter with rocks in his hands and an easy going manner, always smiling.

Gleason matched him against good talent and Nino performed well. He lost on points to the legendary Archie Moore, to Harold Johnson and Bob Baker, but lasted the distance with all and showed he could crack the upper echelon of the division. Critics pointed out that Nino was a good boxer and hard slugger but complained he lacked killer instinct.

Caron Gonzalez, a well-known Cuban trainer remarked in an interview about

Valdes: "Some said he lacked heart but he had plenty of heart. His problem was that he was a very gentle guy and it wasn't his nature to put the hurt on someone who was hurting. If you traded with him he would trade with you like he did with Malibran in those two wars and if he hit you right it was like brass knuckles, but he was slow on the final blow sometimes, like he hoped the referee would stop it. People use that expression about gentle giants. That's what he was."

After the loss to Baker, Valdes turned his career around, beating Omelio Agramonte for the Cuban Heavyweight Title and scoring a huge upset over former champion Ezzard Charles.

The newspapers hyped up stories that Valdes had used a hypnotist to help him prepare for the Charles fight, convincing him that he could not be beaten. When I asked Nino about it years later, the big man smiled.

"When I fought Agramonte in Havana I stopped him in ten," he said, "and Omelio had gone ten rounds twice with Joe Louis and it gave me confidence when I stopped him. I was in very good shape for Omelio and I was not hurt when we fought. Then the offer came for a fight Charles in Miami Beach in less than a month and I did not stop training. Hypnosis had nothing to do with that win. I was in the best shape of my life that night -sharp as a razor- and I felt so strong and so fast that I believed no one could beat me. That night I felt like fighting."

Valdes used his size and weight to neutralize Charles, mauling the former champion, scoring solid punches, winning on points. It was the greatest victory of Nino's career. He returned to Havana as a national icon.

"Charles was a very dangerous fighter," Nino reflected years later, "but I surprised him. I moved on him and used my weight and size and I broke his rhythm and confused him. He hit me a few good shots and I hit him back with a few good ones too. I beat him but Ezzard Charles was something special."

The win over Charles was followed by eight victories, five of them by the quick route. Nino scored knockouts over the eccentric Tommy Jackson and Heinz Neuhaus and won on points over old foe Archie McBride.

At this time Valdes was one of the top heavyweight contenders bidding for a title shot at the crown held by the invincible Rocky Marciano, but an agreement was never reached and Nino did not receive a title shot.

Cuban sportswriters often proclaimed -in their emotional passion- that Valdes was denied a title shot because the Marciano camp was afraid of the Cuban giant. Not so, although it is true that Valdes would have been a younger and much taller foe for Marciano than most of his opponents. It would have been an interesting match between hard punchers with Marciano having a marked edge based on his unbeaten record and crushing power.

Valdes was so popular in Cuba that he was offered endorsements as though he was a world titleholder. Nino filmed television commercials advertising Malta Hatuey, a popular soft drink. A meat company paid him for an endorsement, distributing photos of Nino polishing off huge steaks. Department stores and retail outlets paid him for promotional appearances, while a topnotch tailor traded several expensive suits for the right to use Nino's name and modeling photo in his magazine ads.

For the next six years Valdes moved in and out of the ratings as he won and lost to some top talent. He lost once more to Archie Moore, twice to top contender Eddie Machen and one each to Zora Folley and Bob Satterfield. He also won his share, twice on points over Mike De John, a one round knockout over highly regarded Pat McMurtry and wins over Johnny Holman, Wayne Bethea and Johnny Summerlin.

Valdes harvested his best victories in Europe where Nino decimated the British Empire. Don Cockell fell in three, Dick Richarson in eight, Joe Erskine in one and Brian London in seven.

There were attempts to match Nino with Floyd Patterson but Cus D'Amato did not want his champion giving up twenty or so pounds and three inches in height to a rated contender with a solid punch. Although rated for several years, Valdes was never able to challenge for the world crown.

By 1959, after eighteen years as a pro he was defeated by Sonny Liston, who had won 24 fights and lost only once. Liston and Valdes fought on even terms for two rounds, each man landing some clean shots until a right hand in the third dropped the veteran Cuban to the canvas. His last fight was a satisfying win over Brian London on the first day of December 1959.

"Being hit by Liston," Valdes observed, "was like being kicked by a mule. By the time I fought Liston I was over the hill. I hit him a couple of solid shots and he did not buckle. Sonny was the strongest man I ever fought and he was very tough. When I fought him I still could hit very hard but my reflexes were not there anymore."

The record book states that Nino Valdes fought 70 pro fights in his career, compiling a 48-18-3 record with one no-contest, 36 KO wins and 5 KO defeats. He fought four world champions -Archie Moore, Harold Johnson, Ezzard Charles and Sonny Liston -as well as a score of top contenders

Nino returned to Cuba where he had planned becoming a boxing trainer, but the country was in turmoil. Fidel Castro had seized power and the revolution had carried out hundreds of executions by firing squads -some even televised- in its first year in power.

For a while he attempted living in Cuba, but Valdes soon returned to New York, broke and too old to fight. He earned his living as a bouncer at the 500 Club, a small bar on a side street by Times Square. I visited him there a few times, striking up conversations about his days of glory and Nino, cleanly attired in a turtleneck with a sports coat ensemble, would sit at the bar, drink some juice and talk in that slow, warm voice that was distinct from all others.

Before I moved to Miami in seventy-nine I dropped by to see Nino. A boxing magazine on the bar countertop showed a cover photo of Teofilo Stevenson.

"How would you have done against him?"

He thought about it, sipped some juice and nodded solemnly.

"He is an amateur," he answered, "and I was a pro so it is not fair to compare. Even today, old and overweight, you put me in a telephone booth with Stevenson and I'll be the one walking out of that booth on my feet."

Nino died in New York in June 2001 at the age of 76.

Luis Galvani was a world rated fighter who lived a life of excess.

Florentino Fernandez, Douglas Valliant, Sugar Ramos and Luis Manuel Rodriguez

CHAPTER THIRTEEN; THE END OF AN ERA

The decade of the fifties was the high peak of Cuban boxing. A sterling crop of amateurs joined the pro ranks where veteran talent was of high quality.

The crop of amateurs turning pro during this decade included Luis Manuel Rodriguez, Jose Napoles, Sugar Ramos, Benny Paret and Jose Legra –all destined to become world champions- as well as future world rated fighters and top prospects that included Douglass Valliant, Angel Robinson Garcia, Jose Stable, Pedro Miranda, Florentino Fernandez, Baby Luis, Johnny Sarduy, Chico Veliz, Juvenal Minguez and Tato Menendez.

Among the established veterans who were still fighting in this era the standouts included Kid Gavilan, Nino Valdes, Isaac Logart, Omelio Agramonte, Julio Mederos, Pupi and Lino Garcia, Ciro Morasen, Wilfredo Miro, Diego Sosa, Luis Galvani, Oscar Suarez, Kid Fichique, Baby Colon, Martin –Guije- Rodriguez and many others.

"The fifties," said historian Melchor Rodriguez, "was a great age for Cuban boxing. The amateur program had thousands of boxers and there were hundreds of pros. A dozen cities in Cuba ran regular promotions and the combined quality between veterans like Gavilan and Galvani and the young pros like Luis Manuel and Florentino was outstanding. It was a golden age."

In 1959, Fidel Castro came to power and went about transforming Cuba into a totalitarian communist state. By the end of 1961 professional boxing was banned in Cuba and the fighting pros had to decide whether to resist the new dictatorship, adapt quietly to the system or leave for exile in other lands.

Some resisted, joining in a civil war struggle that stretched for half a decade of irregular warfare. Lightweight prospect Jose Acosta –a butcher by trade- and veteran Tony Armenteros died executed by Castro firing squads; welterweight Marcelino Gonzalez was captured while fighting guerrilla warfare against Castro and was sentenced to a long stretch in a Castro prison. Featherweight contender Pupi Garcia –in line for a fight with Hogan Kid Bassey- and prospect William Roncourt also were sentenced to stretches in Castro's dungeons, accused of being involved with urban resistance groups. Johnny Sarduy and Pedro "Hueso" Gonzalez, hung up their gloves to fight with rifles in the ill fated CIA sponsored Bay of Pigs invasion of 1961. Featherweight Enrique Lamelas fought in the resistance movement and was able to leave the island without facing a firing squad.

Dozens of pros left Cuba, filling up Florida gyms.

"They came in bunches," historian Hank Kaplan said of the impact of the Cuban Revolution on boxing, "And they came looking for Angelo Dundee. Angelo had been going to Cuba for years, taking fighters to the Island, working closely with Cuco Conde and Martinez Connill, who were the top promoters in Cuba. All Cuban fighters knew Angelo and he had a solid reputation having worked with Carmen Basilio and a lot of good fighters. At the time the Cubans arrived, Angie had Willie Pastrano and a young Olympian named Cassius Clay. What he signed up in a few weeks was phenomenal: Luis Rodriguez, Florentino Fernandez, Douglas Valliant, Robinson Garcia and a score of the best talent in the boxing trade."

In Cuba, from 1961 forward, only amateur boxing would be allowed.

Dictatorships love sports if the individual achievements are used to enhance the glory of the government in power. Hitler was enthusiastic in developing a massive sports program in Germany and in Cuba, Castro followed a similar pattern.

A powerhouse of amateur boxing was developed by a team led by Alcides Sagarra –who had learned boxing working corners for his brother, a pro- and by former pros Sal Fuentes –a main event journeyman fighter- and an old trainer named Gabriel Lopez Nunez, born in Panama and raised in Cuba where he had fought preliminaries in the 1920's under the name of Wee Wee Barton.

Some of the former pros who had decided not to resist the new political order –including Paul Diaz, Baby Colon and Diego Sosa- were hired to run local boxing programs and Soviet boxing coaches visited Cuba to teach the new government the nuances of international amateur competition.

Although the Castro government has repeated often that the pre-revolutionary era had lacked quality amateur boxing, even alluding that it was almost non-existent, the amateur program in Cuba had a solid history of performance.

In the 1920's, Havana had no less than eight private athletic clubs that taught boxing and sponsored amateur cards. The Cuban army and navy taught boxing at their bases and almost every town in all six provinces had gyms and amateur teams. During this decade, national tournaments were held often. One young boxer –Aramis Del Pino- won titles in two weight classes in the same year. Del Pino also became a fair pro, trainer, promoter, physical education teacher and boxing writer.

In 1935 Gilberto Bello, a Cuban amateur fighter fought in tournaments in Mexico and El Salvador and won a silver medal in the Central American Games being held in San Jose, Costa Rica.

In 1938 Cuba established a National Golden Gloves tournament, which became the top amateur event of the year. The 1938 team also participated in international tournaments, visiting the U.S. These amateur tournaments highlighted many young men who went on to the pro ranks including Lorenzo Safora, Baby Canzoneri, Chile and Rene Cantero and others.

In the 1940's Cuban amateur boxing teams traveled frequently to international competitions. Enrique Lamela won a Gold Medal as a bantam at the Caribbean and Central American Games and by the middle of the 1950's Cuba had eight thousand amateur boxers registered in clubs and gyms throughout the island. In 1957, three Cubans - Sal Fuentes, Tony Zaldívar and Douglas Valliant-won Diamond Belt Championships in an international tournament held in Seattle.

Under the new Castro political system with no professionalism allowed the "Cuban School of Boxing," as it came to be called relied on two factors: time and quantity.

Melchor Rodriguez, a very knowledgeable boxing historian describes it thus: "In Cuba one of the forms of controlling the population is by having them busy and supervised. So when a child is ten or eleven years old if he's not active in sports he is assigned a sport and told to report for training. This happens all over Cuba. So every year thousands of kids take up boxing and six years later when those kids are seventeen or eighteen, most of them are out of boxing but you probably have a couple of hundred who still compete and they all have over a hundred fights in their ledgers. That core group of teenagers is light years ahead of other countries at a competitive level. Some of the fighters in the national team are in their late twenties or early thirties, which means they are really seasoned pros with fifteen years of ring experience. In the peak years of the Soviet Union, Cuba would have a national team and then a second string team, a third string team and Cuban boxers competed in over fifty international tournaments a year."

Fighter Juan Carlos Gomez –reports journalist Bobby Cassidy- said: "I did not choose boxing. They chose it for me in Cuba. I wanted to be a baseball player. That was always my dream, but you known, in Cuba you are not allowed to make your own decisions."

Sports journalist Melchor Rodriguez stated: "Teofilo Stevenson was listed as being an electrician but he probably never held a screwdriver in his hand. He fought in tournaments in Europe and the Soviet Union almost every month and he traveled the globe. The secret of the so called "Cuban School of Boxing," is no secret. They work on volume to skim the top talent and rely on the longevity of their established stars, which train and are experienced as pros but are still fighting amateur."

"The Castro government always talks about the exploitation of pro boxing, but what do they do? They exploit boxers for medals so they can brag about how their system is so wholesome, produces such great athletes, but after the career ends the fighter is just back to being another slave in the plantation. Some survive with menial jobs as boxing coaches or officials. Others like Hector Vinent –a man with two Olympic medals- were ignored in retirement and Vinent ended up in a prison, convicted for selling goods in the black market."

When pro boxing was outlawed in Cuba, the newspapers –all under government control- published a number of articles interviewing former pro fighters that complained about being exploited by their managers.

One of the fighters called in for an interview was Luis Galvani. The former bantamweight idol was ill and broke, his magnificent physique destroyed by alcohol and years of fast living. In an interview that was never published, Galvani told the reporter: "Look, if you are expecting me to complain about a manager that used me or robbed me, you will wait for a long time, because Pincho Gutierrez always treated me well and gave me good advice and I was the only one to be blamed for screwing up my life."

Ironically, the first Cuban to win an international amateur tournament under the newly established regime became –within hours- a political prisoner.

Heavyweight Marino Boffil won a tournament in Berlin and before leaving Germany attempted to defect to the West, was caught and sent to prison at Cuba's Isle of Pines.

By the late sixties Cuba began its dominance of amateur boxing. Between Marino Bofil's first international win in 1960 to 2012, the Cuban boxing machinery in Cuba produced 34 Olympic boxing champions and scored 67 Olympic medals. In this time frame they also garnered numerous medals in world amateur championships, Pan American Games, Caribbean and Central American Games and international tours, making Cuba the dominant nation in global amateur boxing.

The Cuban boxing system has produced dozens of Olympic, world amateur champions and international stars, including Teófilo Stevenson, Félix Savón, Ángel Milián, Andrés Aldama, Adolfo Horta, Ángel Espinoza, Luis Delis, Maikro Romero, Rolando Garbey, Roberto Balado, Héctor Vinent, Robeisi Ramirez, Arnaldo Mesa, Alexis Rubalcaba, Ramón Garbey, Emilio Correa, Chocolatico Perez, Douglas Rodríguez, Armando Martínez, Juan Hernández, Rogelio Marcelo, Juan Lemus, Ángel Herrera, Julio González, Sixto Soria, José Gómez, Orestes Solano, Orlando Martínez and many others.

How many of these men would have become world titleholders at a profesional level is a question that will never be answered. Certainly many had the talent to become professional stars, while others would fall to the wayside in spite of stellar amateur records.

Perhaps the two best Cuban amateur fighters of the period leading to a new century –although not the most publicized - were Mario Kindelan and Adolfo Horta.

Kindelan, from the city of Holguin, won two Olympics, three World Amateur championships and two Pan American Games as well as dozens of Cuban national championships and international tournaments. His amateur record was 358-22.

Aldofo Horta –from Camaguey- had a 319-27 amateur record. He was an Olympic silver medalist, three times World Amateur champion and was a two time Pan Am Games titleholder. Although Horta never won Olympic gold, he won so many international tournaments that he was considered for several years as one of the top five amateurs in the world.

Both Kindelan and Horta were smooth, fast fighters who could fight at all three distances, combining well and dominating their oppostion with both speed and technique.

Many Cuban boxing experts believe that Kindelan and Horta were "the best of the best" and would have been professional champions had they been allowed to enter the punch for pay ranks.

Cuban boxing, however, has become more identified with heavyweights Teofilo Stevenson and Felix Savon than with any other boxers.

Stevenson is an icon of amateur boxing, an impressive performer who scored three Olympic gold medals, six world amateur titles and an impressive lifetime record of 302-22. Among the men he beat were Americans Duane Bobick, Tony Tubbs, Bill Tate and Michael Doakes. Stevenson had a stand up straight style, known for a stiff jab and a solid, follow up right hand.

Savon –also a three time gold medalist in the Olympics- had a 387-21 record with wins over Andrew Golota and David Izonritei. Almost as good as Stevenson, Savon was a hard puncher and good boxer with a soft chin.

Stevenson and Savon with their great achievements have –however- become a topic of polarizing discussions among Cuban fans due to their politics.

While all athletes in Cuba are expected to toe the line politically, Stevenson and Savon did so with fervor and enthusiasm in their support of Fidel Castro, as they constantly insisted they would never become professionals because pro boxing was exploitative and capitalistic. For their blind support they received uncommon perks, including automobiles, a government gift reserved only for the most politically loyal.

The gifts and perks given to former Cuban athletes are based more on political loyalty than performance. For many boxers who quietly accept playing the political role assigned by the state, there is the rare opportunity to travel beyond the borders of Cuba, where consumer goods can be bought to be sold on their return to the Island, making money on the profitable black market.

In his book "In the Red Corner," British author John Duncan describes a surrealistic scene in which flyweight Maikro Romero, on a trip abroad purchased tires for a Lada automobile, showing up at the airport in his sports jump suit, carrying tires under each arm.

Many boxers who were not as politically loyal or deemed as useful to the system were discarded after their glorious amateur careers. A clandestine documentary by Dr. Darsi Ferrer –a human rights activist in Cuba- titled "Knockout Kuba," (2009) portrayed eleven former Cuban boxing stars that were being ignored by the regime.

Chocolatico Perez, Douglas Rodriguez and Leonardo Alcolea were broken down, impoverished alcoholics. Sixto Soria –who fought Leon Spinks- was convicted of using his private car as a taxi to earn a living, the same as Angel Herrera. Felix Betancourt survived by selling bags of pork rinds in his neighborhood. Osvaldi Riveri –who lost only eight of over 300 fights- lived in a shack –one step above being homeless- in Santiago de Cuba. Jorge Luis Romero –ignored by the government- sat in a wheelchair inside a dilapidated home.

Cuban born Jorge Ebro, respected sports writer for the Spanish version of the Miami Herald believes that politics played a big part in the development of the Stevenson and Savon legends.

"Political allegiance is vital to succeed at any level in Cuban society," Ebro states, "And most Cubans live pretending to be part of a government they dislike. Most athletes go through the motions, playing the pretend game on different levels because to be marked as politically troublesome means to be denied participation in international tournaments and restrictions in your life. A few really believe the propaganda fanatically and defend it, or are very opportunist and pretend to be fanatical."

"The heavyweights are the insignia, the highest symbol of amateur boxing, so it is of huge importance that the most publicized fighters should be the most politically correct communist in the sport. If Stevenson and Savon had not been politically outspoken in favor of the system, their chances of going to three Olympics would have been diminished greatly. When Savon went to his third Olympics, a lot of boxing people thought Odlanier Solis should have been the heavyweight representative. Solis went to the one after but Savon probably went to his third Olympic because of his outspoken loyalty to the regime."

In the seventies, an attempt was made to match Teofilo Stevenson with Muhammad Ali but the Castro government did not permit it and Stevenson gave numerous interviews bad mouthing free enterprise and the evils of capitalism.

"The proposed fight was more propaganda than anything real," boxing historian Hank Kaplan stated, "Castro did not want his prize trophy damaged. Stevenson was a great, phenomenal amateur but styles make fights and Stevenson was made to order for Ali. He was a stand up straight, not very fast, predictable fighter with a left jab right hand basic combination. Stevenson was only aggressive in spots and to beat Ali he would have needed to be a bull, like Frazier. Ali would have played with Stevenson… It was supposed to be a Caribbean version of Hitler and Schmeling, but it was a public relations project from the Cuban government and nothing else because Stevenson did not have the style or speed to beat Ali."

Former NABF champion Frankie Otero said that "I don't believe Stevenson could beat Ali, who had such good mobility and landed very quick combinations. Stevenson was too rigid. Stevenson would have stalked Ali and eaten those combinations all night."

Stevenson was a great amateur fighter but far from invincible.

"In Cuba," states historian Melchor Rodriguez, "he was impossible to beat. A very tough heavyweight named Angel Millian dropped him two or three times and the judges voted for Stevenson."

In spite of all his medals and stellar amateur record, Stevenson lost to Duane Bobick (one out of two) twice to Francesco Damiani and Igor Visotsky as well as defeats at the hands of Craig Payne, Peter Somner, Alexander Krupkin, Bern Adner and Orlando Castillo, all good amateurs but a far cry from the Holmes, Shavers, Lyle, Quarry, Norton, Frazier and Foreman bunch that Ali was facing.

As for Savon, although his record was superb, he was stopped eighteen times in his amateur career, including a loss to a little known Korean heavyweight named Lee Dal Han.

Under proper management and well matched Stevenson and Savon would have both earned fortunes in the pro ranks but no one will know how much greatness they could have achieved. Professional boxing and amateur pugilism vary greatly and there is no guaranteed stardom.

Many outstanding amateurs fizzled and flopped in the pros, the most poignant case being that of Craig Payne. The Michigan heavyweight had a brilliant amateur career, winning a National Golden Gloves title and international tournaments. Payne could boast of being the only fighter in the planet to hold wins over both Teofilo Stevenson and Mike Tyson. Yet as a pro, Payne won 12, lost 20 and drew once, being stopped seven times.

Texas heavyweight Nick Wells had a brilliant amateur career, winning the World Military Championship and the National AAU title, defeating Larry Holmes twice. As a pro, however, Wells only won 13 out of 21 pro bouts.

Argentine boxer Pablo Sagrispanti was a terror in the amateurs winning international competitions, national championships and having a long streak of consecutive victories, yet as a pro he had an 11-23-4 record, being stopped nine times while serving as a punching bag for Oscar Bonavena, Dogomar Martinez and Gregorio Peralta.

Among the Cubans of generations to follow Stevenson some made the big time in the pros while other amateur stars had fair winning records as prelim or club fighters but failed to gain the top tier, including Ramon Garbey, Judel Johnson, Yoandry Salinas, Yordenis Ugas and Yasmany Consuegra.

Amateur medals and trophies are symbols of experience acquired and sharpened skills but do not guarantee automatic success in the professional arena. In boxing one ever knows.

Angel Robinson Garcia fought over 200 pro fights.

Angel and Pupi Garcia

CHAPTER FOURTEEN: ANGEL ROBINSON

The news came down through the Little Havana grapevine that Angel Robinson Garcia died in Cuba.

He was a flawed diamond, a Renaissance oil masterpiece with chili stains. Angel was a fighter of tremendous ability but his lifestyle, which eventually destroyed his liver and kidneys, was what kept him from gaining belts and fame.

Still, even pickled on booze or stoned on weed, in a career that spawned three decades, Angel Robinson Garcia was a ranked contender in two divisions, fighting at least 238 fights in eighteen countries and four continents. He was the second supreme globetrotter in boxing history, after Eddie Perkins. Despite his wild lifestyle the Cuban fighter was never late, nor did he ever cancel a fight.

In 1955, at the age of eighteen, Angel Garcia turned pro, after winning a Cuban national amateur championship. The young lightweight patterned his boxing style after his idol, Sugar Ray Robinson. Thus the handsome young fighter adopted the ring name of Angel Robinson Garcia.

With his flashy moves, Garcia reeled off twenty-five wins out of twenty-seven fights. They were hard fights for small purses. Richie Riesgo, a veteran trainer who worked with Angel Robinson related a memorable anecdote.

"Angel was booked to fight Chico Morales," Riesgo said, "In Santiago de Cuba, and the trip by bus took fourteen hours. When we arrived they had a carnival that had brought thousands of tourists into the city and there were no hotel rooms. So, we went to an all night movie theatre and sat through several showings of the same film, taking little naps but waking up all the time. After that we went to a park bench and that was worse. In the morning we went to the weigh-in, had breakfast and sat through more showings of the same movie. We were exhausted, but Angel Robinson looked very good in the ring that night. He won on points against Morales who was a good prospect."

Between 1955 and 1961, Garcia resided in Cuba, but began his travels by fighting main events in Mexico, Venezuela, Panama and the United States.

"He did not care who he fought," Riesgo said, "all he wanted was to have a good time. Sometimes he trained hard and other times he didn't but he drank and chased women every day. In Cuba the boxing commission for a while suspended him. He was on a winning streak but his adventures became public gossip and the boxing authorities enacted a moral clause. Did he change? No way. He would have sex the night before a big fight, after the weigh-in, anytime and all the time. Money went through his fingers, never in the pockets. He borrowed so many advances from a promoter that after a fight he was still two hundred in the hole. Angel Robinson had a lot of ability and heart but his reason for living was to have a good time."

Young and quick, Angel Robinson fought anybody anywhere. In Venezuela he drew and lost to future junior welter king Carlos Hernandez, a hard slugger. In Havana rings he defeated rated lightweight Alfredo Urbina, split two with future welterweight contender Jose Stable, and drew and lost to another brilliant prospect, Douglas Valliant, who would eventually fight Carlos Ortiz for the lightweight crown. By 1961, Angel Robinson was a fringe contender in the lightweight division with a respectable 42-14-2 record.

Politics intervened. Fidel Castro was on its way to establish a dictatorship in Cuba. Professional boxing was about to be banned. Angel Robinson Garcia did not like communism and an altercation with a Cuban soldier landed him in a prison cell for several days. As soon as he could, the gifted lightweight headed for Miami Beach.

The Fifth Street Gym was in its glory days. A young heavyweight named Cassius Clay and newly crowned light-heavyweight champion Willie Pastrano were two of the stars of the Dundee brothers. Chris and Angelo scooped almost all the Cuban fighters leaving the island.

"Chris had worked with all the Cuban promoters," boxing historian Hank Kaplan said, "and Angelo went to Havana constantly, taking fighters over there and even picking up a working knowledge of Spanish. So when these fighters showed up in Miami they would look for Angelo and Chris to train, manage and promote them and it was a hell of a group. Luis Rodriguez, Jose Napoles and Jose Legra became champions. Florentino Fernandez and Douglas Valliant were top rated contenders and both had title shots and Angel Robinson Garcia was rated as a lightweight and junior welter."

"The first time I saw Angel Robinson," Kaplan said, "he came into the gym dressed in an expensive suit and puffing on a cigar. He was a unique character, always smiling and joking around, a very likable man who could have matched Lew Jenkins at a bar stool."

Angelo Dundee lined up fights geared to take Garcia to a world title. Angel outscored Hilton Smith, a fighter who held a win over Napoles, and beat Jimmy Mackey, a fair Florida club fighter.

"He looked sharp," Angelo said, "and then I get an offer to put Angel in against Rafiu King, a European contender, in Paris. It was one of the big mistakes of my career. I sent Angel over for one fight and he stayed for ten years."

"I could have promoted him to a championship," the late Chris Dundee once remarked, "but he was unpredictable. He had a couple of good wins with us and we were guiding him, making the right matches, keeping him in shape and suddenly he's in France."

Paris was made for Angel Robinson Garcia. Wine was cheap and the nightlife was excellent. Garcia was in his prime, his face slightly marked but still handsome and French girls loved his happy-go-lucky charm. Angel Robinson stayed in Paris, somehow obtaining a temporary residence permit.

French promoters loved his smooth style, which drew crowds that included famous actors like Alain Delon and Jean Paul Belmondo. Garcia was willing to fight anyone on the planet and he fought the best, losing to junior welter champ Eddie Perkins and to the lightning quick Ismael Laguna, but knocking out the highly regarded Ray Adigun in six and defeating Rafiu King in a rematch.

In Paris he married the daughter of a shopkeeper, which meant that for however many days the honeymoon lasted Angel did not go off night clubbing with his new found French buddies, an oversight he remedied quickly.

After his marriage collapsed, the Cuban fighter drifted to Spain where he linked up with a fellow countryman, Evelio Mustelier, known in boxing circles as Kid Tunero. A soft spoken, well mannered, middle-age man, Tunero was the antithesis of Garcia, the wild child of boxing.

In his youth, Tunero had been a ranked contender, an excellent orthodox boxer. He was so good that as a middleweight, he outscored a young light heavyweight named Ezzard Charles. Tunero had settled in Madrid where he was a highly regarded boxing trainer, owned a gym and managed some very good fighters, including another fellow Cuban, the mini-Ali featherweight Jose Legra.

Spain also suited Garcia. He knew the language and wine was cheap. He fought main events but did not mind filling in a prelim to help out a promoter or make enough to cover party expenses. Rolando Fernandez, a young Cuban exile was part of the Tunero team.

"I drove them around," Fernandez, a Miami businessman related years later, "and I worked buckets, whatever. I was young and it was a fun time. Tunero was always booking Legra in cities and towns all over Spain, fighting club fighters and local heroes at very little risk. Angel would ride along even if he did not have a fight booked. We would pull into a town and Angel Robinson would weigh in 'just in case' and inquire where the tavern was located. Twenty minutes in town and he was sitting in a Spanish tavern, puffing on a smoke and polishing off a bottle of wine. Tunero would show up and say something like –there's a fallout but they need a middleweight for an eight and he's fifteen pounds heavier than you are- and Angel would say –I'll take it. I'll be in the dressing room on time.- And after Tunero went back to the arena or bullring, Angel would smile and say –Well, now that I have another payday coming we can order another bottle before the fight.-A couple of hours later with a good wine buzz, he would take out the middleweight. He was unique."

Angel Robinson trained and partied, looking to fight anywhere there was a peseta, lira or guinea to be made. He fought in England, visiting pubs before and after weigh-ins, also traveling to Switzerland for a ten-round draw and a couple of one night stands with easy women. Angel drank good wine before trading leather in Italy, going to war in Belgium, Tunis, Algiers and Finland, where he lost to Olli Maki.

After five years in Spain he became restless. Ever since leaving Cuba he had wandered like a gypsy. Packing his bags Angel Robinson moved to Italy, where he found passionate women and good Chianti. He was no longer young; he had become a mature veteran. His handsome face was slowly flattening and his once smooth eyebrows showed thin lines of scar tissue.

In Rome Robinson Garcia became a local favorite. He won, lost and drew with world rated lightweight Paul Armstead and knocked out L.C. Morgan, a dangerous puncher who held a win over Napoles. Angel lost to world champs Bruno Arcari and Carmelo Bossi.

Growing homesick for his Cuban buddies, Garcia rejoined Tunero and Legra in Spain, where he spent another three years trading leather. He was fading, losing more frequently, but Angel Robinson was by this time a very seasoned, tricky fighter. He was seldom hurt even in defeat. Most of his losses were to top European fighters like Roger Menetrey and Cemal Kamaci.

Deciding to change continents, Angel Robinson Garcia headed back to the Americas. He was in his mid-thirties, no longer rated and showing the wear and tear of his turbulent life. He was offered a fight in Panama against an undefeated young prospect with 21 knockouts in his 25 victories. Garcia hopped on a plane and fought Roberto Duran in the stone man's backyard.

"He was dangerous," Garcia said in an interview years later, "but I knew how to work the ring. I shuffled back and forth and worked angles and kept him out of range, confusing him...I caught him with some good shots but he was too young and strong. He won the decision but after the fight he looked at me and said –Cuban, you know a lot!"

A few months later Angel went the distance with Esteban De Jesus, Duran's nemesis.

Returning to Miami after his ten-year tour of Europe, Garcia contacted Angelo and Chris Dundee once again. In Miami he defeated club fighters Jimmy Hamm and J.T. Dowe before losing in a marijuana haze to Saoul Mamby and Sugar Ray Seales.

Frankie Otero was a world rated lightweight working out at the Fifth Street Gym when Robinson returned to Miami.

"At the time he fought Hamm and Dowe," Frankie remembers, "Robinson was a shot fighter but he was very clever. Even out of condition he knew how to pace the fight, resting in the clinches and with his ass on the ropes, bobbing around and making the other guy miss. He knew every move and trick in the trade and he took advantage of every opportunity you gave him. He was very good and he had a chin like granite. I think he was only stopped a couple of times in over two hundred fights."

Robinson Garcia continued to fight top men. At thirty-nine Angel lost a decision to Wilfredo Benitez, the teenager who was destined to win three belts.

His last moment of glory came in 1976, when a Philadelphia promoter was looking for an opponent to fatten the record of junior middleweight prospect Perry Abney, a seasoned veteran with a good left hook and nine wins in his last ten bouts. The purse was insignificant, only seven hundred dollars, but when no one accepted the grizzled Angel Robinson stepped up to the plate. With a mellow buzz the ancient warrior gave Abney a boxing lesson, stopping the local hero in nine rounds.

In his last years of campaigning, Angel Robinson lost to former welterweight champion Billy Backus, to Clyde Gray, a rated Canadian fighter and to the dangerous Willie "The Worm" Monroe.

Garcia's record is incomplete as his travels took him to far corners of the planet and although he claimed about 300 fights, the accounting so far is 238. His record as far as can be determined was 136-82-20. Of his 135 victories, 54 were knockouts.

Banned from fighting in the U.S. by commissions who rightly argued he was too old and worn out, Angel returned to France. His application for a boxing license was rejected. The man who had fought main events all over the planet had finally lost his trade.

Robinson Garcia was in his forties, but the years of substance abuse, hard fights and daily binges had destroyed his health. His eyebrows were crisscrossed with scar tissue and his face was reshaped from the handsome youth he had once been; his liver and kidneys were failing him, the end result of decades of alcoholic abuse. He could not work.

In France he became a "clocharde," which is an elegant sounding word to describe a homeless panhandler residing in the bowels of the Paris subway. A friend in France wrote to tell me that Jean Paul Belmondo, the great actor recognized the beggar as one of his favorite fighters, interceding on his behalf.

Although the Cuban government did not like professional fighters, Castro has always attempted to maintain a political relationship with European artists and intellectuals. When Belmondo made a request the Castro government allowed the old globetrotter to return home to die. Frail and sick, the nomad fighter returned to Cuba.

He is gone now, the way of all flesh. Angel was the untamed party animal who self-destructed with gusto, yet I feel no anguish at his demise. He chose his road and traveled the highway without the twisted rage of a Tyson or the psychological angst of a Golota. Robinson Garcia enjoyed his smoke, wine and women without regret and did it all with a certain style, with a happy buzz smile and a wink of complicity, always on time, never complaining, always in the fray.

Adios, old warrior.

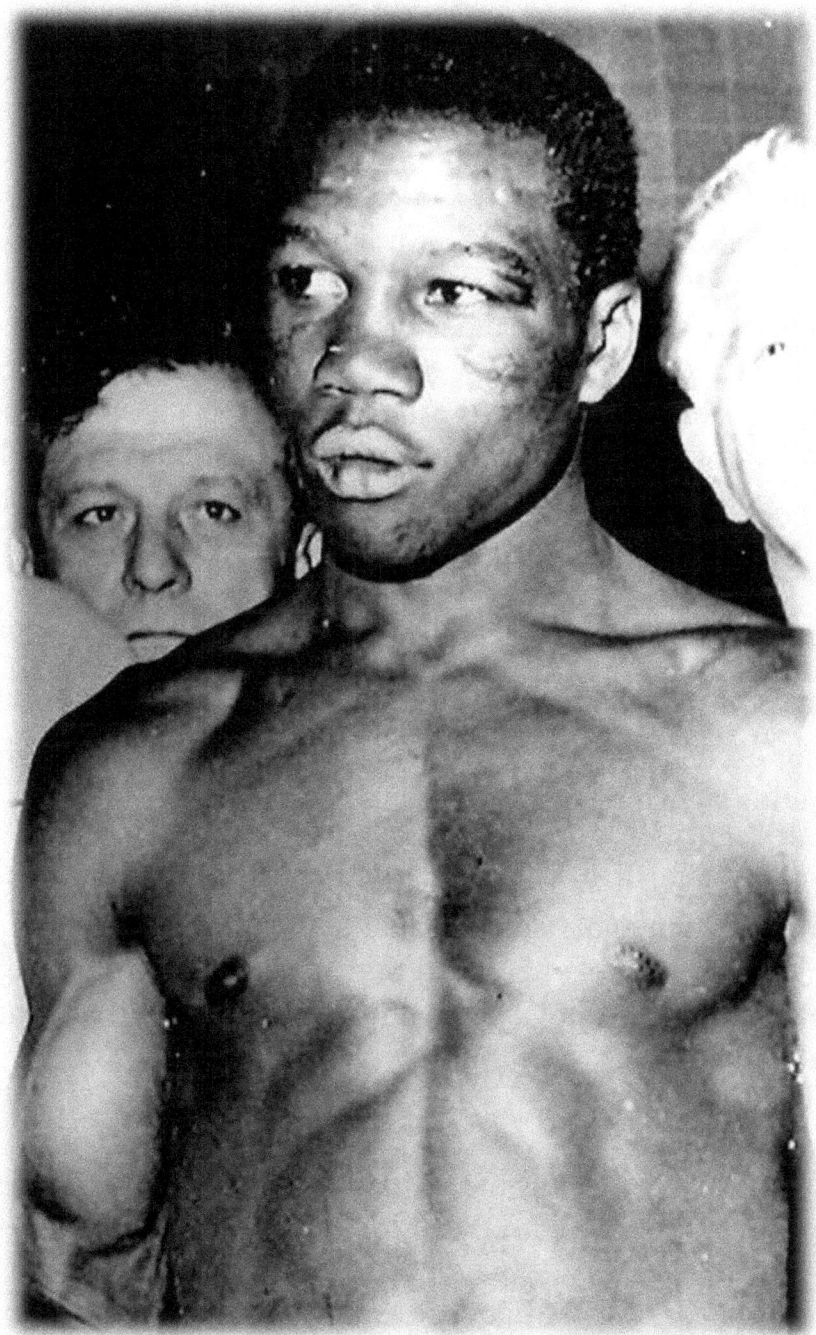
Benny Paret died in a fight because he did not retire as his trainer asked.

CHAPTER FIFTEEN: DEATH IN THE RING

Poor Benny Paret; he was a brave fighter, a good world champion, yet he will always be remembered as the fighter who died on national television.

Benny Kid Paret was born in Santa Clara, the main city in central Cuba. His professional ring record was 35-12-3 with 10 KO victories. At 25 years of age, Paret had twice reigned as the king of the welters and challenged for the middleweight crown but his last title fight ended his life as he was battered to death by a furious Emile Griffith on a nationally televised bout in March of 1962.

Much speculation and commentary has been made of this ring tragedy but the story told by his former trainer Caron Gonzalez has seldom been heard.

Gonzalez, an excellent trainer, worked with Paret since the tough kid from Santa Clara was signed by manager Manuel Alfaro.

"Benny was very tough and had a hard chin," Caron said in an interview twenty years after the Kid's death, "His biggest flaw was that he was not a puncher. He was a brawler, he would trade shots and fight up close, face to face but he did not knockout guys quickly and he took a lot of punishment in every fight. He became champion because he had a lot of heart and determination."

Paret had turned pro at age seventeen after compiling a 28-1 amateur record. Not a pampered prospect, after only eight fights he faced Reinaldo Caballero, a veteran of main events, an experienced pro with a winning record in some fifty fights. The youngster stopped the veteran in three rounds and sportswriters took notice of Benny Kid.

Another young fighter of the time was Rolando *La Plancha* Rodriguez, a soldier with good defensive skills and a good punch. Paret's thirteen fight winning streak ended when Rodriguez landed a big right hand in the second round. Undaunted by the loss, Paret fought Rolando Rodriguez on three more occasions, winning all. Rolando also fought Luis Manuel Rodriguez twice, losing both.

The only Cuban welter that Paret could not beat was Luis Manuel Rodriguez. In 1958 they fought twice and Luis dominated Paret, outpointing him with his usual virtuoso performance.

"Benny was very strong," Luis Manuel said years later, "He had an average punch but he was very aggressive and had a lot of heart. His defense was poor and I won both fights sticking my jab in his face and moving from side to side."

Paret was a determined, very well conditioned fighter who could outhustle opponents who punched themselves arm weary, eventually fading to the will of the fighter from Santa Clara. Benny was not a hard banger but his constant attack wore down opponents and he was able to drop to the canvas even those –like Emile Griffith- who had solid chins.

On his way to winning the title from Don Jordan, Benny twice defeated Argentine junior middleweight Victor Zalazar, twice outpointed tough Charley Scott and fought draws with undefeated Jose "Chegui" Torres and the outstanding contender Federico Thompson.

The Thompson draw was a defining step on the way to a title shot. At the time Benny had a 31-7-2 record with 9 knockouts and the experienced Thompson was 121-9-10 with 65 knockout victories.

"That was a brutal fight," Caron Gonzalez said, "and after that fight the problems started. He was going to fight Jordan for the title but that draw with Thompson damaged him. Benny complained to me of headaches and of occasional blurred vision. That worried me and I went to Alfaro –his manager- and told him that Benny was damaged and should contemplate retirement. Alfaro was not a bad man but he shrugged it off, telling me all fighters get headaches."

"Next I went to Benny and told him he should retire but he refused, telling me he was making more money than ever and could go a few more fights with no problem. He had a family to feed and he was making good money fighting."

"So what could I do? I quit training him and Alfaro hired Maceo and Benny kept on fighting. I tried but no one listened, not even Benny."

After Caron left Benny continued fighting, winning the title from Jordan, defending against Thompson, facing Indian Gaspar Ortega, winning and losing with Emile Griffith and fighting middleweight Gene Fullmer.

The Fullmer fight was particularly brutal, the Utah fighter stopping the Cuban in the tenth round when Paret was dropped three times to the canvas.

"I've never hit a man as hard or as often as I hit Paret," Gene Fullmer commented years later, "but he kept coming and trying and I was asking myself when is this guy going to fall?"

Then came the last fight, when Paret taunted Griffith for being homosexual and Emile became truly furious. It was a real grudge fight with enormous intensity , Griffith going down in the sixth but coming back fighting, peppering Benny Kid with combinations until the final seconds when Paret received eighteen consecutive blows, dropped tangled on the ropes and began nine days of sleeping darkness before drawing his last breath.

No one listened, not even Benny.

Pupi Garcia in battle against tough Guije Rodriguez.

The very popular Antonio Pupi Garcia

CHAPTER SIXTEEN: PUPI WAS SPECIAL

Antonio Garcia grew up in a poor, blue-collar neighborhood in Havana during the decades that were marked by an international economic depression and a World War.

Nicknamed Pupi -- pronounced "pooh-pee" in Spanish -- he was a shy, soft-spoken child who dropped out of school at the age of eleven to earn a living running errands, hawking newspapers at busy intersections or cleaning and dusting mausoleums at Colon Cemetery in Havana.

Life was tough but there was opportunity and the Garcia family was hungry to improve their lot in life. Older brother Lino tried boxing and began well, scoring a string of impressive wins over local featherweights before moving up to main events, winning and losing to world class contender Miguel Acevedo.

Pupi decided to follow his brother's path. While smooth boxing Lino was stopped by Sandy Saddler and traded leather with Orlando Zulueta, Lulu Constantino and Diego Sosa, little brother Pupi was making his own name heard in the amateurs, where he reeled off nine wins before losing on points in the final bout of the Cuban national Golden Gloves tournament. As Lino's career eclipsed, Pupi Garcia turned pro. The two brothers who had a strong family bond were as different in the ring as fire and rain. Lino was slick and Puppy explosive; Lino had smooth combinations and Pupi a crunching body attack. Lino was liked and Pupi adored.

Oh, he was shy and would not talk much in interviews; praises embarrassed him and he did favors without publicity, but charisma flowed from him when he climbed through the ropes to work at his trade.

From the very first time he laced on a glove, Pupi Garcia gave his best and then some. He fought fast and hard, tearing hooks into his opponent's ribcage while taking plenty in return. He had soft white skin, the kind that turns pink in the sun and cuts easy in the ring; he bled often but the warm blood flowing from a busted eyebrow only made him more determined as he brought up the fight a notch, to a higher level of will and pain.

How popular did he become? In the fifties, Cuba had quality fighters: Kid Gavilan, Nino Valdes, Luis Rodriguez, Jose Napoles, Benny Paret, Sugar Ramos, Ciro Morasen, Angel Robinson Garcia, Florentino Fernandez, Orlando Zulueta, Isaac Logart and dozens of other headliners -- young prospects and old veterans – which made Cuba a boxing hot spot.

With all that talent around, the biggest ticket seller was Pupi Garcia. With the exception of a Kid Gavilan world title fight, Pupi Garcia was the single biggest gate attraction in Cuba, consistently selling out 6,000- or 8,000-seat venues even when the bout was nationally televised.

His career was meteoric. He came out of the amateurs a hungry, sixteen-year-old featherweight who fought with grim determination and transferred some of his energy to the crowd, electrifying in his performance, magnificent in the face of adversity.

After only fourteen pro fights, Pupi faced top gun Pappy Gault, who had 29 wins in 33 fights. Pupi stopped Gault twice, both times with constant body blows.

More wars followed. A win and a loss to Jimmy Cooper and a loss and a win against Charlie Titone were battles raged in front of sold out stadiums.

"Titone cut me in the first bout," Garcia stated in an interview, "and the blood caused the stoppage at a time when I was getting to him, so I was very anxious for a rematch. I went for him right away and I hit him with a hook to the body that was the hardest I ever hit a man and he made a sound of pain -- a surprised moan -- and dropped to the canvas for the full count."

One of Pupi's finest nights took place in 1954, when he faced Luis Galvani, one of Cuba's premier fighters. Luis was talented but had a never-ending thirst for booze and a self destructive lifestyle. By the time he fought Pupi, the former world rated Galvani was the shell of a once top fighter. His record only showed seven loses in sixty three bouts, but his reflexes had faded and he figured to be another notch in the Garcia record.

There are still some old timers from the era that claim Pupi liked Galvani and did not want to humiliate him, so he made the fight exciting enough to give fans their money's worth, yet allowed the old veteran to go the distance. Pupi won by a shutout but did not stop the fading Galvani.

Pupi was stopped in nine by former world lightweight titleholder Lauro Salas in a grueling war of attrition but drew a standing ovation from the crowd for his gallantry in the fray.

Pupi had three thrillers when he clashed with smooth boxing Ciro Morasen, a legendary fighter who lost only 13 times in more than 100 pro bouts. The jabbing Morasen beat Pupi twice, the third being a No Contest that ended with a small riot, bottle throwing and a burst of gunfire -- from a soldier's machine gun -- being fired at the roof of the arena.

Pupi won, lost and drew with tough Venezuelan Victor "Sonny" Leon, selling out arenas in Caracas.

In 1958, a mature, seasoned Pupi Garcia squared off against a flashy youngster -- with a 31-3 pro record -- named Angel Robinson Garcia. Handsome Angel was destined to become a supreme globe trotter in the history of boxing, but at that time, he was still a young fighter with very clever moves.

Miami sportscaster Sarvelio Del Valle said of the fight: "I am not a betting man but I made a bet on Pupi beating Angel. I had seen them spar each other at the gym and Pupi had a style of infighting and body attack that bothered Angel Robinson. Pupi could impose his will on Angel and Angel could not impose his will on Pupi."

The fight occurred as Del Valle predicted. Angel Robinson Garcia had the speed and the flashy combinations but Pupi cut the ring, moved inside, smothered Angel, hooked and hooked again, brawling for ten rounds and winning on points.

Pupi had it made. Labor union leaders provided him with a good paying job with the Cuban Electric Company, where he acquired technical skills while his boxing income provided security away from the poverty of his youth. Furthermore, Miami promoter Chris Dundee was negotiating a world championship bout for Pupi to tangle with Hogan Kid Bassey at the Orange Bowl.

In 1959, his life changed forever. After two years of guerrilla warfare against Fulgencio Batista, Fidel Castro came to power in Cuba, greeted by millions as a liberator until he unleashed his own brand of Jacobin Marxism on the island. Almost fourteen hundred Cubans were executed by firing squads in the first year of socialist terror and over four thousand more over the next four years. By 1960, the revolutionary government controlled all media and began the elimination of all private enterprise in the island. By 1961, all professional sports -- including boxing -- were banned and thousands of Catholic priests and nuns were expelled from Cuba, accused of being subversives.

The country became a Cold War battlefield. Thousands of anti-Castro guerrillas were active in all six provinces of Cuba and urban resistance units functioned covertly in every city and village in the island. Bombs exploded daily, Cubans shot other Cubans everyday and all jails in the island were packed with political prisoners.

At the age of twenty-seven, waiting for a world title fight, Pupi Garcia had to decide between his career and his country. He only fought three times in 1959, winning all, one of them over Hilton Smith, who followed his loss to Garcia with a win over Jose Napoles.

Pupi did not fight pro again. His final ledger reads 36-8-4 with 17 KO wins and four stoppage defeats. Pupi Garcia retired from the ring, but not from fighting, for by 1960 he was involved in the resistance against Fidel Castro, transporting weapons, hiding covert operatives, driving cars in urban guerrilla operations.

Sportscaster Sarvelio Del Valle tells of visiting Garcia at a time when Cubans were being executed for being active in the resistance.

"I told him, Pupi, I have a problem, I have two men on the run that I'm hiding and I have to find a way to get them out of the country- and Pupi looked at me and said: now they are my problem."

"That's the kind of man Pupi Garcia was," Del Valle said, "and he saved those two men."

In 1961, Pupi was arrested by State Security and sent to Isle of Pines Prison, which at the time housed several thousand of the hardest core anti-Castro political prisoners.

Castro's guards attempted to break the political prisoner's will by offering two options. If a political prisoner was willing to join a "rehabilitation plan," he could have his sentence reduced and receive a few privileges, such as better food and additional family visits. The "plan" required a prisoner to issue a public apology asking forgiveness for opposing the revolution, attend Marxism classes and if requested to teach the ideology to other prisoners.

Pupi Garcia could not publicly renounce his convictions. It never entered his mind the same way he never considered diving to the canvas to ease his pain inside the ropes. So he went with the second option: he declared himself a prisoner in rebellion -- "plantado" -- and braced himself for a taste of hell on earth.

Francisco Chappi, a former prisoner at Isle of Pines, stated: "In order to force us to join The Plan, the guards became more sadistic than ever. We were roused from our beds in the middle of the night, beaten with rifle butts and machetes. Sick 'plantados' were denied medical care, fed bowls of rice crawling with worms, locked up in solitary confinement for disobedience. Men in solitary spent months confined to rooms with little or no light, unable to shower, expected to shit in a small hole in the floor without toilet paper. They slept on the floor without pillows or blankets, and in their own urine. Rather than submit, many died in attempts to retain the last shreds of human dignity."

The prison guards hated Pupi, hated the fact that a national sports icon had become a resistance fighter and a prisoner in rebellion, willing to live naked and sleep in his own filth rather than accept the new imposed socialist order.

All Cuban political prisoners were beaten and tortured but Pupi Garcia received more than his share of blows over eight years in Castro's prisons. A rubber truncheon pounding to his kidneys caused him to urinate blood for days; eyebrow scar tissue from ring wars was ripped open by the kick of a boot during an interrogation, an ankle was fractured during another beating.

Roberto Martin Perez, who spent 28 years in Castro's concentration camps stated that "Pupi received more beatings in prison than he ever did in the ring."

The guards tried to tempt him, telling him that with a nod of the head he could have a uniform to wear instead of filthy undergarments, a plate of food without maggots and an end to the beatings. Pupi refused the offers and was locked for days in a cold room without clothing or blankets.

"It was about dignity," he said, "If I surrendered my dignity, renounced my belief in democracy then I had nothing left. I could not live a lie and offer allegiance to a government that was destroying my nation."

Pupi was in rebellion for almost nine years, coming out of jail in 1970, unbroken. He worked odd jobs in Cuba for a decade, arriving in the United States as a Mariel boat lift refugee in 1980. In Miami he worked as a security guard for a few months until word got around that the little featherweight was in town.

Cuban exiles -- politically powerful in South Florida -- set Pupi up as the sports director of the Parks and Recreation department in Sweetwater, one of the cities in Miami-Dade County.

Pupi lived in Miami for almost two and a half decades, retiring from his job in Sweetwater, attending local club fights where boxing fans shook his hand and old timers pointed him out to the younger fans.

In his seventies, he developed stomach cancer, but did not talk or complain about his illness. A few weeks before he died of a stroke at a local hospital, he attended a local boxing show, where promoter Richard Dobal -- a young Cuban born after Pupi had retired -- had a plaque for the little featherweight with a big heart. The crowd gave him a standing ovation and the old warrior, in the ring for his final bow, smiled with shy embarrassment.

Rest in peace.

A wonderful human being: trainer Luis Sarria

CHAPTER SEVENTEEN: LUIS SARRIA

Sports historians enthralled with the Ali legend have written little about Luis Sarria. There are reasons for such apathy. Sarria knew little English and his well-mannered, soft voice and quiet demeanor were overshadowed by the ranting of Bundini, the brilliant glibness of Pacheco and the blue-collar appeal of Angelo.

The sports historians missed out on a treasure find. Luis was one of the most interesting characters in the game, considered among Cubans to be the greatest fight trainer the nation ever produced. He had wit and a dignified manner that was the mirror of his good soul.

Luis Sarria was born on the 29th of October, 1911, in Cumanayagua, a farming town in central Cuba. His childhood was marked by poverty, hunger, illness and death. One of his sisters died before reaching adulthood. A brother - with whom Luis shared a bed - died in his sleep by the age of twelve,

Sarria was an orphan who wore hand me down clothes and had known gnawing hunger in his belly. Many years later, when a journalist made a casual remark about having skipped lunch and feeling very hungry, Sarria smiled and said softly: "You don't know what going hungry is like. Son, when you are hungry you can eat melted lead."

He was on his own by the age of thirteen, working at shining shoes in a street stall in the southern city of Cienfuegos. As he grew in size and strength he made good wages for very hard work during the season of the sugar harvest, wielding a sharp machete under the hot Cuban sun. He also worked in the tobacco fields of Las Villas Province, in central Cuba.

Luis Sarria started in boxing at the age of thirteen, fighting in amateur smokers where a hat would be passed for the fighters and winning bettors would tip their favorites. After a few fights - mostly victories - Sarria turned pro, beating an American fighter named Ernie Balin in a four-round fight.

"The money was not there," he said about his prelim fights. "They paid a peso a round, so it was four pesos for a four- rounder. That was very little money but when I did not have any money at all, a peso could buy me a couple of cheap meals to get by another day."

Sarria fought in Cienfuegos and Santa Clara, winning most of his bouts, then headed for Havana, a very active fight center, where he set up a shoe shine stand in the porch of a café named "El Polo." He lived in a cheap boarding house and trained at a boxing gym after working a full shift to earn a few bucks.

Sarria shined shoes and sold newspapers, fighting prelim bouts for a few pesos. He scored a win over Pedro Canales and was a known fighter in undercards at Cuba's famed Arena Cristal, a venue that had featured Kid Chocolate as one of its headline performers.

For his first main event, Sarria was paid fifty pesos in 1938. His opponent was Ramon Rodriguez, an established journeyman welterweight with a decent punch and a difficult southpaw style.

"It was the toughest fight of my life," Sarria recalled in a rare interview, many years later. "He hit very hard, dropping me early, but by then I knew how to survive and it took all my skill to last the ten rounds, losing on points."

Sarria realized that his career as a boxer was going nowhere. He was a good boxer with a fighting heart, but he lacked power and his chin was ordinary. His last fight took place in 1939, when he faced Domingo Govin, a young welterweight with a hungry attitude. In the first round both men threw hard right hands and both went down in a rare double knockdown. Both lifted themselves groggily from the canvas, but Sarria was the worst of the two as their seconds worked over them in their corners.

"I lost by TKO in two," Sarria said, "Referee Benitez stepped in and that was my last, my thirtieth pro fight. I won nineteen."

Luis Sarria continued to shine shoes but began a new career as a boxing trainer. A pattern was soon established: Sarria's fighters won most of their fights. The young trainer did not allow his students to climb through the ropes unfit, nor did he overmatch them to make a quick buck. Green kids became proficient inside the ropes, and his amateur team picked up medals at tournaments.

By 1943, Luis Sarria was the trainer and corner for the legendary Kid Tunero, an old Cuban pro who defeated four world titleholders, including Ezzard Charles; by 1948, Sarria was named trainer for the Cuban amateur team, winning three gold medals at the Guatemala Central American Games.

The fifties established Luis Sarria as one of Cuba's best trainers. He was the teacher and corner for three future Cuban world champions: Luis Rodriguez, Sugar Ramos and Jose Legra. Sarria also worked with world contenders including his amateur star turned pro heavyweight Julio Mederos, Spanish welterweight champion Ben Buker, lightweight Douglas Vaillant and national flyweight titleholder Amado Mir.

Life was good. Luis was a respected trainer making a modest living, keeping his belly full while working at his favorite trade, but his world changed in 1959, when Fidel Castro took power in Cuba. As Cuba entered the Cold War, with guerrilla fighting and resistance movements opposing the Marxist revolution and thousands being executed by firing squads, Luis Sarria contemplated leaving his country to live in a foreign land.

"Luis Rodriguez and I came to exile together," Sarria said in an interview. "When Castro took over Cuba he abolished pro boxing but it took him a couple of years to get around to doing it and boxers were allowed to fight in other countries. Luis Rodriguez and I traveled to the United States several times. Once, after a fight, we were both alone in the dressing room and I told him, "You go back alone this time." Luis looked at me and said "Sarria, are you staying?" And I said to him: "Yes, I cannot go back to that crap." Luis Rodriguez looked at me and he nodded, and then said, "I am staying also. I feel the same way."

In Miami, Sarria started life once again. He was flat broke, an exile in a strange land, but he had a good reputation as an honest trainer and he had a friend in Angelo Dundee. The Dundee brothers had spent over a decade importing and exporting Cuban fighters for their Miami Beach cards. Angelo spoke chopped up Spanish and his gym was filling up with new exiles: Luis Rodriguez, Florentino Fernandez, Jose Napoles, Angel Robinson Garcia, Sugar Ramos, Jose Legra, Douglas Valliant, Johnny Sarduy and a dozen other top talents.

Sarria became Angelo's right hand man at the Fifth Street Gym. He worked with prelim fighters and future champions, as a second to Angelo and on the road with the journeymen pugs and contenders. Muhammad Ali was then Cassius Clay a brash youth who idolized and studied Luis Rodriguez in the gym, studying the Cuban welter, copying some of his moves.

"I was training Luis…" Sarria said, "And Ali spoke to me, but I do not speak English. Then he spoke to Angelo and he told me Ali wanted me to massage him…Our friendship started that day." Sarria's big hands kneaded Ali's muscles. The Cuban trainer was not licensed as a masseur but decades of gym work had taught him where every pinched nerve could be softened, how to break down the body fat, how to release tension. His large hands did their magic on the fighter from Louisville and Ali understood that the soft spoken Cuban was in a league of his own.

Sarria only learned a few phrases of English and Ali could say a few words in Spanish, but their language differences did not prevent both men from becoming friends, using their own sign language to communicate. Sarria became Ali's conditioner, training the Great One, running him through endless hours of sit ups and knee bends, tuning his body while Dundee prepared the strategy for the upcoming bouts.

"The Ali years were unbelievable," he said, "I worked with him for all but two of his title fights. I was there from beginning to end. Ali treated me well. He gave me a down payment for my house and paid me a good salary, but many people around him were leeches. Angelo and the sparring partners earned their money but there were many in the camp that earned high salaries and did absolutely nothing…Few cared for him as a human being."

The sixties and early seventies were the best years of Sarria's life. He traveled the planet with Ali, Willie Pastrano, Jimmy Ellis, Luis Rodriguez, and a squad of top talent that included top rated middleweight Florentino Fernandez and lightweight contenders Douglas Valliant and Frankie Otero. He met presidents, kings, celebrities - including The Beatles - and intellectuals including Norman Mailer and Budd Schulberg. Sarria ate at the finest restaurants in Europe and the Orient and bunked at excellent hotels in all corners of the globe. The shoe-shine prelim boy from Cumanayagua became a celebrity himself, being photographed and filmed as he worked in the gym with the Great One or stood at the corner of contenders and champions. He rode in motorcar parades in Africa, walked the ancient streets of Rome, visited the presidential mansion in Manila, felt the snow under his boots in Toronto, visited the Statue of Liberty in New York, gazed upon movie sets in Hollywood and swam the beaches of Puerto Rico, the Bahamas and Florida.

He was there - at the corner of the ring with Angelo and Ferdie - when Ali fought Frazier, Foreman, Chuvalo, Norton and Spinks. Sarria was there when Rodriguez faced George Benton, Rocky Rivero, Rubin Carter, Curtis Cokes and Emile Griffith, when Frankie Otero traded leather with Buchanan and Florentino Fernandez landed big left hooks on opponents' chins.

"It was incredible," he once said, "I have a lot of tremendous memories… In Manila it was exciting. In the middle rounds Frazier hurt Ali very bad and he was in pain…Working the corner was a lot of pressure in that fight but Angelo is very smart at working a corner…I first met Angelo in the fifties when he went to Cuba almost every week for the fights…He was not rich or famous then. Like most trainers he was barely making a living."

One of the sad days of his career came when Luis Rodriguez lost a title bid to Nino Benvenuti. "Luis was a great fighter," Sarria said, "one of the greatest I ever saw, but he was shop-worn from more than a hundred fights, yet he gave the Italian a boxing lesson until Benvenuti threw that left hook. That was the hardest punch that man ever threw. It caught Luis on the side of the jaw. When I saw Luis go down, I knew he wasn't going to stand up that time."

In the eighties Sarria contemplated retirement. He had a home, a family and several dogs, a social security pension and Medicare, but he needed the fight game to stay alive, to feel useful. By then, the Fifth Street Gym was too far to travel for an old trainer with increasing arthritis. He needed a place closer to his North Miami home. Besides, the Fifth Street Gym had changed. Ali and the top guns of the sixties and seventies had retired, melting back into civilian life. Angelo was still active but had moved his base of operations away from Miami Beach. Ferdie Pacheco was doing TV commentary for big fights and writing books while Chris Dundee was still active with sporadic promotions and booking some fighters, but the aging Chris no longer produced the weekly fight shows that had made the gym the bubbling cauldron of pugilistic activity of its heyday.

Enter Caron Gonzalez, an old friend from the time Sarria was a prelim pug. Caron was a muscular black man who had been a sparring partner of Kid Tunero and had become a very good trainer after an unspectacular and brief pro career as a welter. Caron had worked with Benny Paret and Jose Stable and was a very good teacher of infighting. Gonzalez was opening up a gym in Miami's Allapatah neighborhood - only a block away from where Jack Britton had owned a drugstore - and Sarria was offered a chance to earn a few bucks and stay busy. Caron and Luis ran the gym for several years. Roberto Duran trained there for the "No Mas" fiasco with Ray Leonard, as did other champions including Happy Lora and Wilfredo Vazquez. Gonzalez and Sarria kept busy working with fighters like Puerto Rican lightweight Juan Arroyo, Cuban lightweight Pedro Laza and a small army of prelim fighters hailing from all corners of the Caribbean. Sarria trained fighters, massaged bodies and worked corners. He would pace himself, taking breaks in which he sat ringside, puffing on a pipe, waiting for the arthritis to ease so he could stand again, to continue teaching the nuances of the jab or hook. Eventually, he stopped working corners, for it hurt too much to climb the few steps into the ring.

That was the beginning of the end of the Sarria story. All good things come to pass and so do good men. Luis Sarria is no longer among us, but those who knew him will never forget his big smile, his large hands, his soft manners and his bearing that Ferdie Pacheco equated with "the dignity of an African Prince."

Not bad for a poor shoe shine boy from Cumanayagua.

Luis Rodriguez with a Cuban flag the day he won the welterweight crown.

Luis Manuel: roadwork at the race track

Luis at work against Joe Shaw at Madison Square Garden, 1968.

Rodriguez stops Ricardo Falech

CHAPTER EIGHTEEN: A CHAMPION'S FUNERAL

Mourners began arriving at the Bernardo Garcia-Brake Funeral Home in the early evening, while the Miami sun still bathed Seventh Street with a dim light.

In the lobby, a black board with plastic stick-on letters announced that the mortal remains of Luis Manuel Rodriquez could be viewed in Room Nine.

Frankie Otero, former junior lightweight contender stood next to me as we gazed down on a withered corpse, neatly dressed in suit and tie. The body in the casket had a stone expression.

"It doesn't look like Luis," Frankie said.

"It's because he's not smiling," I answered, "you are not used to seeing him not smiling."

I turned away. I did to want to remember him like this, crated for eternal sleep.

The first time I saw him, I was a little kid, and he, a dozen years older, was then a young pro, undefeated in Havana rings. He stood on the sidewalk and performed for the children who recognized him, shadowboxing, soft shoe dancing and capping off the performance with an opera aria sung with a clear, crisp voice. Then, he shook our hands and walked away, laughing. He was cool by anyone's standards.

Luis Manuel Rodriguez was born in Camaguey, in Western Cuba in 1937. By the time he was eighteen he had won several televised talent shows, as a dancer and crooner. He had also become Cuba's top amateur boxing talent, winning the national amateur title with ten straight knockouts.

He was a natural, Luis Rodriguez with his thin legs, round chest, wide nose and flashing smile did not look intimidating, but the black welterweight from Camaguey was a slick boxer with a crisp punch, dazzling speed and a cement chin.

Rodriguez turned pro two weeks before his nineteenth birthday. In thirty months, being matched against good foes, he racked up eighteen wins and one no-contest, a bout stopped by rain at an outdoor arena. His undefeated ledger shows victories over two tough young fighters –Guillermo Diaz and Rolando Rodriguez –beating each twice. Luis also scored two wins over future world champion Benny Paret, as well as a triumph by knockout over spoiler Charlie Austin, a win on points over future British Empire Middleweight Champion Gomeo Brennan, and a clear victory over Kid Fichique, winning the national welterweight title.

The year 1959 was sweet. Luis out-slicked former welterweight king Virgil Atkins, and scored six other wins over top-rated fighters. Joe Miceli, a veteran of over a hundred bouts was stopped in five rounds; Cecil Shorts was finished off in nine. Isaac Logart, a fellow Cuban who had fought for a world title was out boxed by Luis in ten.

The time was coming to leave Cuba. Fidel Castro was executing opponents by the thousands and laying out the foundations of a Marxist dictatorship. Luis Rodriguez headed to Miami, where thousands of his fellow countrymen had sought exile over political repression.

In the three year period from 1960-1962 he fought twenty-five times. He lost two close fights with Emile Griffith and Curtis Cokes, while outscoring Cokes in a rematch. He beat former champion Akins a second time, out-pointed and stopped dangerous middleweight Yama Bahama in two matches, knocked out tough Gene Armstrong in a televised bout, outfoxed top rated contenders Federico Thompson and Chico Vejar, and became the first fighter to stop brawler Ricardo Falech.

In his corner, the flashy Cuban had a trio of legendary fight men: Angelo Dundee, Luis Sarria and Ferdie Pacheco.

"He was an incredible fighter," Ferdie Pacheco told me, "Luis could fight on the inside or from a distance. He could attack or counter punch. He had a terrific jab and he would fire quick shots to the body then switch to the head. He slipped punches with ease, and he was very difficult to hit. Even when one could nail him in a solid shot, the follow up was impossible. Luis would slip and dance and bob and weave. If you were really good, you could hit Luis Rodriguez a clean shot, but it was almost impossible to nail him twice in a row..."

"Ali studied Luis," Angelo Dundee said, "When Luis was sparring you would see Ali watching, studying how Luis would step in and throw an uppercut or how he would move at an angle to make the guy miss. Ali respected Luis a lot because Luis was the complete package. He could box outside or fight inside or at middle distance. Luis was a complete fighter."

When Pacheco went on a ten city radio tour to promote his books, he was invariably asked to name the best fighter -besides Ali- that he had ever worked with and the answer over the radio, on ten occasions was: Luis Rodriguez.

"At the Fifth Street Gym," Frankie Otero remembers, "Luis sparred with fighters that were ten, twenty, thirty pounds heavier. Guys like Florentino Fernandez and Willie Pastrano, and Luis Manuel was trouble for anyone."

The greatest moment of his life came in Los Angeles, in 1963, when Rodriguez outscored nemesis Emile Griffith to win the welterweight crown. Less than three months later, Rodriquez lost his title in a hotly disputed fifteen rounder in New York, Griffith's hometown.

"I won the fight and lost the championship," Rodriguez stated several years ago, "It was New York. You need a flamethrower to beat Griffith in New York."

Rodriguez was not one to cry about a defeat. Nine weeks after losing the crown, he squared off against Denny Moyer in a Miami Beach ring. Moyer, a former junior middleweight champion, was a veteran of forty-six pro fights. Moyer had wins over a distinguished group of champions including Emile Griffith, Johnny Saxton, Virgil Akins, Sugar Ray Robinson, Benny Paret and Tony De Marco. The Oregon fighter had never been stopped.

Luis Rodriguez turned the trick. The Cuban out boxed Moyer, winning the lion's share of the first eight rounds. Attacking sometimes and countering others, Rodriguez decked Moyer in the ninth, stopping the Portland fighter.

"The Moyer fight was a magnificent performance," remembers Hank Kaplan, "then Luis had another heartbreak squeaker with Griffith. But what was really amazing was the way Luis plowed right through the middleweights. He fought the top fighters in the world in their backyards, spotted pounds, and licked them. Those that wanted a second shot, he gave a rematch, and licked them again."

Ruben Carter was a feared middleweight knockout artist. The muscled, skull shaved, Fu Manchu mustachioed ex-convict had scored clean first round knockouts over Emile Griffith and Florentino Fernandez.

Luis Manuel fought Carter at Madison Square Garden in February of 1965. In the seventh round a hard hook by Carter dropped Luis Manuel to the canvas for the first time in his career.

"Luis Manuel got up and nodded slightly as he looked towards our corner," said Luis Sarria, "when the round was over Luis sat on the stool and said – That is not going to happen again…. he gave the Hurricane a boxing lesson and a few months later came a rematch in Los Angeles and Luis Manuel won again."

Skeeter McClure was a full-fledged unbeaten middleweight, a Gold Medalist from the 1960 Olympic Games. Luis decked McClure and beat him twice.

George Benton was a top contender that champions avoided. The crafty and solid punching Benton was no match for Rodriguez. Benton was stopped on cuts, for the first time in his career.

Rocky Rivero was a knockout puncher from Argentina who had a 55-14-3 record with 45 knockouts. A fearless slugger, Rivero had fought Florentino Fernandez in four brutal wars, each man winning one on points and one by knockout. Rivero had also stopped Wilf Greaves, beaten Hurricane Carter on points and had lost to Dick Tiger and Joey Giardello.

"Rivero was made for me," Luis Manuel said years later, "He was a tank, very strong and a solid, hard puncher, but he was not fast and he telegraphed his punches. I put a leather factory on his face. I punched and counterpunched and he missed me all night."

Benny Briscoe was the hottest prospect in the middleweights, a tough left hooker from Philadelphia, destined to fight a draw with Carlos Monzon. Rodriguez beat Briscoe twice.

Future light heavyweight king Vicente Rondon won the first bout but Rodriguez won the second match.

"Luis was unfazed," remembers Hank Kaplan, "he was never bothered by how big a fighter was or how many knockouts he had. . . he was a welterweight fighting middleweights and light-heavies, and if they would have let him, he would have fought Ali."

After losing on cuts to Curtis Cokes in a title bout, Rodriguez concentrated on the pursuit of the middleweight crown. On November 22, 1969, he toed the scratch against Nino Benvenuti, in Rome.

For ten rounds, Rodriguez outfoxed the Italian. He seemed headed for a second title belt, until a desperate Benvenuti threw a tremendous left hook that exploded against Luis' chin in the eleventh round. Rodriguez was stopped cold.

"It was the best punch Benvenuti ever threw," Luis Sarria told me, "and when it landed, I knew it was over. That punch would have knocked down a heavyweight."

Luis Rodriguez continued fighting for three more years. He still beat some top fighters, losing and winning to Jose Gonzalez, barely out pointing tough Bobby Cassidy and knocking out Tony Mundine. Back to back losses to club fighter Mike Lancaster and prospect Donato Paduano convinced the thirty-four year old Rodriguez to hang up the eight-ouncers.

His 107-13-0 and 1 NC record included 49 knockout wins, and only 3 kayo losses.

After retirement he trained amateur boxers, owned a bar, worked in a warehouse, and discovered booze. The last two years of his life were a nightmare of dialysis treatments. He was fifty-nine years old when death came to him in a Miami Beach hospital, not far from the Miami Beach Convention Center, where he had beaten Denny Moyer and a score of other good fighters.

Near the coffin there was a painting of a young Luis Rodriguez, wearing a title belt and boxing trunks. It was a Ferdie Pacheco original, brought by the fight doctor as a gift to the family.

In the picture, Luis was smiling.

Johnny Sarduy was a good fighter, a patriot and a smart entrepreneur.

CHAPTER NINETEEN: BANTAM JOHNNY SARDUY

Johnny Sarduy was born in Ranchuelo, a farming community in central Cuba.

"In Ranchuelo where I was born," said Johnny Sarduy, "Most people either worked at a cigarette factory that provided hundreds of jobs in town, or they did agricultural work at the farms in the region."

Ranchuelo also had a boxing gym where a few amateurs and prelim pros trained.

"I came from poverty," Sarduy has stated. "But we survived without complaining and I had a happy childhood. How poor were we? I tell you, I did not eat a steak until I was an adolescent and I had a boxing career…the only meat I had eaten up to then was ground beef mixed with white rice – *arroz con picadillo*- and even that dish was infrequent in our menu….I did not learn to eat with a knife and fork until I was well into boxing because poor people eat with spoons. Everything we ate you could eat with a spoon: soups, cornmeal, rice and beans…"

"I was young but I was already working in a shoe repair shop in town, learning the trade and when I decided I would try amateur boxing my parents did not want me to fight but my father allowed it figuring that as soon as I was hit a few times I would retire quickly…He was wrong."

As a flyweight, Sarduy won 31 of 33 amateur fights, becoming Cuban National Golden Gloves champion. At the end of his amateur career, Sarduy met Benito Fernandez, the man who would become his manager and mentor.

Fernandez was a wealthy businessman who owned real estate, a garage and auto repair shop as well as an auto parts wholesale distributorship. Above all that, Fernandez was a fanatical lover of boxing and was already managing two young prospects: William Roncourt –who would become a main event fighter- and future world monarch Sugar Ramos.

Fernandez was not into boxing for the money but for the sheer pleasure of being involved in a sport he loved. He treated all his fighters very well but his relationship with Sarduy transcended boxing. Fernandez became a father figure to Johnny.

Don Benito did not make a penny from Sarduy, on the contrary, he spent a considerable amount of money on the young fighter. Money from purses was deposited in a saving bank account under Johnny's name. Fernandez also paid all his training expenses, gave him a job pumping gas, provided him with additional spending money and eventually even moved him into his own home, treating Johnny as a son.

Fernandez also moved the Sarduy family to Havana, providing jobs for Johnny's father, three brothers and a sister, whom he also enrolled at a business college, paying the bill.

Johnny Cruz, hired as Johnny's trainer, was a former main event fighter who had fought Kid Chocolate twice and other champions and contenders including Freddie Miller, Chino Alvarez and Tommy Spiegal. Cruz trained him intensely for seven months before turning him pro. By then, eighteen year old Sarduy had grown into the bantamweight division.

Johnny won his first two bouts, settling for a draw in the third against *Huesito* (Little Bone) Gonzalez, a tough club fighter known for his heart and durability.

The draw was followed by fourteen more wins, earning Sarduy mention as a Ring Magazine prospect. The fourteenth win was over a hungry fighter named Felix Gutierrez, who beat Johnny on points in the rematch.

Sarduy bounced back from defeat scoring a knockout over Florida's Ken McCurry.

In 1958, Sarduy impressed the boxing community with two wins over Eloy Sanchez, considered one of the top Mexican fighters in the bantam division. Johnny also won and lost with Miguel Lazu, a good, experienced Cuban fighter.

1959, which began with the arrival of Fidel Castro to power, was a down year for Sarduy, winning two, losing three and drawing in another two. He was stopped by knockout in a Mexico ring by hard hitting contender Jose Medel, the only time in his career he would be stopped.

In 1960, Sarduy twice faced Orlando Castillo, better known as *Gallito del Ring* (Rooster of the Ring). The rooster was a good boxer who had been a top main event fighter for years. Castillo and Sarduy drew in their first bout and Sarduy won the second one on points.

Sarduy's mind was no longer into boxing but into concern for the civil war that was tearing Cuba apart. He joined a resistance group and after months of risking being caught and executed by the communist authorities, Sarduy made his way to Florida.

In January and February of 1961, Johnny won two bouts, defeating a Puerto Rican club fighter named Hector Rodriguez. Those would be his last two pro fights, as Sarduy retired from the ring with a 33-7-4 record with 6 KO wins.

Benito Fernandez, then exiled in Mexico, was not there for Sarduy's last two fights.

A few days after announcing his retirement, Sarduy went into training again, this time at a CIA base camp in Louisiana, where Assault Brigade 2506 had been assembled for what became known as the Bay of Pigs Invasion. One of his fellow recruits was *Huesito* Gonzalez, the tough little fighter he had faced in the ring.

The invasion was a dismal failure and Sarduy was back in Miami before the end of 1961. He worked in restaurants as a waiter to pay bills, married an exiled Cuban girl and proceeded to raise a family.

From the restaurant job, Sarduy moved to the construction field. He learned to use the spray texture "popcorn" machines for ceilings and calculate cost and labor for bids. Making a good living, he eventually partnered with a friend, creating his own company, then, a few years later, he opened a second company all by himself.

By the 1980's, Sarduy had become one of South Florida's largest drywall contractors, with over sixty workers on its payroll, bidding contracts on high rises and office buildings. The boy who had not known how to use a fork and knife had grown up to be a wealthy millionaire.

By the beginning of the new century, Sarduy retired, passing down his business to his children.

Benito Fernandez, his beloved mentor, died in Venezuela in 1978.

"Much of what I am today," Sarduy said, "I owe to him…I never dreamed that I would have all that I have….real estate properties, houses, a prosperous business that has put food on the table for many families… Success –in the ring or out- is something one has to sweat and what I have, I earned working hard –in and out of the ring- and I firmly believe that he who seeks to triumph will eventually triumph."

Sugar Ramos in training.

Promoter Cuco Conde and Ramos in church praying for Davey Moore.

CHAPTER TWENTY: SUGAR RAMOS

Some men are destroyed by adverse destiny while others confront it and manage to survive emotionally.

Ultiminio –Sugar- Ramos has managed to overcome the crushing emotional burden of having killed a man in the ring at the age of sixteen, and a second by the age of twenty-one.

Fatalities occur in boxing as they do on any sport but few have been the cases in boxing history that one fighter killed two men in the ring. Yet, in spite of the traumatic experience, Sugar Ramos has survived as a human being, enjoys life and is proud of his lifetime accomplishments.

"When I killed Tigre Blanco," he told me in a Canastota interview, "I was going to quit boxing forever but his parents told me that they did not consider it to be my fault, that it was an accident, that it could have been me instead…then with Davey Moore –the night I won the title- came more anguish but although I blamed myself for a time, I came to understand that they were accidents and a man has to accept what destiny brings…"

Ramos was born in Matanzas, the son of a father that sired 32 children with two different women, Ultiminio turned pro at the age of fifteen, with a knockout over a prelim fighter named Rene Arce.

He went through the featherweight division like a ball of hot flame. He won eleven –nine by KO- before he stopped Jose Tigre Blanco in that tragic night in 1958.

Convinced by Blanco's family that he was not to blame for the fighter's death, Ramos was back in the ring only one month after the tragedy, scoring another knockout.

Between his pro debut in 1957 until the end of 1961, Ramos went undefeated in 34 fights with 31 wins and three draws and his first defeat was a controversial disqualification against an ordinary journeyman named Rafael Camacho.

By the time in 1963 when he faced Davey Moore for the world crown –WBC and WBA versions-, that DQ was the only loss for Ramos in a forty two fight pro career.

On his way to the title, Sugar Ramos had scored wins over Alfredo Urbina, Sonny Leon, Jesus Santamaria, Orlando –Rooster of the Ring- Castillo, Danny Valdez, Kid Anahuac and Rafiu King.

"My fight with Davey Moore was very hard," Ramos said years later in an interview, "He was a phenomenal fighter and I am sorry for what happened. When they took him away I was saying to myself –Not again, please God, not again…"

An investigation on the death of Moore came to the conclusion that the fatal blow happened when the fighter's brain stem was damaged by whiplash as his head hit a low rope of the ring, but for the exonerated Ramos the personal pain remained.

The new champion defended against Rafiu King in Mexico, winning on points before travelling to London to finish off Sam McSpadden in three rounds, followed by two more over the weight wins before defending his title in Japan against Mitsunori Seki, an experienced boxer with an awkward southpaw style and fair punching power. Seki had a 42-5-1 record and 24 of his victories had been by knockout.

Angelo Dundee –working with Ramos- has said that on the day before the match he went to the Kokugigan Arena to inspect the ring, which was in fine condition. Dundee, however, worried that there were no chairs in the large hall.

"When are you going to set up the seating?" Angelo asked the promoter.

"Oh, no," the promoter responded, "We do not use chairs. Japanese prefer the floor."

The following night, when Ramos dropped and stopped Seki in six rounds, Angelo reflected that the promoter was right, Japanese prefer the floor.

By then, the muscular, well proportioned Ramos was having trouble making the featherweight limit, for his body had matured and added additional muscle. He was weakening himself to maintain the weight to defend his crown.

The next fight took place in Ghana, facing local Floyd Robertson. Ramos picked up an early lead but weakened in the last third of the fifteenth round fight, being cut in the mouth and dropped to the canvas for a count in the thirteenth stanza. The result ended in controversy. The judges voted Ramos as winner but the Ghana boxing authorities declared it a no contest, later recognizing Robertson as champion, a position that crumbled when the WBA and WBC supported the original judges' vote awarding a split victory on points to the Cuban.

In his next defense, Ramos lost the title to Vicente Saldivar, a tough Mexican southpaw. The bout was a war of attrition, a bloody brawl in which Ramos retired from combat at the end of the eleventh round.

Moving up in weight, Ramos won five in a row and challenged Carlos Ortiz for the lightweight crown. The Puerto Rican fighter won by cutting up Ramos but the boxing bodies demanded a rematch in face of a controversial long count in Ortiz' favor. The rematch brought a second Ortiz victory, also by TKO, this one in four, a round faster than the first bout.

Ramos –although still young- had peaked and lost his edge. He still had enough to beat very good fighters including rough and tough Raul Rojas and Mexican Chango Carmona, but he was no longer an invincible slugger.

He lost a bloody battle against Mando Ramos and also lost on points to Antonio Amaya. He drew with prospect Jimmy Robertson, scored a knockout over Lyle Randolph and ended his career with a humiliating stoppage at the hands of journeyman Cesar Sinda.

The former featherweight king retired with a 55-7-4 record with 40 KO victories.

His ring fortune was spent in some partying and expensive clothing and in supporting his Mexican family. Ramos had left behind another family in Cuba and his Mexican family would eventually grow to seven children, making overhead expenses high for the ex-fighter.

He decided to become a professional musician and entertainer. The idea was not new to former fighters. Kid Gavilan had tried, flopping as a dancer and Jose Napoles had a band for a while that eventually broke up, forcing the fighter to hock his instruments and sell his van.

Ramos, however, succeeded where others had failed. For almost four decades he has earned a living as a musician, playing drums or congas with his own band in nightclubs, weddings and private parties all over Mexico, or playing back up for well known Mexican performers.

"I did not make big money in music," he told me when inducted to the International Boxing Hall of Fame "but I have worked steadily, made an honest living and I've enjoyed it. I love music and being paid to play music is sweet."

The Hall of Famer has performed in dozens of nightclubs and catering halls in all corners of Mexico, has appeared in a movie and several television shows, lives in modest comfort with his family and continues to dress impeccably in suit and tie.

Jose Legra: The Pocket Cassius Clay

CHAPTER TWENTY-ONE: THE POCKET ALI

In the sixties Jose Legra was nicknamed "The Pocket Cassius Clay," because of an uncanny resemblance to the Great One. Had Legra weighed eighty pounds more and gained seven inches in height, he would have convinced anyone that he was Ali's twin brother.

Beyond the physical resemblance both men fought with similar styles; both had dazzling footwork, lightning speed and flashy combinations.

A Spanish journalist, noting the comparison, asked Legra if he had patterned his style after the heavyweight champion.

"No," responded the smiling Cuban fighter, "If anyone copied anyone, he copied me because I turned pro before he did."

Jose Legra was born in the town of Baracoa, on the eastern tip of Cuba in 1943, one of seven brothers. His father was a dockworker and his mother a cleaning maid. By the age of eleven, Jose was earning money to help out, shining shoes or working as a street vendor, peddling newspapers, bags of peanuts or fruits.

Baracoa had a gym with a few prelim pros and amateurs and Jose joined up. He was poor and there was money to be made, even as an amateur. In the amateur cards grateful gamblers tipped the winners and promoters generally paid a peso to each fighter, as expense money and not to be considered a professional purse. Legra fought 23 times and lost only one, to an experienced amateur from Santiago named Vicente Nunez.

At the age of sixteen Legra left Baracoa and hitchhiked to Havana to make his fortune in the ring. He signed up as a pupil to master trainer Luis Sarria, but was turned down for a professional license for being anemic, being forced to wait a full year before passing his next health exam.

He turned pro in 1960, about a year and half before Fidel Castro banned pro boxing in Cuba, enough time to develop quickly into a main event fighter.

One of his most important bouts at the time was against Baby Luis –real name Emiro Duvergel- a very smooth boxer with solid power, who beat Legra, dropping him twice in the process.

Baby Luis was the son of a good club fighter of the same name who had trained his child well. The young fighter had all the talent of a champion but was attracted by the fast life and easy money.

Dr. Ferdie Pacheco tells an anecdote of flying to Mexico to locate Baby Luis for a fight with Howard Winstone in 1964.

After searching Mexican gyms for days, Pacheco finally found Baby Luis, who had bloodshot eyes and needed a shave. Pacheco asked him where he had been and Baby answered by saying a Mexican friend had given him a bag of marijuana and he had sat on a hill seeking the meaning of life.

"Okay, I'll bite. What is the meaning of life?" Pacheco asked.

"I ran out of marijuana and I want some more," answered Luis.

Besides smoking weed, Baby Luis worked in the drug trafficking business, being eventually murdered in Miami when a deal went sour.

After Castro abolished boxing, Legra headed to Mexico and Florida but was not comfortable in either place. In the United States blacks were still discriminated and the Civil Rights bill had not yet become law. Legra was shocked and humiliated when he boarded a public bus in Miami and was ordered to sit in the back rows.

The young Cuban fighter decided to try his luck in Spain, under the guidance of Kid Tunero, one of Cuba's ring legends. Tunero was a former middleweight contender who had beaten four world champions, including Ezzard Charles. He was exiled in Barcelona where he was training some Spanish prospects. Tunero's assistant was a former Cuban light heavyweight- Cheo Morejon – who had some eighty pro fights including a draw with Nino Valdez and had earned a living for awhile as a pro wrestler.

The Tunero-Legra combination grew into a solid, trusting relationship with excellent timing. When Jose Legra arrived in Barcelona he was already a seasoned professional with thirty three fights on his ledger, an experienced ten round fighter who had good skills, yet despite all the experience was only twenty years old.

"I loved Tunero," Legra said of his manager, "He became family to me."

Legra won nine in a row before fighting a draw with Kid Tano in 1964. Tano was a deaf mute and his corner would indicate to him a round was over by flashing a light at his face. Before the year ended they fought two more times with Legra outscoring the Spanish featherweight champion on both occasions.

From October 1963 to May 1965, Legra fought thirty times with 28 wins and two draws, before losing on points to clever Welshman Howard Winstone.

He followed the loss with forty straight wins. Many of his victories were over ordinary club fighters but he also scored quality wins over British Commonwealth and African Champion Love Allotey, over Don Johnson, a former contender from California, Jose Luis Torcidas –light welter champion of Spain- and Rafiu King, an established star in European rings.

Always in condition, he was making fair purses packing arenas in different cities in Spain. He happily admitted being a womanizer but did not drink, smoke or do drugs. The skirt chasing never interfered with his professional work ethic.

In December of 1967, in his 110th professional fight, the twenty four year old Cuban –by then also a citizen of Spain- became European featherweight champion by dismantling Yves Desmarets in only three rounds.

He did not defend his newly acquired crown for only seven months after beating Desmarets, Legra faced old foe Howard Winstone for the WBC Featherweight title.

Legra started out very fast, surprising Howard, who was knocked down twice in the first round by right hand blows. Legra set a fast pace, peppering the Welshman with combinations until the fight was stopped due to Winston's left eye being closed shut, impairing his visibility. The young Cuban from Baracoa had become a world champion.

Legra was by then an international boxing star and very famous in his adopted nation. He was invited to meet Spanish strongman Francisco Franco in a private audience in which he was given a new Oldsmobile as a gift. He had endorsement contracts that fattened his bank account; he was also invited to a number of television shows in which he made a good impression because he spoke well, had a warm personality and dressed well, making a reporter state that no one in Spain wore a suit and tie better than Legra.

He picked up two good paychecks beating Bob Allotey and Felix Brami before losing the crown to Australian boxer Johnny Famechon, who used a hit and run tactic to outpoint the Cuban. The Spanish press howled robbery but Legra accepted the defeat and continued to fight.

The Pocket Cassius Clay won two tune-ups and travelled to California where he dropped Vicente Saldivar to the canvas but lost on points at the Inglewood Forum.

Jose Legra returned to Europe and won six bouts, including a victory over British Champion Evan Armstrong, before challenging for the European featherweight title against Italian Tomasso Galli.

Legra outpointed Galli to become king of the European feathers, defending it successfully five times before receiving an opportunity to fight Clemente Sanchez for WBC featherweight title in Mexico.

Sanchez lost the fight at the scales and Legra –who did make weight- became world champion once again, stopping the Mexican by TKO in ten rounds.

Again, Legra lost in his first defense as the iconic 37 year old Brazilian, Eder Joffre, managed to outpoint him by split decision.

Now thirty years old, his lightning reflexes fading, Legra only fought twice. He beat Jimmy Bell in ten and travelled to Nicaragua where a highly rated youngster named Alexis Arguello knocked him out in the first round.

Legra hung up his gloves and retired from the ring. He had invested in real estate and in a partnership of a sports clothing manufacturing company. He won and lost in the real estate business but kept enough to have a source of income and a roof over his head. The clothing business did well for some time until the partnership dissolved and Legra went to work as a public relations executive for a Barcelona company, a well paying job he held for years until his retirement.

The now seventy year old Legra –still active in the business world- is still one of the most elegantly well dressed men in Barcelona.

Jose Angel –Mantequilla- Napoles

Napoles as a junior welterweight

CHAPTER TWENTY-TWO: SMOOTH AS BUTTER

Santiago de Cuba is a city with a solid boxing tradition. From Santiago came the flashy globetrotter Ramon Castillo, the three time National Cuban heavyweight champion Goyito Rico, tough middleweight Eliseo Quintana who beat three fighters in one card and Ciro Morasen, a world class featherweight.

The Napoles family of Santiago de Cuba was very involved in professional boxing from the late thirties when Sergio Napoles –who fought under the name Kid Guarina began a fifteen-year career as a journeyman bantam.

Sergio was followed into the ring by a squad of sons and nephews. They entered the pro ranks but most were mediocre. Pedro Napoles lost more than he won but could boast of having survived four rounds with hard banging Florentino Fernandez. Light heavyweight Miguel, featherweight Luis and lightweight Israel were all willing, but limited prelim fighters.

Jose Angel Napoles changed all that.

From the beginning he showed natural ability and was blessed with an outstanding teacher, a lean, black ex fighter named Juan Sierra but known throughout Cuba as Kid Bururu.

Bururu's career had stretched for over twenty years when he had headlined many shows in Havana and Santiago de Cuba with occasional jaunts to Panama, Mexico, Venezuela and Guayana. A light puncher with a good chin, Bururu had won the Cuban National Lightweight Championship from Joe Calixto and lost it in 1948 to Orlando Zulueta in a close, controversial decision as reported by Ring Magazine. He lost twice on points to Kid Gavilan had a draw with contender Humberto Sierra and wins over Santiago Sosa and Dan Calcagno. Bururu was well regarded by Cuban fans for his defensive skills and technical boxing displays.

Bururu trained Jose well and the young boy proceeded to defeat anyone within ten pounds of his weight at the amateur level.

Bururu sent his prize pupil to another old friend in Havana, Alfredo Chavez who had fought as a featherweight under the name of Kid Rapidez.

As a fighter Rapidez had been an adequate club fighter who had twice challenged for the national featherweight title; as a trainer he was outstanding, handling a group of prospects that included Sugar Ramos and Baby Luis.

At eighteen, Napoles first pro opponent was Julio Rojas, a local featherweight that was stopped in the very first round. Napoles won his first seven fights – five by KO- before losing on points to Hilton Smith, a lightweight from Tampa. He would not be defeated again for almost five years.

Although a brilliant performer, Napoles apparently felt that he was not being acknowledged enough by sportswriters who raved about the power sluggers like Florentino Fernandez and Sugar Ramos and wrote reams of print about the masterful Luis Manuel. Although Napoles was praised, he felt relegated to a second level and resentment built as he also toiled daily as a bus driver to pay his bills.

Johnny Sarduy was another young fighter at the time. Sarduy was a country boy from the town of Ranchuelo, in central Cuba. He had won a national amateur title at flyweight and as a pro had scored an impressive string of wins at the time. Sarduy -a very smooth bantamweight- was destined to finish his career with a 33-7-4 ledger. Years later, Sarduy, by then a wealthy construction contractor in Miami related an unflattering Napoles anecdote.

"We trained in the same gym," Sarduy remembered, "but we were not close. My closest pal in the gym was William Roncourt, a young featherweight…. I had just won a fight at the Trejo Arena and the Havana newspapers had printed articles stating how I had won every round… On this day, Roncourt and I were sitting at the massage table in the gym, just talking, when Napoles showed up, looking upset…To my surprise he looked at me and said: You little white piece of shit you make headlines and get praises just for being white…His words surprised me and I laughed and it made him angrier. He spat at me and I was so surprised that I did not react immediately but William –who was black- did, coming off that massage table swinging at Napoles… It was an ugly moment… to me it wasn't about black or white.

I thought we were all brothers, all poor, hungry kids trying to make a living in a very tough trade. Napoles was a brilliant fighter but to me, a real son of a whore of a human being."

After the loss to Hilton Smith, Napoles won thirteen in a row in Havana rings including two victories on points over the flashy Angel Robinson Garcia and one triumph over Bunny Grant, a very good Jamaican fighter.

By 1962, exiled from the Castro government, twenty-three year old Napoles became a resident of Mexico, where he became well known as "Mantequilla" for being smooth as butter in the ring.

Over the next seven years he fought often. He lost on points to Mexican lightweight champion Alfredo Urbina and gained revenge by knocking out Urbina twice in rematches. He defeated veteran L.C. Morgan three out of four.

The fight that impressed the boxing world took place in Caracas in 1964, when Mantequilla faced Carlos "Morocho" Hernandez –destined to become Venezuela's first world champion- a hard puncher that top fighters ducked, with a ledger that included KO wins over three world champions or future titleholders : Davey Moore, Joe Brown and Carlos Teo Cruz.

In a hard fought fight, Napoles outscored and outpunched Hernandez, stopping him by TKO in the seventh round with a brutal, well aimed left hook.

Mantequilla was beating all the top lightweights and light welters but champions Carlos Ortiz and Sandro Lopopolo were unwilling to risk their crowns against the slick boxer-puncher from Cuba.

Mantequilla fought the magnificent Eddie Perkins –a former world champion- in Juarez and won a unanimous decision, dropping Perkins to the canvas in the eighth round.

In 1968, Mantequilla could still make 140 pounds but moved to the welterweights seeking a title shot. On April 18, 1969, five days after turning 29 years old and after 11 years as a pro with more than sixty bouts, Napoles got his title shot against Texan Curtis Cokes.

Mantequilla dominated Cokes from the first bell and the champion was unable to answer the bell for the fourteenth round. Two months later, Napoles made his first title defense, offering Cokes a rematch, stopping him in the tenth round.

When asked his opinion of Napoles after their second meeting, Cokes said: "He's a better fighter than Curtis Cokes."

After his first bout with Cokes, Napoles was invited to meet Mexican president Gustavo Diaz Ordaz. In the meeting, Napoles expressed his desire to become a Mexican citizen and the president personally notified Mexican immigration authorities to expedite Mantequilla's citizenship.

Before 1969 ended, Napoles defended his title once more, against the great Emile Griffith, knocking down the New York fighter on the way to winning a 15 round decision.

In 1970 Napoles defended his title twice. He defeated tough Ernie Red Lopez by TKO and lost his title on a cut to Billy Backus.

Backus, from Canastota, New York, also came from a fighting family. His uncle was the great Carmen Basilio, one of the roughest welters of all time. Backus had inherited his uncle's valor but was not considered much of a threat to Napoles. Billy came into the ring with a 29-10-4 record with 15 KO wins. The contenders he had beaten included Manuel Gonzalez and Percy Pugh.

Backus pulled an upset, opening a cut over the champion's eyebrow that earned him a victory and the coveted crown, which he held for only six months, Napoles stopping Backus by TKO-8 and regaining the crown.

After regaining the title, Mantequilla defended his crown against Hedgemon Lewis, a clever boxer managed by comedian Bill Cosby, against Ralph Charles, Adolph Pruitt, Ernie Red Lopez –for a second time- European champion Roger Menetrey and Canadian Clyde Gray, defeating them all.

Mantequilla was at his peak and the days of hunger and bread and butter purses were part of the past. He made $85,000 for the Pruitt fight, $70,000 for Gray and even the four over the weight non-title fights he used as tune-ups in this time frame brought paychecks of ten to twenty thousand dollars apiece. There was additional income from public appearances and endorsements.

Napoles bought dozens of suits, expensive shoes, fast wheels and wore a thick solid gold bracelet adorned with diamonds. He went night clubbing, drank with gusto and enjoyed his money without salting away a single peso.

Still, he trained hard and retained his will to win.

A French promotional group headed by famous actor Alain Delon, offered Napoles the then considerable sum of $120,000 to face the mighty Carlos Monzon for the middleweight crown and Mantequilla accepted.

"The fight looked attractive," boxing historian Hank Kaplan said years later, "because it was a match between the two best pound for pound fighters active, but it really was a bad match. Napoles was a junior welter who had been fighting as a welter and Monzon was a big, solid middleweight with power and a very long reach."

Monzon gave the game Cuban a solid beating, stopping him.

Napoles was still welterweight king. He beat Hedgemon Lewis again, followed by a knockout of Argentine Horacio Saldano and two wins over California's Armando Muniz. Besides being a top contender for years, Muniz was a college graduate who went on to have a productive, long career in the educational field.

The money kept coming in and quickly disappearing. Napoles was drinking and partying but he was also professional enough to train hard to defend his crown.

Mantequilla was thirty five years old when he defended his title against European and British champion John H. Stracey in a ring set up in a Mexican bullring.

A very likeable extrovert with a fine singing voice and sharp sense of humor, Stracey was not a foe to be taken lightly. At the time he challenged Napoles, he had a creditable 42-3-1 record with 34 knockouts.

It was Napoles' last fight. Both men scored knockdowns, but Stracey used his jab as an offensive weapon, throwing dozens every round. His constant jabs busted up the older champion. By the beginning of the sixth round, Napoles' face showed a nasty cut over the right eyebrow, his left eye was almost closed shut and his right eye was surrounded by swelling.

Mantequilla tried to rally but the British fighter kept pumping the left into his bruised face until the third man in the ring stepped between them, making Stracey the new king of the welters.

Years later Stracey –interviewed by journalist Garth Davis- said of that fight: "The night itself is still very clear to me. The feeling of getting knocked down in the first round, and thinking "right, he's hit me with his best shot", then in the third round, knocking him down with a left hook. That said my jab was the winner. I had sparred with Napoles three years earlier in a gym in Hampstead. Terry Lawless had told me to jab Napoles if I ever fought him. So that night in Mexico City, we had our plan, in front of 27,000 Mexicans and 23 fans from London. Funnily enough, I could hear my fans all the way through the fight. I had been there for a month, but had boxed there seven years earlier at the Olympic Games. I knew what was needed to be prepared."

Stracey eventually retired with a 45-5-1 record with 37 knockout victories, and has done well as owner of a sports bar; he has also acted in British films and television, has been a boxing choreographer for films and has performed –to acclaim- as a singer-comedian in numerous cabaret performances.

Napoles (81-7 with 55 KO) announced his retirement from the ring. He acted in a Mexican movie, invested in a nightclub and continued to live as a high roller.

He attempted to make money. He allowed his name tobe used to endorse a nightclub for a monthly fee, made a few dollars on public appearances for retail businesses and sports festivals and attempted a career as a singer with his own band called *El Negro Santo* (The Black Saint).

Within four years after retirement he was flat broke.

For a while the musical group made a living, playing private parties and small clubs in different Mexican cities and towns. They dissolved, arguing among themselves while performing in Juarez, where Napoles eventually sold his van and the instruments to pay his own food bills.

By the summer of 2011, an aged, sick Napoles and his wife were living in a room in the back of a filthy, run down Juarez gym, their only source of income being a few dollars a week earned for teaching private lessons to a few amateur boxers, a small, occasional handout from boxing politico Jose Sulaiman and the Mexican Social Security pension.

The gym is located in a neighborhood where dozens of men are killed yearly in a constant battle between drug cartels.

When a Mexican journalist named Manolo Coss attempted to interview Napoles, the old champion answered: "What for? I no longer exist."

Florentino Fernandez lands a hook to Johnny Featherman's jaw

Fernandez and Rocky Rivero had four brutal wars, each man winning two.

CHAPTER TWENTY-THREE: THE OX

His friends remember Florentino Fernandez as a good humored easy going man who loved his family and enjoyed playing dominoes or hanging out at the dog track with friends. His foes remember him as a man whose good nature disappeared between the ropes, killer instinct unleashed into an attack that neither gave nor asked for quarter, his left hook breaking bones and dropping opponents to the canvas.

Florentino Fernandez –Floro to his friends and fans- was born in Santiago de Cuba, on the southeastern tip of the island, on the sixth of March 1936.

"As a kid I dreamed of being a baseball player," Floro stated, "but I was a skinny little kid and kids being kids, there was always a bully around looking to harass me. I did not pick fights but I did not run away either. When I was ten, eleven years old I was street fighting kids who were older and bigger than me and almost all fights ended with a single punch from my end. I would hit them once and they would be stretched out on the sidewalk.

Sometimes they guy I beat would have an older brother who would come looking for me and I decked him also. All my friends started telling me that I should take up boxing and by the time I was a teenager I was training seriously to become a fighter."

As a thin, wiry lightweight he travelled to Havana, where he was trained by Higinio Ruiz, a legendary trainer. Ruiz had been a club fighter in the thirties, but in the fifties –when Floro arrived in Havana- Ruiz was a gym owner with an impressive record as a corner and trainer for Cuba's best fighters, including the popular brothers Lino and Pupi Garcia.

"My most important amateur fight was against Luis Manuel Rodriguez," Floro stated, "and I caught him early in the fight and dropped him, but he had an iron chin and picked himself up from the canvas and put up a tremendous fight. I beat him on points and we never fought again. We became very good friends, sparred together, trained together and for years, when one of us fought, the other one was usually at ringside cheering him on. Luis was a great world champion, a very skilled, smooth boxer and a good guy. He was a true friend."

"Floro and Luis were both very competitive," former lightweight contender Frankie Otero said, "Although they never fought as pros they did –over the years- spar hundreds of rounds at the Fifth Street Gym and it was a thrill to watch them…. they would talk to each other. Luis would move, slip and hit Floro with a combination and say something like –you did not see that coming- and Floro would later tap Luis with a short hook and answer –you felt that one didn't you? and they liked each other and were good friends but even in the sparring there was that competitive edge…."

Fernandez turned pro at the age of twenty –in 1956- at Cuba's biggest boxing venue, *Palacio de los Deportes* (Sports Palace), demolishing Pastor Burke, a club fighter from Cienfuegos. Luis Manuel Rodriguez fought on the same undercard, also stopping his foe.

The Cuban press loved Floro's raw brutal power, nicknaming him "The Ox."

Promoter Cuco Conde loved Fernandez. The Ox did not care who his opponent would be, for he was willing to fight anyone as long as the pesos justified the contract. In his seventh pro bout Fernandez faced Marino Gonzalez, a seasoned club fighter with 25 pro fights, experienced in main events and owner of a winning record. Floro took him out in three.

The Ox became sports front page in Cuba as he continued blitzing all who faced him. Ray Estepa, who had a good record in almost thirty fights, went out in two. Veteran journeyman Rocky Randell –with 70 wins in over 100 pro fights- managed to last until the fifth round. Wilfredo Hurst, a slick boxing young prospect, fell in three, as did Alberto Bisbe, a former Cuban national light welter champion.

One of Fernandez most impressive performances took place when in January of 1959, the Ox -undefeated in 17 fights with 14 KO wins- faced Baby Diogenes Sagarra, who had a record of 20-2 with 11 KO wins and held the national light welter championship. The clever Sagarra eluded Floro the first round, peppering him with quick combinations, opening a deep cut that threatened to end the Ox's unbeaten streak.

In the second round a desperate Fernandez rushed Sagarra, landing an explosive hook to the throat that dropped the fighter for the ten count.

"They could have counted to fifty," stated sportswriter Andres Pascual, "Florentino damaged Sagarra's vocal cords and from then on, Sagarra sounded hoarse every time he talked."

Floro continued banging, stopping former world champion Paddy De Marco in four, Stefan Redl in seven and wining two back to back fights on points over tough welterweight contender Gaspar Ortega.

"De Marco had been a world champion when I was still an amateur," Floro said about the fight, "and the win meant a lot to me because it proved to all that I belonged at the top. It was not a hard fight because I came out fast and did not give him time to set up a rhythm and my punches were hurting him from the first round. I really hit him hard and often."

Life was good. Floro drove a convertible, ate well and had pesos to spend. His televised fights in Cuba had made him into a national celebrity, recognized in the street by even those that did not follow boxing. With his easy going attitude, Fernandez endeared himself to his fans by always talking to all strangers as though they were old friends.

Then Floro faced his first defeat. A Manila slugger named Rocky Kalingo stopped him in the first round and Floro got his revenge stopping Kalingo in two in a wild rematch. After the Kalingo victory, Floro beat Ralph Dupas in Florida before returning to Cuba to dispatch Gerald Gray in four.

"He was a promoter's dream," sports editor Sarvelio Del Valle said of Fernandez, "In the ring he was a savage beast with a ton of courage and a brutal punch. He scored sixteen straight knockouts which became a national record for straight knockouts and most of those fights were against some pretty tough fighters. Outside the ropes he was a gentleman and gave very good interviews and was liked by all."

The Gray fight was his last fight in Cuba. By April of 1960, when this bout took place, Fidel Castro was well into converting Cuba into a satellite state of the Soviet Union and a hot spot of Cold War conflict. Almost fifteen hundred Cubans had faced the firing squads by then and civil war was raging in the island, with guerrilla uprisings and urban resistance groups fighting the new communist government.

Although Fidel and Raul Castro and Che Guevara had attended his fights, proclaiming that they were his fans, Fernandez was soon convinced that the new system was tearing apart his beloved country.

"Leaving Cuba hurt a lot," Florentino stated in several interviews, "It was not because I knew that pro boxing was going to disappear in Cuba that I left my country…the executions, murders, the destruction of the whole country. I left and it was one of the saddest days of my life. I have never returned and will not return until Cuba is free."

By the time he settled in Miami he was almost a full fledged middleweight. He lost on points to welterweight great Emile Griffith weighing 149, then became a top middleweight contender scoring three knockouts in a row over top competition. Phil Moyer, Rory Calhoun and Marcel Pigou all became victims of the Fernandez hook and the Ox signed a contract to fight Gene Fullmer for the middleweight championship and a fifteen thousand dollar paycheck, the biggest purse of his career.

Fullmer was a very tough champion who had only lost four of his fifty nine pro fights. He had split three –winning, losing and fighting a draw- with Sugar Ray Robinson and had stopped the formidable Carmen Basilio twice. A hard man to beat under normal circumstances he had the edge of defending his title in his hometown of Ogden, Utah.

"We knew it was a bad situation," Ferdie -The Fight Doctor- Pacheco stated, "but we also figured that Florentino could –over fifteen rounds- rip apart Fullmer. Florentino had a puncher's chance and it was a world title fight."

Angelo Dundee said "Nobody could punch like Fernandez. He was a converted southpaw so his left hook was murder. He broke Gene Fullmer's elbow with a left hook during that middleweight title fight. Florentino could hurt anyone with any kind of punch no matter where it landed. I have seen him rock heavyweights in the gym with training gloves on."

At the end of fifteen hard, brawling rounds, one judge voted for Floro and the other two gave the victory to Fullmer.

"I have seen the video of that fight many times," Florentino has said, "And there's no way I lost that fight. I fractured his elbow and I landed all the harder blows. I was denied the title belt but I know I beat him. I know it. I don't have anything against Fullmer and I respect him because he was very tough, a real hard bone. In my heart I know I really won the championship that night."

In an interview years later, Fullmer said: "I have fought some very hard punchers in my day but no one hit like Fernandez. Every punch he hit me, I felt it vibrate up and down my spine."

Fernandez lost two more in a row. Tough Nigerian Dick Tiger fractured his nose, winning by a TKO and Joey Giambra also won on a cut. Floro snapped the losing streak by repeating a win over Phil Moyer and signed to fight top contender Hurricane Carter.

Carter was like Fernandez, a left hook artist. They clashed and Carter won by a fulminating one round knockout in a bout that many experts predicted would be the final chapter in Fernandez' career. Floro sailed through the ropes and landed on a concrete floor, the fight concluding with a knockout victory for the Hurricane from New Jersey.

"Carter won because he landed first," Ferdie Pacheco said, "Carter started fast and Florentino always started a little slower. Everyone thought that was the end of Florentino's career but they were wrong."

The Ox won two fights over fair competition and in his third comeback bout faced Jose "Chegui" Torres, an unbeaten Puerto Rican destined for greatness, a future world light heavyweight titleholder. Chegui had been an Olympic silver medalist and was unbeaten in 27 pro fights, with 21 KO wins.

The fight took place in Puerto Rico, Torres' backyard. In front of a large crowd at Hiram Bithorn Stadium, Florentino stopped Chegui by TKO in the fifth round.

In an interview –years later- Torres reflected on the fight: "Cubans were my jinx. I drew with Benny Paret and Fernandez was the only one that ever stopped me… I hit him very good, clean shots and he was right there in front of me and hitting back very hard. My punches did not seem to bother him. He knocked me down twice and I remember the first time but I don't think I remember the second one. The referee stopped the fight and I argued but he was right. At the time he stopped the fight I was hurt…. He was a very good fighter. I have seen him when I visit Florida and I like him very much and joke with Florentino and ask him for a rematch."

"It was one of my best fights ever," Floro said in an interview years later, "I was sharp and in great condition and I could feel that I was hurting him with my punches. I could feel him getting weaker but Torres could take a very good shot. It was a real good win for me."

The win –the biggest of his career- made Fernandez an idol in Puerto Rico and set off a four fight series with a tough Argentine slugger named Juan "Rocky" Rivero.

Rivero, -a brutal slugger- and Fernandez fought twice in Puerto Rico and twice at Madison Square Garden. Fernandez won one on points and one by KO and Rivero did the same.

"They were wars," promoter Tuto Zabala said, "Of hundreds of fights I promoted those stand out as the most thrilling real wars. They hit each other from bell to bell. They were like two bulls locking horns, trading bombs and both fought exactly the same, throwing hard hooks and uppercuts. Those four fights –two of which I promoted- were thrillers."

In the early sixties Frankie Otero was a teenager who dreamed of being a boxer.

"Boxing was everything to me," Otero said, "I ate and slept boxing and Florentino was one of my heroes that I saw on television. Every Cuban in Miami knew Floro by sight. One day I was with my father in downtown Miami and we see Florentino walking towards us. My father stopped him and I was embarrassed because I was a shy kid. So my father says to him –My son admires you and wants to be a boxer but I tell him he should forget about boxing and study in college. What do you think? – and Florentino smiled and answered –My father said the same thing to me but I have done very well in boxing…. Needless to say, my father was not pleased with Florentino's answer."

Otero –who did go to college- also did well in boxing winning an NABF title and being a top ranked fighter for three years in a sixty bout career.

By the mid sixties Florentino Fernandez was past his peak. He continued knocking out fighters but began losing more frequently. Jose "Monon"

Gonzalez beat him twice, cutting him badly in one of those fights. Andy Heilman outpointed him and Jimmy Lester broke his jaw.

After a loss to Nicaraguan Lou Gutierrez, Fernandez was now ending his career as a light heavyweight. Matched carefully he scored seven wins and a draw before facing Vernon McIntosh, his last ring opponent.

McIntosh was a twenty three year old journeyman club fighter with a deceiving record of nine wins and eight losses. The young fighter had fought high quality men of the ring, including reigning light heavyweight titleholder Bob Foster and top contender Gregorio Peralta. A few years before, McIntosh would have been considered cannon fodder for Fernandez but in 1972, the journeyman was a very tough opponent for the thirty six year old Ox.

World rated junior lightweight and former NABF champion Frankie Otero was sitting ringside for Fernandez last bout.

"McIntosh was very young, had a lot of heart and Florentino was an old veteran by then," Otero said, "Florentino knocked McIntosh down in the first round and was winning almost every round but McIntosh was hanging in there, giving him a hard fight and making him work, until by the tenth round Florentino had nothing left and was wobbling around the ring when Eddie Eckert stopped the fight, awarding McIntosh a TKO win."

"Dad fractured a hand early in the fight," Virginia Pascual, Florentino's daughter said of her father's last fight, "and he fought most of the fight with a broken hand."

Florentino Fernandez final ledger reads 50-16-1 with 43 KO wins. He was stopped on ten occasions, most of them on cuts.

After retiring from the ring Fernandez lived happily married and content in raising his family, becoming a tender grandfather and occasionally training fighters or working corners.

In retirement his face bore the marks of his former trade, with some scar tissue and a nose thickened by hundreds of blows, but Floro was not addled, talking clearly, his conversation spiked with a solid sense of humor. His body was still hard, carrying only a dozen pounds more than it did decades ago, when he was the most feared puncher in the middleweight division.

He often showed up at the local club shows in Miami where his introduction was followed by warm applause. An icon among Cuban exiles in Little Havana, Floro was stopped by fans on the street thirty years after hanging up the gloves and he always chatted with the fans in his amicable way.

At a local show in Miami, when Fernandez was close to seventy years of age, he sat at ringside talking to a reporter as he watched two local middleweights brawling in the ring.

"I could take those guys," Floro said to the journalist.

"Oh, sure," the sports scribe answered, "In your time it would have been easy."

Fernandez shook his head.

"Not in my time," Florentino said, "I mean now. All I need is one round each."

The journalist nodded in agreement.

In 2009 Florentino Fernandez was inducted into the Florida Boxing Hall of Fame.

The clean living Florentino, whose splendid health seemed to make him immune to even common colds, died from a stroke on the morning of the 28th of January, 2013 at the age of seventy-six.

"The only regret my father had," his daughter said, "was that he was never able to return to a free Cuba. He mentioned it every week. It was the only thorn in his heart."

Jose Stable: talented but emotionally fragile welterweight

Stable Vs Emile Griffith for the welterweight title.

CHAPTER TWENTY-FOUR: JOSE STABLE

Jose Stable was born in La Maya, a small village on Cuba's eastern tip.

From an impoverished background, Stable would later jokingly claim that he was a pro by age six, for he would be paid a dime or a quarter for winning amateur fights on improvised rings set up in empty lots, small dance halls or cock fighting arenas in Oriente Province.

His father –a laborer- died when he was ten and little Jose shined shoes and worked as a messenger boy to help his family eat. At fifteen he won the first of three Cuban National Golden Gloves titles and by the time he was eighteen he was representing Cuba in the 1958 Pan American Games.

He turned pro in 1959, managed by Manuel Alfaro, who also handled Benny Paret. Alfaro turned the young fighter over to Caron Gonzalez, a master trainer who had been a sparring partner for Kid Tunero.

"Stable was the best of the best," Caron said of his pupil, "he had more raw potential than Paret….He was poison, a very good infighter, who could do wonderful work up close…He had excellent aim with his hooks and uppercuts and it was a pleasure seeing him at work. He slipped punches really well and trained hard, but emotionally there was always a problem with Jose. His everyday life was a constant problem. He had women problems, money problems. One woman was married, another was jealous, he either owed money or money was owed to him…everyday was a headache with Stable. He was a very good fighter but emotionally complicated and very fragile."

By the end of 1959 –his first pro year- Stable was already fighting eight rounds. He lost for the first time in 1960, a ten rounder against the clever Angel Robinson Garcia, whom he beat in a rematch.

By the end of 1960 Stable –like so many others-left Cuba never to return. Within months of his arrival he outscored Kenny Lane at St Nick's Arena, impressing the New York boxing crowd. Three more victories followed before losing a controversial decision to British champion Dave Charnley in Liverpool.

After the Charnley defeat came nine straight victories over quality fighters, making Stable the top contender for Emile Griffith's welterweight title.

It was an impressive string of victories. Stable won unanimously over future welterweight champion Curtis Cokes, outpointed top prospects Stan Hayward and Dick Turner, stopped former New York Golden Gloves champion Vince Shomo and also derailed up and coming Gabe Terronez. The muscular welterweight from La Maya seemed unbeatable.

In 1965, the twenty four year old Cuban faced Emile Griffith for the welterweight championship of the world and a $10,000 payday, the biggest of his career.

Hall of Famer Griffith, a superb fighter, survived a hard Stable hook in the first round before figuring out the Cuban's style. Emile took control of the fight, beating Stable to the punch. By the eleventh round the fighter from La Maya was wobbly but refused to fall. He managed to survive but lost on points to Griffith by a clear margin.

The fragile psyche of Jose Stable came unglued after his defeat by Griffith. He fought on, eleven more fights, winning one, fighting a draw and losing nine. His final ledger reads 27-12-2 with 10 KO victories.

"He lost confidence in his own abilities," Caron Gonzalez said, "I would see him now and then after he quit boxing and he was surviving working menial jobs and his problems were bigger….no money…bills to pay…problems with women….drinking….street arguments…going to court…paying lawyers."

In November 1981 he failed to appear in a Miami court. When an arrest order was issued, Stable –using a shotgun- shot the police officer who attempted to serve the arrest warrant to the ex fighter. The officer was paralyzed and Stable was condemned to life imprisonment by the state of Florida.

Jose Stable, prisoner number 085680, has now served over thirty years in the Florida penal system and will die behind bars.

Frankie Otero was NABF Junior Lightweight champion.

Otero beats Joe Cartwright

Three Cuban icons: Frankie Otero, Luis Manuel Rodriguez and Florentino Fernandez at the legendary Fifth Street Gym.

NABF champion Frankie Otero was a very popular Miami fighter in the seventies.

CHAPTER TWENTY-FIVE: THE CUBAN BOMBER

In boxing, which is a business based on bullshit excuses, Frankie Otero has carved a reputation as an honest man. Frankie always tells the truth, which is one of the endearing qualities that made him a local hero in Miami during the late sixties and early seventies.

There was an interview after the first bout against Ken Buchanan, which Frankie lost on points, when a reporter thrust a microphone in front of the Cuban lightweight.

"Do you think you were robbed?" the reporter asked.

"No, He beat me fair and square. He's a terrific fighter."

"How about the knockdown?" the reporter insisted, "It looked like a slip to me..."

"Oh, no," Frankie interjected, "it was a clean shot. He hurt me. It took some effort to get up. As a matter of fact, I usually fight better after I get knocked down. Maybe I should be knocked down early every time I fight."

The Otero honesty and humor, combined with a mop of curly dark hair, a pleasant smile and an elegant, flashy style, made the Cuban exile a popular drawing card in Miami Beach arenas.

The record books will tell you Otero had sixty pro fights. His 49-9-2 record includes 31 knockout victories and 4 defeats by the quick route. He was ranked number one in the world in his division, was an NABF junior lightweight titleholder, fought on network television, and scored wins over Love Allotey, Kenny Weldon, Bill Whittenburg. Felix Figueroa and Jimmy Trosclair. He lost to Ken Buchanan, Alfredo Escalera, Vilomar Fernandez, and Jose Petersen.

In his sixth pro fight he faced Willie Sands in Key West. There was no Florida boxing commission at the time and the local appointed officials were inept. In the dressing room, a corner man started wrapping Frankie's hands with a roll of electrical tape.

"What are you doing?" Frankie asked.

"No inspector here to supervise this," the corner man answered, "so with this, you will hit like you have bricks in your hands."

"Wow," Frankie answered with his usual wit, "You better run to Sand's dressing room. I wonder what they are taping him with..."

Otero was one of Chris Dundee's most popular fighters, packing small arenas in South Florida. When he broke into the ratings, back in the days when the world had less than a dozen champions, Chris Dundee rushed into the gym to tell his fighter the good news.

"So," Frankie answered, "Does that mean I have to fight really tough guys from now on?"

Hank Kaplan, the world's top boxing historian, saw almost every one of Otero's fights, from prelims to the top crust.

"Frankie was a tiger," Hank recalls, "When they knocked him down he got up and fought back hard. He had a lot of talent, boxed well, was quick, avoided punches, could fight inside and he had heart. Frankie fought some real tough guys, like Buchanan, Escalera, Jose Luis Lopez, Kenny Weldon and Victor Ortiz. The fans loved Frankie."

In his first year fighting main events, Otero twice beat a tough New Orleans lightweight named Jimmy Trosclair, a former Southern US Golden Gloves champion.

"The first time I saw Trosclair, I was impressed," Otero remembers, "The guy had a rosary tattooed around his neck. He looked tough. I remember thinking -what the hell are you doing in this ring, Frankie? You are a middle class college kid from a good family and you are going to fight this guy with a rosary tattooed on his neck? You should be playing golf. I beat Trosclair twice, outpointing him both times."

"Bill Whittenburg was another very tough guy. He had been a pretty good amateur winning a bunch of regional titles but as a pro he had a lousy record because he had fought a lot of tough guys and champions in their hometowns on short notice… He had lost to world champions Pedro Carrasco and Bruno Arcari and to top contenders like Sammy Goss and Edwin Viruet and to Bruno

Arcari in Italy… Whittenburg was strong as a bull. If he had been properly managed and promoted he would have done very well….He knocked me down but I got up and won the fight. Sometimes I fought better after I was tagged. It woke me up. I hit him a lot of good shots and I won but it was one of my hardest fights."

"My biggest win was over Kenny Weldon who had won 24 of his 28 fights and I beat him for the NABF title. He was a good fighter but I had more speed and power than he did and I won on all three scorecards…Kenny is a very nice guy and has become a good boxing trainer…"

"Another huge win for me was my victory over Love Allotey. He was a strong, muscular African who had held the British Commonwealth Lightweight title and had fought for the world title. He had been in the rankings for nine years and had fought everyone. I caught him at the end of his career but he was still strong and dangerous."

"Ken Buchanan was very strong and a great champion. I was a junior lightweight and he was a lightweight with lots of upper body strength. The first fight was close. I made him miss a lot and tagged him some nice shots in the first five rounds, but he won it on the second half. In the rematch he stopped me in six. I just didn't have it that night."

Dr. Ferdie Pacheco who was in Frankie's corner from beginning to end, remembers an incident from the first Buchanan fight.

"Going into the last round," the fight doctor stated, "I emptied the ice bag inside Frankie's cup, to cool him down. He went rigid, his eyes opened in surprise and he said- Now, Doc, was that absolutely necessary?"

"I had a great team," Frankie remembers, "Richie Riesgo was my trainer, and Pacheco and Luis Sarria worked my corners. Chris Dundee was my promoter. I trained at the Fifth Street Gym and I sparred with champions like Luis Rodriguez."

One afternoon a young fighter from Panama named Roberto Duran showed up at the Fifth Street Gym. Chris Dundee attempted to match Duran and Otero in a main event.

"Chris and I were watching Duran spar with Vinnie Curto who was a top middleweight with an iron chin. Chris was telling me -I'll make this match.

You can take this Duran guy- Just as Chris finishes saying this, Duran drops Curto. Now understand this, no one dropped Curto, not even top ten middleweights. He had a chin like reinforced concrete. And Duran, who was a lean, little lightweight put him down with one shot, with sparring gloves. I looked at Chris and he shrugged. -You fight him, Chris. -I said. Roberto and I became friends, but we never fought."

After retiring from boxing, Otero earned a living as a real estate broker and residential appraiser. He owns a three bedroom townhouse and a couple of investment properties. Nancy, his lovely wife, works at Miami International Airport. He did return to the ring, winning a couple of prelims before realizing that age had dimmed his reflexes ending his career with a 49-9-2 record that included 31 KO wins.

The boxing bug remained in Frankie's blood. Besides his real estate, Otero became a matchmaker for promoter Walter Alvarez, trainer and part manager of a couple of fighters and occasional road traveling corner man. Frankie has worked corners in Brazil, the Bahamas and Europe. He has even bumped into fans who remember his glory days.

"I was in London, at the Thomas A'Beckett pub and gym and the promoter tells me -Hey, we have a celebrity here today, a movie star-... and suddenly this guy enters the room, looks at me and says -Hey, it's Frankie Otero, how are you doing?... I look and I don't know who the hell he is, but he's happy to see me... -Frankie-he says -it's me, Phil, from the Fifth Street Gym. Don't you remember me? I look at him and I remember this young amateur that was one of my biggest fans, used to follow me around the gym...I say hello to Phil, and I'm wondering what he's doing in London, and the promoter turns to me and says -I didn't know you are a friend of Mickey Rourke.... I just stood there, nodding my head. So Phil became a movie star. Go figure."

Otero's only regret is not having fought for a world title, although he was ranked number one in his division for a year.

"Negotiations fell through," he says, shaking his head, "Back then there was only one world champion. Today with all the alphabet soup groups, I would have been a champion. Still, there's something to be said. I did very well at a time when there were some good fighters punching around."

Amen.

Cuban-American Walter Alvarez promoted the Alexis Arguello Vs Aaron Pryor at the Orange Bowl, establishing an attendance record in Florida rings.

Former amateur boxer and bank executive Ramiro Ortiz has promoted over forty boxing cards in South Florida, many involving Cuban boxers.

Pedro Laza had a good career in which he faced Cornelious Boza-Edwards.

Isidoro Moreno was a good prospect until stopped by a tough club fighter.

CHAPTER TWENTY-SIX: THE BOATLIFT FIGHTERS

The 1980 Mariel boatlift brought 125,000 Cuban refugees to America in one summer and some tried their hand at pro boxing.

The Mariel crop of fighters included some fair talent but none that attained a title or were considered serious contenders.

Flyweight Luis Kid Monzote was the only boatlift fighter to fight for a world title when he was stopped in three rounds by Humberto "Chiquita" Gonzalez. Monzote started out badly, losing his first four but turning his career around he managed to win twelve of his next fourteen, including a victory over faded former WBC champion Prudencio Cardona, earning him a title shot at Gonzalez. Monzote retired after he lost three more fights, in one of them being stopped in five by Michael Carbajal.

The best of the boatlift fighters was "The Magician" Pedro Laza who was trained by Caron Gonzalez. Laza had fought some ninety amateur bouts in Cuba, winning regional championships. A very smooth boxer who lacked power, Laza compiled a 30-7 pro record with 12 KO wins and 4 KO losses. He was stopped by Cornelious Boza Edwards and Tony Baltazar. Laza retired and has made a living employed in the construction industry.

Another promising fighter of the era was Mauricio Rodriguez (39-3 with 14 KO), a slick boxing light welter who managed himself and never challenged a top tier fighter, preferring to perform at club fight level. Rodriguez had talent and an engaging personality but ended his winning career with a long prison sentence for drug dealing.

Flyweight Alcides Morales (10-1 with 5 KO), a former top amateur in Cuba showed great promise but attempted to manage himself and retired after constant arguments and fight cancelations with Florida promoters.

One of the most popular fighters of this crop of arrivals was Raul "The Cuban Fury" Hernandez (22-30-5 with 3 KO), a light hitting but entertaining prelim fighter who became a crowd favorite in spite of his losing record. Hernandez was stopped by Bill Costello, Julian Jackson and Bobby Joe Young.

Other Cuban club fighters from the boatlift included welters Isidoro Moreno and Remigio Carrillo, light welter Eduardo Lugo, flyweight Mario O'Farrrill, featherweights Gavilan Gonzalez and southpaw Carlos Albuerne who after retiring became a trainer for several good fighters, including Shannon Briggs.

Gavilan Gonzalez became the first fighter in the United States to use the thumb attached boxing glove when he faced Ray Denis in a prelim fight in Fort Lauderdale on September 30, 1981. The card was promoted by boxing historian Hank Kaplan and Cuban American banker Ramiro Ortiz. The promoters invited Uruguayan journalist Jose Laurino as their guest and although Gonzalez lost the bout, the thumb attached glove eventually was accepted as standard in the boxing game.

Some of the best Cuban fighters of the eighties did not arrive via boatlift, but were Cuban Americans who had competed in the Golden Gloves tournaments of Florida.

Jose "Nino" Ribalta (39-17-1 with 28 KO) was born in the town of Rodrigo in central Cuba but grew up in Florida.

The Ribalta name has a Cuban boxing legacy. In the forties and early fifties, Rodolfo "Pototo" Ribalta was the first of the clan to appear in the record books as a club fighter who lost more often than he won but did pull a few remarkable upsets. The featherweight from Santa Clara won twice and drew once with National Kid who was champion of Cuba. Ribalta also drew with Humberto Sierra -who became a world rated fighter- and with the popular Lino Garcia.

In the sixties the Cuban fight scene –by then strictly amateur- had a good Ribalta representative. Jose Felipe Ribalta was a top heavyweight who fought and lost two highly disputed bouts against Teofilo Stevenson.

Jose Felipe had younger brothers that left for America and the Ribalta tradition continued on US shores. Jose Agustin Ribalta won the Florida Golden Gloves and turned pro as a welterweight, fighting four bouts before retiring as a participant to become a trainer.

The third brother also named Jose –Nino- Ribalta fought as an amateur in Florida, winning in the Sunshine Games as well as state championships in Golden Gloves and AAU competition. Nino turned pro in 1982 at the War

Memorial Auditorium in a card promoted by Hank Kaplan and Ramiro Ortiz, scoring a one round knockout over J.C. Richardson.

Nino Ribalta was a tall fighter with a good jab, solid boxing skills and a fair punch. In a busy career Ribalta faced twelve world champions and a cluster of top contenders.

Ribalta's most famous fight was a losing effort against a young Mike Tyson, lasting into the tenth round at a time when fighters were toppling over in one or two assaults against Iron Mike. The short, hard hitting Tyson had trouble with the tall Cuban who used his jab effectively and made the young heavyweight work hard to impose his will and stop Nino in the last stanza.

Ribalta's career highlights included a one round knockout of former heavyweight champion Leon Spinks and a victory on points over a feared puncher named Jeff Sims. He was the victim of hometown judging, most notoriously in a battle against former champion James –Bone Crusher- Smith.

A likeable man, Ribalta retired from boxing with some modest real estate investments, worked as a security guard for Miami Dade County's board of education and trained some professional and amateur fighters.

Another heavyweight was New Jersey based Carlos –Rocky- Hernandez (18-6-1 with 14 KO) a cruiser who grew into the heavyweight division. Hernandez did well at prelim and club fight level but never made the front tier. He retired after being stopped by George Foreman by a four round TKO.

A Cuban American fighter active in Florida rings was Braulio Santiesteban (20-4 with 11 KO), a Hialeah lightweight with elegant boxing moves but lacking when it came to breaking into the top tier, retiring from the ring after losing to Puerto Rican Juan Nazario.

THE PROMOTERS

At the time –with the exception of Chris Dundee in Miami and Ernie Letiziano in Palm Beach- most boxing promoters in South Florida were Cuban-Americans including Tuto Zabala, Ramiro Ortiz, Julio Martinez and Walter Alvarez.

Zabala, former bank executive was the best connected of all the Cuban American boxing entrepreneurs, with experience promoting in Puerto Rico, Florida, Dominican Republic and Colombia, having represented a number of champions in his career including Carlos Teo Cruz and Vicente Rondon.

Ramiro Ortiz, a bank executive who would later become president and CEO of two of Florida's largest banking operations was a former amateur boxer who joined with Hank Kaplan to promote boxing at the War Memorial Auditorium in Fort Lauderdale. In some thirty promotions, Ortiz launched the careers of Jose Ribalta and other local fighters. In later years he returned to promoting boxing at the Magic City Casino in Miami and also served a term as Florida State Boxing Comissioner.

Julio Martinez, a former US Army boxer who became mayor of the city of Hialeah ran his first promotion in a warehouse with a ring and several hundred folding chairs set up for the audience, before moving up to a picturesque Milander Auditorium, where he promoted pro boxing fairly regularly for several years, featuring Pedro Laza, Mauricio Rodriguez, Jose Ribalta and his brother Jose Agustin, Robert Daniels, Steve and Ken Whetstone and other popular Florida fighters of the eighties and early nineties.

Walter Alvarez, a young engineer who loved boxing and was a close friend of fighter Frankie Otero, began his boxing career by managing two local Florida fighters: Joe Medina and Mad Dog Martinez. Medina was a good looking welterweight who retired from the ring after scoring six knockouts and Mad Dog went from local prospect to journeyman status but Alvarez was learning the business and surprised the boxing world by jumping into the world of big time boxing with two huge promotions: the first Alexis Arguello vs Aaron Pryor fight and the Tommy Hearns vs Roberto Duran clash.

The Arguello vs Pryor promotion, which Alvarez co promoted with Bob Arum drew a live crowd of 23,800 fans at Miami's Orange Bowl, making it the biggest live gate boxing promotion in the history of Florida boxing. Alvarez continued in boxing after the Hearns vs Duran bout with a few promotions, occasionally managing or representing a fighter and as proprietor of a gym in the Doral section of Miami Dade County.

Elvis Yero was a good fighter claimed by the streets.

CHAPTER TWENTY-SEVEN: ELVIS YERO

The first time I saw Elvis Yero was in 1984, when I attended an amateur show at the Virrick Gym in Coconut Grove.

The gym was located in an old Coast Guard armory overlooking Miami's Brickell Bay, the boxing arena sharing a parking lot with a seafood restaurant; the scent of salt spray from the bay mixing with the crisp aroma of conch fritters and breaded shrimp.

I follow and enjoy the pros more, but there's something very pure and clean about an amateur show. The fighters are young -some still children- but they are eager, compensating their lack of experience with enthusiasm.

In an amateur show everyone is a dreamer. Fantasy collides with reality, but fantasies are sometimes fulfilled.

Elvis Yero was the featured dreamer of the night.

Havana born and Miami grown Elvis -named after the man from Tupelo- loomed as a promoter's dream.

He was a handsome teenager with chestnut hair and a soft smile, articulate, extremely polite and well mannered, a boy who enjoyed sketching and painting. Even while still attending high school, he already seemed marked for greatness.

He could fight.

The slim, good-looking surfer-type was a natural. He laced on a pair of boxing gloves at the age of fifteen and won his first tournament a few weeks later. Yero stormed through the amateurs winning two Florida Golden Glove titles back to back, the Sunshine Games, and the AAU regional. By his senior year in high school Elvis Yero was the 1984 United States Amateur 139-Pound Champion, a feat accomplished with a streak of wins over the best prospects in the nation, many of them full grown men. Previous U.S. champions in this weight class included Tommy Hearns -in 1977- Don Curry -in 1978- and Johnny Bumphus in 1980. It was royal company for a high school boy.

The first time I saw Yero fight he arrived at Virrick Gym followed by an entourage of high school cronies that included very young girls with very short skirts and very young boys with loud attitudes. Elvis moved among them as royalty, clearly enjoying being the center of attention without being perceived as vain -a difficult feat for a high school kid.

In the ring he impressed. His moves were fluid, well-balanced, jab working at good distance, hooks thrown without telegraphing. His opponent, a muscular, squat fighter -who learned to box in the state penitentiary gyms and the smokers at the migrant worker camps of Belle Glade- crumbled in the second round.

After the victory young girls surrounded Yero and he smiled, probably feeling invincible and immortal as all adolescents feel, particularly when they are well known, tasting the fame of press conferences and interviews.

Fame is a harsh mistress, particularly for one so young. Behind the smile and polite manners, beyond the artwork and the ring performances, Elvis Yero was a tortured soul, a vulnerable boy who hid his demons well.

His first arrest came while still an amateur. A man by the name of Diegstad, the husband of a county judge, argued with Elvis on a street corner and Elvis placed him in the hospital.

Yero spent four months in Dade County jail awaiting trial, for his family could not post bond. At his jury trial he was acquitted, but the downward slide had begun.

Elvis liked the limelight; the backslapping friends, the naked bodies of young girlfriends and the drugs that made him feel mellow or invincible. The harder drugs took over and the man-child became a cokehead by the time he was out of high school and ready to turn pro.

How fast hard drugs can deteriorate a young body was exemplified in the case of Elvis Yero. The lightning quick, gifted prospect of the amateurs looked like a worn-out old pro while he was barely out of his teens. His manners were still impeccable and when given advice he would confess to being a fool. Yet, he continued to slack off in training, disappeared for days on drug binges, was arrested for being intoxicated in public, for lewd behavior, for possession of drugs. He went to jail for a few weeks and then went back to the streets to repeat his self-destructive cycle.

Former lightweight contender Frankie Otero featured Elvis in four of his boxing promotions.

"He was a tremendous talent," Frankie says, "he was the full package, a good-looking Cuban fighter, a hometown hero with a following and talent of world class potential, articulate and nice. Everyone liked Elvis."

"He fought for me four times," Otero continues, "And he won all four but he did not look like the same fighter who we saw in the amateurs. He was never in shape. Even when he trained hard he was using drugs and staying up nights and he looked like an old man real fast."

"In one of the cards I scheduled him to fight Jesus Perez, who is a tough prelim fighter, the kind that fights rarely but spends a lot of time in the gym sparring with everyone."

"Then Elvis disappears a week before the fight and no one can find him for four days. He comes back and beats Perez but he has scary moments winning that fight. Perez nails him some clean shots that he would have avoided in his amateur days. Elvis looked slow that night, very sluggish and he was in his early twenties."

"After that fight, when I was making out the checks for the fighters, Elvis insisted on being paid in cash. He was usually very soft spoken but that night he was agitated. Not rude. Elvis was never rude. He said he needed the cash to pay the rent so he would not be evicted that night, but he probably needed the money to get high."

Yero, who fought pro as a welterweight and junior middleweight, lost on points to Kenny Ellis in a six round slugfest and continued his downward spiral.

More arrests followed, for panhandling, drinking in public, disorderly conduct, grand theft auto, dealing in stolen property, domestic violence, selling and using marihuana and cocaine. His rap sheet would compile over 50 arrests in less than two decades.

"He would go to jail for a few weeks," Frankie said, "and come back out and train for a while, have one fight and then go back to jail for a few days. I'll tell you one thing about Elvis: he was tough."

"He was just a kid when I sent him to spar with Aaron Pryor for two weeks. Pryor was in some island -I think it was Saint Martin- and he needed a sparring partner for a couple of weeks, so I offered Elvis the chance. Most kids that age would have a moment's hesitation before traveling to an unknown place to trade shots with a world champion, but Elvis just nodded and thanked me for the opportunity. Pryor later remarked that they had worked hard and Elvis held his own. He was a tough guy."

In 1990 Yero was shot in the hand during an incident in which he tried to sell twenty dollars worth of crack to an undercover police officer.

"Even then," Frankie says, "he came back and beat Johnny McClendon, but he was winning at the six round level against club fighters when he should have been fighting main events against champions and contenders."

In 1993 Elvis was shot in the stomach during a street mugging over drugs. Yero survived in spite of damaged lungs and liver but his boxing career ended with that shootout.

His only moments of achievement and pride had been in the ring, where he maintained a winning record in spite of his lifestyle. When his boxing dream disappeared, his last shred of will power went also. The championship dreams were traded for a constant numbness induced by crack and alcohol.

Elvis Yero disappeared from the boxing scene in 1993.

He died on Saturday, October 13, 2001 -of a crack overdose- in room 212 of the Gold Dust Motel, a loud blue and white two-story structure on the edge of a harsh Miami ghetto, next door to a strip theater. Elvis Yero was thirty-six years old.

The story does not merit a headline. Crack junkies die every day, the lucky ones, anyway. There's Robert Ayala, an undefeated Hialeah welterweight of the late sixties who mixed the wrong pills with the wrong booze and spent over a decade and half as a vegetable, before dying.

Frankie Otero and I have talked about Yero often in the last days, saddened when we see life and talent wasted, promise abandoned.

"There's a poem that applies here," I said.

"So how does it go?" Frankie asked.

"Of all the sad words / of tongue or pen / the saddest are these / It might have been."

"Who wrote that?"

" I think it was John Greenleaf Whittier. Correct me if I'm wrong."

"Like I would know," Frankie answered with a smile, "but it does apply."

"Yeah," I said, "because in real life, the saddest thing is to stop dreaming and trying."

Tuto Zabala was a top international promoter guiding Vicente Rondon, Teo Cruz, Happy Lora and Wilfredo Vazquez, among others, to world titles.

CHAPTER TWENTY-EIGHT: A GREAT PROMOTER

For four decades he was a promoter and manager of fighters. He handled world champions, contenders and four round pugs, traveled the world and knew the fight game as few others ever did.

The story begins in 1960, at a time when Felix Zabala, known to his friends by the nickname "Tuto," was a young bank executive in Havana. The former university basketball player had an easy manner and warm smile that hid his dangerous double life.

Havana in 1960 was a dangerous place to live. Fidel Castro's new dictatorship had tightened the screws of repression, the firing squads executing over a thousand resistance fighters in little over a year since the revolution had gained power. In the cities, resistance fighters bombed electrical plants and oil refineries, torched government warehouses and gunned down informants and Castro's police officers. In the countryside, anti-Castro guerrillas fought militia forces, burned down crops and blocked highways. The nation was involved in a civil war while the Bay of Pigs Invasion and the October Missile Crisis loomed in the near future.

Tuto Zabala, smiling bank clerk and former basketball star at the University of Havana, was a member of the anti-Castro resistance, processing paperwork by day and transporting weapons or hiding hunted resistance fighters by night. Suspected of links with the resistance cells, Tuto was detained and interrogated by the feared State Security agents.

Realizing that his days as a secret conspirator were ending, Tuto Zabala left Cuba before the State Security interrogators caught up with him once more. Without an exit visa or passport, he devised a clever escape plan, assisted by underground contacts. Dressed as a KLM Airline employee, clipboard in hand, Tuto walked down the runway, stood stiffly while passengers for a flight walked past him, then nonchalantly followed them, boarding the outbound plane to freedom.

Once in the United States, Zabala settled in Puerto Rico where he became a charter member of Alpha 66, an anti-Castro paramilitary organization that launched commando raids and infiltration teams into Cuba.

Residing in San Juan, the former bank executive turned revolutionary was flat broke, with a young wife and children recently arrived from Cuba that needed feeding, so Tuto became a boxing promoter, nailing posters to telephone poles, hawking tickets, matching fights and cutting deals.

It did not take Zabala long to out hustle the competition. The six-foot three rookie promoter learned the trade quickly, giving the fans what they desired, which happened to be middleweight Florentino Fernandez.

Florentino was a Cuban middleweight who compiled a career 50-16-1 record with 43 knockouts facing champions such as Jose Torres, Gene Fullmer, Emile Griffith and Dick Tiger. Fernandez had a left hook that crushed jawbones and Zabala matched him against other sluggers in ten round wars. Hiram Bithorn Stadium was packed when Fernandez knocked out Dulio Nuñez and future champ Jose Torres, while winning and losing with tough Argentine brawler Rocky Rivero.

Fernandez and Rivero fought four wars, two in New York and two in Puerto Rico. Each man won two and each stopped the other once. Both middleweights were sluggers with vicious left hooks, a no retreat strategy and a marked disdain for defense. They locked onto each other's body as targets and dropped their bombs without much concern for exploding flack coming their way. There was little footwork and zero jabbing. Hooks were lead weapons, followed by nasty uppercuts and looping, clubbing rights.

Rivero, billed as the South American middleweight champion, had a habit of holding up promoters for more money. Zabala had a signed contract for Rivero to fight Fernandez for five thousand dollars, which was a very fair purse in 1963, a thousand more than the standard fees for network television shows.

The day Rivero was due to arrive in San Juan, Zabala received a phone call from Buenos Aires. With less than a week to go for the highly publicized fight, the Argentine refused to fight unless the fee was doubled.

"Very well," Tuto answered, "You got me in a bad position. Come in tomorrow and I'll give you half at the airport."

Rivero thought he had hustled Zabala, but after the fight, when the Argentine asked for the second payment, Tuto shook his head.

"The receipt you signed at the airport for five thousand is an acknowledgement of full payment as stipulated in the original contract," Zabala answered, "I suggest you go back to Buenos Aires."

"Those fights between Floro and Rocky were some of my best promotions, big packed houses," he once told me, "and the profit all went to Alpha 66."

Tuto's first champion was Dominican Republic native Carlos Teo Cruz, a busy lightweight with a good chin and a light punch. The shrewd Zabala knew how to match Cruz and the fighter obliged, beating Frankie Taylor, Grady Ponder, Frankie Narvaez, Vicente Derado, Chico Veliz and a score of top guns of the time. Cruz was champion in 1968-1969, beating Carlos Ortiz and losing to Mando Ramos. Teo Cruz had a 42-13-2 record in a career that stretched from 1959-1970.

Tragically, Teo Cruz and his family died in an airplane accident in 1970. Zabala always referred to the accident with sadness.

"It was such a waste," he once said, "Carlos bought a farm with his ring earnings. He had bananas and different kinds of fruit trees, hogs, chickens and milking cows. He had a nice wife and two beautiful kids and they all died in that accident. It was one of the saddest days of my life, to see a young family vanish. Teo was a very nice man. He deserved better."

The next Zabala champion was Vicente Paul Rondon, a competent Venezuelan fighter who was WBA Light-heavyweight Champion from 1971-1972. Rondon, a fighter who enjoyed nightlife and alcohol, compiled a 40-15-2 record, making and spending a small fortune before heading back to a life of poverty in Caracas.

"Rondon was a good fighter," he remarked about the Venezuelan, "but he would not listen. As soon as he had a couple of dollars he'd go partying."

From the early sixties to the late seventies, Zabala promoted several hundred pro cards in San Juan, booked Puerto Rican fighters to fight in Europe and the United States, traveled the world, trained fighters, worked corners and was involved in a dozen world title fights. Besides Florentino Fernandez, Teo Cruz and Vicente Rondon, Tuto Zabala promoted Alfredo Escalera, Angel Espada, Jose Gonzalez, Pedro Miranda, Sammy Serrano and a legion of main event fighters and prelim club fighters.

By late seventies the seasoned promoter moved to Miami. He began by signing up a dozen Mariel boatlift refugees with amateur experience in Cuba. All of the prospects fizzled, quit or were relegated to prelim status within a couple of years, but Zabala became established in Florida during the elimination process.

I met Tuto in the early eighties. At first our relationship was limited to a few nods or pleasantries. After a few years as an amateur light heavyweight I stayed active in boxing writing for almost all of the trade magazines. My knowledge of the sport and the hours spent hanging out at Caron's or at the Fifth Street Gym led me to book a few fighters and manage others. I did occasional matchmaking and was involved in public relations work with three promoters, including the famous Chris Dundee. My hobby had turned into a full time job while I worked at a free lance writing career.

"How come you work with every promoter except me?" Zabala asked me, point blank when I attended one of his fight cards.

"Because you never asked me," I answered and he laughed in response.

I became Tuto's matchmaker and was involved in twelve world title fights and some eighty local shows over a six year period. Sometimes the money was good and sometimes there was no money, but it was never boring.

Once, as I sat on a stool in his kitchen, sipping the extremely powerful concoction we Cubans call coffee, I heard Tuto complain about his finances, bemoaning that the last cards had dented his reserves at the bank.

"In fact," he said, "I'm flat broke right now."

I did not know what to say. I was doing fine but I'm not a believer in lending money to friends because money between buddies leads to complications.

"So," Tuto went on, "what we need is a title fight to generate some money. Let's make a few phone calls."

He got his title fight and enough cash flowed in to bankroll a couple of more shows and build up future contenders.

In the eighties and nineties in Miami, Zabala promoted Wilfredo Vazquez, Miguel "Happy" Lora, Baby Rojas and dozens of other top fighters, most of them in the lower weight classes.

Competition in promotions was tough, so very tough that a competitor set up Zabala with a false arrest on drug charges.

Willie Martinez, a stereotype drug dealer with all the trappings of the trade (sleek limousine, gold chains, trophy babes and bodyguards) entered the boxing game and after a short lived partnership, locked horns with Zabala. Willie Martinez later admitted in court that he hired two corrupt Metro Dade Police officers to stop Tuto and arrest him for a planted bag of cocaine.

In TV interviews Zabala had accused Martinez of being a drug dealer and the gold bejeweled Willie did not take kindly to the adequate adjective. After several death threats and the fake drug bust, Zabala survived as Martinez traded his silk threads for prison denim.

Tuto did land in the joint, for a two-year stretch starting in 1989. The promoter who was often strapped for cash accepted a promotional partnership with a California jeweler named Robert Alcaino, who turned out to be a laundering link for the Medellin cartel. One promotion later, Zabala paid the price and learned his lesson. In 1991 he returned to boxing, his promotional company still active thanks to his son, who had continued to promote Caribbean heroes and local prospects.

Tuto was a real promoter, not to be confused with the network executives or the closed circuit super promotion types.

Zabala hustled tickets to taverns, barbershops and restaurants. He distributed posters and leaflets, attended local radio talk shows, delivered his own press releases and argued dollars with managers over the phone. In between promotions of his cards in Miami and Puerto Rico, Tuto booked fighters, shipping them off to Las Vegas or Europe.

Every club fight show was taped, with journalist Carlos Fournier and I doing the color commentary. Copies of the tapes were sold to local TV in Puerto Rico, Colombia or any other country at rates that ranged from a few hundred dollars to a few thousand.

During our tenure together we survived all the conceivable horrors that could occur in boxing promotions.

The Happy Lora-Wilfredo Vazquez weigh-in was a shambles in which all the under card disintegrated as some fighters did not attend the weigh in because they were sick or in jail while those that showed flunked physicals for high blood pressure or their fights were scratched when they came in overweight.

In the afternoon of the title bout the only fight holding up was the main event, I called every gym in South Florida leaving the message that any unattached fighter should show up at the arena door, ready to fight. Minutes before the doors opened Tuto showed up at the arena with a duffel bag containing an assortment of spare trunks, used boxing shoes and protective cups. We stood by the arena door as the crowd trickled in, convincing any prelim fighter that showed up to go a few rounds with another local boy.

The show was a success and the prelims were exciting. The tension of the moment did not compare to our trip to Barranquilla, Colombia to co-promote the Happy Lora-Albert Davila title bout. Lora was mobbed like a rock star and a naked woman, a fan with few inhibitions, was arrested as she knocked on the champion's door, begging to be allowed to show her gratitude towards "el campeon."

Everywhere we went, soldiers with automatic rifles protected us from possible kidnapers (an entrepreneurial fad in the country) or Marxist narco-guerrillas (a permanent national sore) and being pointed out as member of the Lora team guaranteed free refreshments at any local pub.

Zabala was an extremely clever promoter, a man who knew how to gain psychological edges. Tuto would not fix a fight but he knew how to carry out a war of nerves on the opponent of his own house fighter.

I worked a dozen title bouts with Zabala and a particular one will be memorable.

The champion was coming to Miami to defend his crown and travel arrangements made by Tuto were somehow jumbled up and after a couple of days of back and forth, the champ had to come on a flight with a layover of a couple of hours in Atlanta, arriving late at night.

His accommodations were on the first floor of the hotel, near a noisy nightclub in the lobby area and the champ and entourage were unable to get a good night's sleep. This was followed by an early morning press conference in which a beat up club fighter whispered to the champ that Zabala was short on money and might not be able to pay the full purse, which made the champ extremely upset -- you get the picture. Three days later, unable to concentrate on the fight, he was the ex champ and Zabala controlled another top gun.

Am I excusing this behavior? No. In a perfect world it would be different, but Zabala's actions were no different than those of thousands of corporate heads of American enterprise. He loved boxing but it was also his livelihood and he was better than most at the fight game.

Promoters are supposed to be cold and unfeeling, yet Zabala was always good for a touch. When he had money he picked up the tab and when he was broke he also picked up the tab. He was generous with money but ruthless when he believed someone was attempting to take a slice of his pie.

A stroke ended his career and the once big and loud promoter is now a sick man who sits in silence and has little speech or movement. It is sad to see him that way, for I much prefer to remember him hoisting Wilfredo Vazquez off the canvas, picking him up as though he were a child, or arguing with a member of the boxing commission at a weigh-in, trying to convince him that a last minute substitute was qualified to fight a six round bout.

That's the Tuto I remember.

CHAPTER TWENTY-NINE: THE BUILD UP

Jorge Luis Gonzalez looked like a real deal; he stood six foot seven inches and weighed –in shape- around 235 pounds. He looked fierce, with a Mongol type hairstyle and thick, muscular arms.

He came to Florida with an impressive resume. He had compiled a 220-13 amateur record, winning gold in two Pan American Games, gold in the Central American and Caribbean Games, several Cuban national titles and scoring amateur wins over Riddick Bowe, Tyrell Biggs and Lenox Lewis.

He had the goods, but no dice. He made headlines before turning pro by signing with Tuto Zabala and Luis De Cubas two separate contracts that became a lawsuit well discussed in the Florida media.

In his pro debut Gonzalez fought William Campudani, a cruiserweight moved up to heavyweight level with a record of two wins and four losses. Although it was obvious that the fight was an easy victory for Gonzalez, the public was turned off by the big Cuban's antics.

Gonzalez showboated, taunted and played with his inferior opponent and in doing so he portrayed himself as a bully to the fans. He demolished Campudani in three rounds but did not make fans in the process.

The thousands of Cuban American boxing fans in Florida liked their boxing idols to be cheerful in their bragging, gentlemen in their demeanor and elegantly dressed. The smiles of Luis Manuel and Sugar Ramos, the sartorial elegance of Chocolate and Legra, the gentlemanly aura of Kid Tunero did not compare with the loud, vulgar Gonzalez, who looked like a nasty villain in a B movie.

Minito Navarro, a Miami sportswriter with a lifetime experience in boxing was extremely critical of Gonzalez, resulting in a loud confrontation between both men at a press conference in Miami.

"You will be a great champion," the old sportswriter said to Gonzalez in the press conference, "when I become an astronaut."

More easy fights followed for Gonzalez. Panamanian heavyweight Adolfo Morel –who was vanquished in two rounds- had only won one out of four fights; Larry Fortner -a first round victim- had won two out of nine fights.

In communist Cuba, where government is the only employer with absolute power to reward or punish, Gonzalez had to adhere to discipline to remain in the national boxing team or face spending the rest of his life cutting sugar cane under a burning sun to be taught a political lesson.

"I once missed a week of training because of serious family problems," middleweight Mario Iribarren said, "And they disciplined me for six months. I was not allowed to compete or travel with the team for a half year."

In the United States, discipline disappeared. Gonzalez' management provided a car, a roof over his head, a refrigerator full of food and weekly spending money and the fights were very easy, so the big prospect –who liked being spoiled- began sampling various brands of beer, missing gym sessions, arguing and changing trainers while continuing to alienate fans with his antics.

Carefully matched, the undisciplined heavyweight racked up 23 wins, all but one by knockout. A club fighter named David Greaves survived an eight round fight, losing to Gonzalez on points.

Highlights of this winning streak included knockouts of worn contender Renaldo Snipes, of also former contender Phil Brown –who had six losses in a row- and over one time prospect Olian Alexander. They were good wins but made better by marketing, while Gonzalez moved up the ratings more based on politics than on the quality of his opponents.

In 1995 Gonzalez was signed up to fight Riddick Bowe for the WBO version of the heavyweight title. By then, Gonzalez was living at the MGM Grand Hotel in Las Vegas, where the title fight was scheduled to take place.

Bowe was a hot and cold fighter, who could either destroy swiftly or coast through rounds contentedly. For the Gonzalez bout the usually placid Bowe was truly enraged. Besides the typical Gonzalez insults in which the Cuban heavyweight promised to eat Bowe's heart, the level of bad taste reached a new height when Gonzalez told Bowe's pregnant wife: "I am going to kill your husband before your baby is born."

The usually easy going Bowe climbed in the ring with a burning desire to pound his former amateur foe into hamburger and did so in a methodic, destructive fashion. Round after round, Bowe connected with straight right hand, hooks and uppercuts, dropping Gonzalez for the full count in the sixth round with a long right hand blow.

After the Bowe fight, Gonzalez was finished as a serious contender. He fought fifteen more times, winning eight and losing seven. Although he did post wins over Alex Stewart and Greg Page, six of his seven losses in this time period were knockouts or TKO.

It was said that Gonzalez became a security guard at the MGM Grand after leaving the ring, but Joel Casamayor told a different story.

"I heard he got religion," Casamayor told me as we ate lunch at a recent press conference, "I heard he walks around with a Bible under his hand, but if he is like that, he's not in Vegas anymore, because I know every inch of that strip and I know the boxing people there very well and I haven't seen Gonzalez in years and I don't know anyone who has."

Hurtado was a likeable, competent champion who almost beat Whitaker.

CHAPTER THIRTY: THE TALENTED HURTADO

Diosbelis Hurtado, a twenty two year old amateur star defected from the Cuban national boxing team as it toured the United States in 1994.

The well mannered Hurtado had an impressive 221-20 amateur record that included victories of Olympian gold medalist Joel Casamayor and winning two Cuban national titles and a world amateur championship.

Hurtado came from a village near Santiago de Cuba, from a poor family with eleven brothers and sisters living in poverty, in a shack without running water or electricity, where his boxing talent had been his key to escaping from a lifetime of picking produce or cutting cane.

As a national champion he had lived in Havana, graduated as a physical education teacher and travelled the world, seeing free societies unlike the one in which he had grown. His leap to exile, escaping from his hotel room, evading the vigilance of the sports security detail, was a calculated risk that would cost him dearly, for although gaining his individual freedom, the Cuban government would not allow him to return to the island to see his relatives.

He would not step back on Cuban soil for thirteen years, during which time his grandparents, three brothers and his father died, Diosbelis being refused entrance to the country to attend their funerals.

Alone in exile, Hurtado had a promising beginning. He won his first twenty pro fights -13 by KO- including an impressive stoppage in the first round of Puerto Rican Antonio Rivera.

In his twenty-first bout he faced the talented Pernell Whitaker for the WBC welterweight title. Critics implied that Hurtado was not a welter but a light welter and his twenty victories – with the exception of Rivera- had been over second and third rate club fighters. In both instances critics were right but Hurtado entered the ring hungry for victory and looking for a good payday.

To the surprise of the critics, the Cuban dropped Whitaker in the first round. The champion stood up but had problems solving Hurtado's style, for the Cuban was attacking in spurts and not allowing the champion to set his own rhythm. In the sixth, another well delivered blow dropped Whitaker to the canvas for a second time but the champion rallied in the next three rounds. As the eleventh round started, Hurtado was ahead in all three scorecards and the title belt seemed close for the young exile.

In desperation, Whitaker launched an attack. A tired Hurtado went against the ropes, where he was stopped by TKO, after receiving nine consecutive blows from Whitaker.

The loss enhanced Hurtado's reputation. The Oriental Kid —as he was called because his village is in Cuba's Oriente Province- sent money to the island to build his mother a modest house and continued fighting. He won eight more, including notable knockouts over Jaime Balboa, Leonardo Mas and Darryl Tyson, all fighters with good credentials, before becoming a substitute in a light welter world title fight against Kostya Tszyu, the feared Mongol destined to become a Hall of Famer.

The first round was explosive and surprising. Before a minute had passed, Hurtado was dropped to the canvas by a Tszyu hook. Standing up, Hurtado then scored a flash knockdown over the Mongol with a right hand. An unfazed Tszyu stood up and attacked but was again dropped by a Hurtado right hand.

Tszyu, an excellent boxer with solid power, imposed his will and strength stopping Hurtado by a five round TKO.

Although highly regarded, most of Hurtado's fame derived from his defeats, having decked and almost beaten Whitaker and Tszyu, two of the biggest names in boxing. At the time, Hurtado was part of Team Freedom, a group of Cuban fighters based out of Florida, managed by Cuban exiles Luis de Cubas and former Hialeah mayor Julio Martinez.

After losing to Tszyu, Hurtado fought seven more times in search of a title shot. One bout was a technical draw with Ricardo Mayorga due to an accidental head clash, while the other six were victories, three of them significant wins over Lonnie Smith, Cosme Rivera and Ricky Quiles.

In May of 2002, in San Juan, Puerto Rico, Hurtado received an opportunity to fight Randall Bailey for the vacant WBA Junior Welterweight Championship. Bailey —a former WBO Champion- had a 25-1 record and all his victories had been by knockouts.

The hard hitting Bailey floored Hurtado but the Cuban rallied, winning the title with a volley of punches, stopping Randall in the seventh round. After a long road, Diosbelys Hurtado had finally become a world champion.

His royal tenure was short lived, for five months after winning the crown, in his first title defense, Hurtado was stopped in two rounds by a hungry challenger from Guayana named Vivian Harris.

The loss depressed him. Hurtado fought three more times and apparently retired from boxing, leaving Miami to settle in the Canary Islands, a beautiful Spanish territory off the coast of Africa, where he was reported to have bought a townhouse and opened up a gym geared to upscale businessmen.

In 2007, Hurtado received news from Cuba that his mother had died. Fidel Castro's government had not allowed him to return to his own country to visit, but this time, because of requests of the Spanish government and the International Red Cross, Hurtado was allowed a brief visit, although his mother's funeral had to be delayed eleven days while requests and approvals were shuffled back and forth.

At the end of 2007 Diosbelys returned to the ring but up to the summer of 2011 he only fought five times, winning them all bringing his ledger to 43-3-1 with 26 KO wins and all three losses by the same route.

By the summer of 2011 it was announced that the 39 year old Hurtado would –before year's end- fight for the little known WBF junior middleweight championship but by the following year nothing had occurred and most believed that the former champion had retired to his home and to his health gym in the beautiful Canary Islands.

CHAPTER THIRTY-ONE: THE BLACK PANTHER

Juan Carlos Gomez has been underrated as a fighter. As an amateur, the "Black Panther" had a 158-12 record which included a win over Antonio Tarver and a loss to Sven Otke. Gomez won several Cuban national championships and the 1990 World Junior Amateur Championship

As a pro, the southpaw from Havana claimed a 55-4 pro record with 40 KO wins and one No Contest. As WBC Cruiserweight champion, Gomez defended his crown successfully ten times between 1998-2002, abdicating to move up to the heavyweight division, where he challenged but did not win the title.

His exile began in 1995, when Gomez found asylum in Germany while on a boxing tour with the Cuban amateur team. Three years and 22 fights later, he challenged and won in his bid for the cruiserweight title –WBC version- against Marcelo Dominguez in Argentina, whom he defeated via a 12 round decision.

Ten title defenses followed, as Gomez imposed himself on Imayu Mayfield, Napoleon Tagoe and others, including a chunky Argentine veteran named Jorge "The Locomotive" Castro, who had lost only six of 124 pro fights.

Looking for the big money, Gomez moved up to heavyweight, where he scored wins over Alfred Cole and Samil Sam, but also lost for the first time, after having scored 37 wins in a row and having stayed undefeated for nine years.

In what was expected to be a tune up fight, fellow Cuban Yankee Diaz –a club fighter with a 10-1 record- scored a surprising TKO over Gomez in the opening round.

Gomez, who had been confronting the German government overdue taxes, returned to the ring, scoring two knockouts before facing Oliver McCall. The Cuban won on points, outscoring the former heavyweight king, but the result was changed to a No Contest based on Gomez urine test after the bout, which proved positive for cocaine.

It was the low point in Gomez' career; he claims to have never used cocaine or any other drugs and hinted that the alleged drug test was a conspiracy against him, also claiming that he had converted to Islam, a religion that provided him with a purpose and inner peace.

"I don't know Gomez," the clever and witty former NABF champ Frankie Otero said, "but I find it hard to believe that any Cuban would give up eating roast pork."

Five more wins followed, including a win in a rematch with McCall, setting the stage for a heavyweight title bid against Vitali Klitschko.

Gomez –a bulked up cruiser- was no match for the six foot seven Ukranian. From the first round, Vitali Klitschko dominated the Cuban, methodically chopping him down with a stiff jab and right hands, stopping Gomez in nine stanzas.

After his second defeat, Gomez stayed busy winning over journeymen fighters, waiting for another chance to challenge for the heavyweight crown. After five wins he lost to Darnell Wilson on points, stopping the Maryland heavyweight in a rematch. He won six out of his next seven before retiring at the age of 41, as a German resident.

Casamayor fought top talent and was a worthy world champion.

CHAPTER THIRTY-TWO: TEAM FREEDOM

Team Freedom was an entity created in South Florida to project Cuban refugee fighters onto the international stage. The promotional group included as key figures Julio Martinez –a former mayor of Hialeah with boxing promotional experience- Luis DeCubas, a young Cuban American boxing manager, Rene Gil, and a well known local businessman and attorney Leon Margules.

The number of fighters in Team Freedom varied as some retired early and others came and went seeking better contracts, but at any given time Team Freedom had near a dozen pros ready to fight.

Its first champion was Diosbelys Hurtado and Joel Casamayor became its brightest star.

Other Team Freedom members included:

Elieser Castillo (32-8-2 with 18 KO) left Cuba on a raft at the age of 24, after a good amateur career where he obtained a bronze medal in the international Cordova-Cardin Cup, Cuba's premiere amateur tournament. As a pro he did not win a world title but did obtain several regional championships, including the NABF heavyweight title. Castillo had some solid wins in his career. He knocked out Andrew Purlette –who was undefeated in 32 fights- also stopped then up and coming Lawrence Clay Bey and defeated Paea Wolfgramm, a former Olympic silver medalist, on points. Castillo also drew with well regarded Russian Alexander Zolkin and lost to Chris Byrd and Fres Oquendo.

Eliseo Castillo (20-3-1 with 16 KO) Elieser's brother fought mostly as a cruiserweight. As a heavyweight he scored an upset by outpointing an out of shape Michael Moorer, which led to a fight with Vladimir Klitschko in which Eliseo was easily stopped in four rounds.

Ramon Garbey (19-4 with 13 KO) was a disappointment as a pro. He had been a magnificent amateur winning several world amateur tiles, knocking out the great Sven Ottke and beating Chris Byrd. Yet as a pro, his career fizzled as he lost to Fres Oquendo and James Tonney.

Ivan Ledon (12-12-1 with 11 KO) a super middleweight, never went beyond preliminary status.

Mario Iribarren (23-4-1 with 18 KO) was a middleweight southpaw who started out well but was unable to penetrate the first tier of the middleweight division.

Giorbis Barthelemy (25-9-2 with 10 KO) was a junior middleweight southpaw who lacked power but boxed well. In 2011 he was still active, beating Derek Ennis and losing to Charles Whittaker at the age of thirty eight.

Rene Valdez (10-3 with 5 KO) was a gutsy prelim fighter who did not make the grade at main event level.

Anselmo Felipe (13-1 with 10 KO) was a junior middleweight who started out very well but retired after his first loss.

Alex Barcelay (8-8-3 with 3 KO) was a lightweight club fighter who had little or no previous amateur experience when he joined Team Freedom.

Ramon Ledon (13-1-1 with 10 KO) had a short career as a super featherweight, losing by KO to Roberto Garcia in an IBF title bid.

Juan Carlos Suarez (16-5-2 with 6 KO) had a fair career as a journeyman super feather, losing to Daniel Attah and John John Molina.

Hicklet Lau (20-21-2 with 9 KO) was a gutsy junior middleweight who faced top guns and always gave a good performance even in defeat.

The super star of the team, however, was a flashy lightweight from Guantanamo named Joel Casamayor.

Casamayor was a southpaw who accomplished an amazing 363-30 amateur record, winning Olympic gold in Barcelona, a gold and bronze in world amateur championships, a silver medal in the Goodwill Games and a bronze in the World Cup Amateur Tournament, as well as a half dozen Cuban national titles.

Casamayor had been sent to the Barcelona Olympics as a last minute substitute by the Cuban government, not being expected to win gold. Upon his return to Cuba, the young fighter received a bitter surprise.

"The Olympic Committee gave all gold medal winners a check for twenty thousand dollars. I had never seen a check or a money order in my life. I did not know what it was. The Cuban government officials asked me to sign it and turn it over to them and I did…they gave me three hundred dollars back, as my share. They robbed me….then, in Cuba, they told me they had a surprise for me and I figured it was a Lada –a Soviet car- which some athletes and government officials had, but no, no car for me…they gave me a Chinese bicycle. That's when I decided I had to leave Cuba if I wanted a future."

Casamayor traded the bicycle for a pig to feed his family and began looking for an opportunity to defect on a boxing trip abroad. The opportunity presented itself on a trip to Mexico, where the Guantanamo fighter and his stable mate, Ramon Garbey, sneaked past the Cuban state security officers who travelled with the team to prevent defections.

"I love Cuba and I'm proud of being Cuban," he said after starting his pro career, "To me, I always represent Cuba and wear the flag on my trunks."

Turning pro, the Florida based Casamayor reeled off twenty wins in less than four years -12 of them by KO- before fighting undefeated Korean Jon Kwon Baek for the WBA version of the junior lightweight championship. The fighter from Guantanamo demolished the Korean in five rounds, being crowned champion.

Joel was nicknamed *Cepillo* (The Brush) and although several different explanations have been given regarding its meaning, there is only one. In Cuban jargon *dar cepillo* (brush him) can be interpreted as "kicking his ass," or even "killed him," so the nickname translates to the "ass kicker."

Casamayor defended his crown five times, losing a unanimous –and somewhat controversial- decision to Brazilian Acelino Freitas. Casamayor fans felt that a slip had been ruled a knockdown favoring Freitas and the third man in the ring had favored the Brazilian.

Casamayor bounced back from defeat by winning the IBA Junior Lightweight title and the WBC Lightweight title in a thrilling, classic three fight series with Diego "Chico" Corrales.

Casamayor won the first bout by TKO, his well aimed punches ripping an ugly lip cut on Corrales' face. Chico was knocked down but took a split points win in the rematch and Casamayor won the third bout on a close decision. There was no fourth meeting, for seven months after their third bout, Corrales riding his motorcycle fast on the Las Vegas strip, died as he collided with an automobile at a busy intersection.

"Corrales was a very good fighter," Casamayor said in an interview, "but I boxed better than he did and I also had more power. He was tall and had long arms and a lot of heart but he lived a crazy life and he paid the price very young."

By 2007, boxing scribes were speculating that Casamayor was past his peak but he showed he had plenty left when he stopped Michael Katsidis in ten rounds of a scheduled twelve, in a California ring. Casamayor was knocked down in the sixth while the tough Katsidis –a top contender- was decked three times by the Cuban southpaw.

Fighting infrequently, Casamayor dropped two –one by TKO and the second on points- to Juan Manuel Marquez and Robert Guerrero, while beating Jason Davis and Manuel Leyva. In his last bout of 2011, Casamayor was stopped by unbeaten Tim Bradley, bringing his record to 38-6-1 with 22 KO wins and two KO defeats.

"He's a fighter worth admiring," promoter Ramiro Ortiz said, "He fought his best, had talent and did not hide from anyone."

Yan Barthelemy, Odlanier Solis and Yuriorkis Gamboa made the leap to freedom

Yuriorkis Gamboa, an all action performer.

CHAPTER THIRTY-THREE: A GREAT ESCAPE

In the first decade of the Twenty First Century, the Cuban boxing exodus to exile grew enormously. Some left the island in rafts made of tire inner tubes, others sneaked away from the team on tour of a foreign country, while a few were smuggled out of the country in covert style, well funded operations.

In 2006, three Olympic gold medalists –Yuriorkis Gamboa, Odlanier Solis and Yan Barthelemy- left the Cuban team while on a tour of Venezuela, crossed quickly into Colombia, then ended up in Germany, all within a matter of days. Their arrival in Germany coincided with an announcement that the three men would fight professionally under contract for Arena Box Promotions, a German promotional entity.

It was speculated that the whole escape plan had been prepared and financed by the promoters, something rather obvious because of the efficiency and speed of the operation.

It was big news in the sports and political world. Three of the brightest stars of Cuban boxing had fled the system together. The Castro government accused the men of being greedy and selling out but they were in search of an individual freedom not available in a totalitarian society. Furthermore, they felt used and manipulated by a government that praised publicly but ignored them privately. Gamboa –nicknamed the Guantanamo Cyclone-claimed to have sold his Olympic gold medal to a collector, in order to feed his family.

Gamboa told journalist Anson Wainwright in an interview that: "We had won Olympic gold for our country but I didn't even have enough money to buy a birthday present for my daughter. I asked myself: Why should I stay in a country where the ruling class doesn't care about me even though I represent my country in the best possible way? It just didn't seem to make any sense."

In spite of being a national hero in his homeland, Gamboa had not been happy for he lived in a repressive society. In Fidel Castro's Cuba, opponents of the system have been jailed for such crimes as using the Internet, owning a fax machine, buying food on the black market or simply being considered a danger to the socialist system.

Gamboa grew up understanding the rules of the Marxist game. He kept his mouth shut and kept on winning fights but silently questioned the rules of the game. When he was forced to sell his Olympic medal to a collector in order to pay for a birthday party for his little girl, the Guantanamo featherweight began considering escaping Fidel's fiefdom, following the footsteps of another local Olympian named Joel Casamayor.

It was a tough choice. The unforgiving government would brand him a greedy capitalist puppet and he would be separated –perhaps for years- from his family and friends, but the idea grew in his mind until it became an obsession.

"You wait for the opportunity to escape," Gamboa.said, "and if you are lucky you get one chance and you take it and do it; there are no second chances."

The three men had superb amateur records. All three were Olympic Champions; all had been multiple times Cuban national champions and had picked up numerous medals in international tournaments.

All three turned pro on April 27, 2007 in Hamburg, Germany, winning their bouts. A fourth Cuban –heavyweight Pedro Carrion- headlined the main event on the card, also winning. Carrion had been fighting in Germany for over a year and had a brief career in which he fought a draw with Franz Botha.

After a few bouts Gamboa and Barthelemy relocated to Miami, while Solis continued to reside in Germany, commuting to America.

Their highly publicized million dollar contracts placed great pressure from the promoters on the fighters for they were to be moved swiftly in search for the mega money purses.

Top Cuban trainer Roberto Quesada said that "Being an amateur star does not mean you are immediately ready for a world title. There's a big difference between amateurs and pros. They have to adapt to fighting more rounds, pacing themselves different…there's no bobbing and weaving in the amateurs and very little infighting. It takes time to adapt and develop a good amateur into a good pro."

Cuban American promoter Ramiro Ortiz agrees with Quesada: "The amateurs are about scoring points, the pros are about winning the fight in a manner that will bring the crowds to see the fighter. It's a different game in strategy, in rounds, in conditioning and although the amateurs give one a great foundation the pros are much harder, demanding a different mentality."

Bantamweight Yan Barthelemy –a clever boxing southpaw- became the first casualty. As an amateur the little southpaw had won an Olympic gold medal in 2004 that included a victory over Chinese amateur icon Zou Shimming. After winning his first six pro bouts, Barthelemy dropped a decision to a club fighter, which soon after led to the cancelation of his big money promotional contract. Under new management, Barthelemy continued fighting, winning on ESPN cable TV shows but also losing again, compiling a winning but not impressive 13-3 pro record with 4 KO wins

Gamboa's rise was meteoric. A good puncher with blinding speed, he was an aggressive slugger who could box well but was careless in his defense at times and had a suspect chin. Adailton De Jesus knocked him down but Gamboa roared back to stop the Brazilian in six. Marcos Ramirez dropped Gamboa in the first and the Cuban came back to score a KO in the second.

Yuriorkis became the toast of the town in boxing circles. As his star rose and his earnings increased, the fighter purchased a home, a Rolls Royce, a Bentley and a considerable amount of gold jewelry. Gamboa was spending heavily but was also being paid very fat paychecks.

In 2009, Gamboa stopped Whyber Garcia to become featherweight champion –WBA version- defending it against Rogers Mtagwa and Jonathan Barrios before facing tough Orlando Salido for the vacant IBF title and the WBA Super World Featherweight title.

Gamboa beat Salido by a wide margin and defended against Jorge Solis – stopping him in four- before running against the body politics of the alphabet soup organizations which, in a confusing statement, stripped him of his belts in June 2011.

Undefeated in twenty one fights –with 16 KO wins- Gamboa was no longer a titleholder but was still a huge box office draw with the expectancy that his career would extend a profitable few more years, but by 2012 the Cuban fighter was involved in a career threatening dispute with Bob Arum's Top Rank and his German management team. Ill advised, Gamboa wanted to break his contract and become independent but his management threatened legal action in a conflict that could extend for years, bleed his earnings and put his career in deep freeze.

Eventually agreements were reached and the Cuban fighter ended up being managed by Fifty Cent, a well know recording artist with lots of money and little knowledge of the fight game. In 2012 and the first half of 2013 Gamboa fought only twice in two uninspired performances, failing to score knockouts and losing some of his recently acquired megastar status. By the closing of 2015, the Guantanamo fighter had a 25-1 record with 17 KO wins but had only fought five times in four years and was stopped by Terence Crawford in a lightweight title bid. Although still a name in the fight game his lack of activity and legal battles had withered his luster.

Odlanier Solis started his career well. As an amateur he had all the credentials for an outstanding pro career. He had a reported 347-12 amateur record that included an Olympic gold medal, Pan American Games gold, five world amateur championships and six Cuban national titles. Dubbed *La Sombra* (The Shadow) for his clever boxing ability, Solis beat Felix Savon two out of three and also defeated Sultan Ibragimov in the amateurs.

Solis was fed a steady diet of good journeymen with winning records, increasing the level of opposition gradually. He defeated seasoned Monte Barrett and Carl David Drummond before winning –by DQ- over a shop worn Ray Austin.

Set to face Vitali Klitschko for the WBC title, critics wondered if the Cuban heavyweight was up to the task. Although he had won all 17 of his pro bouts -12 by KO- Solis had failed to impress by his lack of condition. As a young amateur in Cuba his best weight had been between 220-225 pounds. As a pro he had apparently discovered American cheeseburgers and German pastries, for most of his fights had been fought in the 250-270 pound range.

The fight did not last long. Solis' knee gave way in the very first round and the Cuban was unable to continue, giving the Ukrainian champion the easiest victory of his career. For Solis it was a heartbreak moment that denied him his title opportunity as well as being out of the ring for months, while recuperating from an operation to repair his knee cartilage. He did not have to worry about paying the rent for he received 1.8 million dollars for the bizarre round with Vitali Klitschko.

Since losing in his title bid, Solis returned to the ring winning three fights in 2012 and the first half of 2013, looking to try for another title shot, but his opportunity vanished after being twice beaten by 43 year old veteran contender Tony Thompson, the first one on points and the second bout being an eighth round stoppage.

Guillermo Rigondeaux

Erislandy Lara

CHAPTER THIRTY-FOUR: LARA AND RIGONDEAUX

On July of 2007, two Cuban amateur boxers became international news.

Gullermo Rigondeaux and Erislandy Lara attempted to defect from the Cuban government while expecting to compete in the Pan American Games being held in Brazil. Unable to make the proper connection to leave Brazil for a third country, they were arrested at the city of Cabo Frio and sent back to Cuba.

At first, the Cuban government announced that both men had returned to the island willingly and pledged their loyalty to the revolutionary system, but both were taken off the national boxing team and banned from boxing competition even at a local level.

The news of their ban was criticized by human rights groups internationally.

Journalist Alan Mota wrote: "Castro and his regime seem to like the old dictatorial strategy of restraining the liberty of the ones they need the most. This infantile tactics does nothing more than spur revolt in the competitors, who have a glimpse of a more comfortable life every time they leave Cuba for an event, only to come back to their inferior practice conditions and salaries. Fidel might think the athletes are ungrateful, but the government seems to be the most ungrateful of all, treating their champions this way."

Fidel Castro's answer to all the critics of the harsh treatment against the boxers –depriving Rigondeaux of a possible third Olympic medal- was to publish an article from his own hand, in the front page of the national newspaper, calling the boxers "mercenaries" and "traitors" who had sold out to an "international mafia"

Castro's fury had reached boiling point. The flight to exile among athletes was staggering, in spite of strict security, purging those not politically in tune with the system and constant implied threats of suffering for those close to the fleeing athlete.

Dozens of well known baseball players had fled the island, to the point that the *Industriales* -Cuba's premier baseball team-, lost seven of its players, including their two starting pitchers. The volleyball team lost six players in

2001 and the team captain and two players skipped off to exile in 2010. Soccer players, swimmers, judokas and other athletes were leaving in rafts, paying off smugglers or using trips abroad to evade their traveling security to flee Castro's rule.

As a result of the desertions, Cuba, who had been a medal powerhouse in Olympic competition being ranked as high as fifth place in Barcelona 1992, dropped to 28th place at the 2008 Peking Olympics.

Castro chastised Lara and Rigondeaux, angry that every athlete that fled the island represented a political statement against his regime.

Both men were world class amateurs. Lara was the 2005 world amateur champion in the welterweight division while Guillermo Rigondeaux -who had a 374-12 amateur record - was a two time Olympic gold medalist and three time world champion with a winning streak of over 140 fights, being considered at the time the best amateur pound for pound in the planet.

"Castro accused us of betraying Cuba," Lara said in an interview years later, "We were banned from boxing and told we could never set foot in a boxing club again... I wasn't worth anything to them anymore. They cast us both aside... I knew then that there was no future for our family in Cuba. There was no future for me in my own country. I had to try escaping once more.."

Although it took time, almost a year for Lara and almost two for Rigondeaux, both men were able to leave Cuba clandestinely, in a smuggling operation where speedboats smuggled them to Mexico in search of political asylum.

Lara turned pro in 2008 and by January 2011 had racked up a record of fifteen wins –ten by KO- and no defeats, becoming a top prospect in the junior middleweight division. A draw with rated Carlos Molina was followed by a fight with Paul Williams.

Tall and hard hitting Williams –a former world champion- was the favorite to win the match, having lost but twice in thirty nine bouts. To everyone's surprise, Lara seemed to shut out Williams, even out boxing the taller man from long range. Yet, to the amazement of millions watching on HBO, the three judges –all inexperienced- voted a win for Williams.

It was described by many as one of the most outrageous robberies in the history of boxing, with such public protests that the New Jersey State Boxing Commission indefinitely suspended all three officials, something that had never before happened in the history of pugilism.

"It wasn't three blind mice out there; it was three corrupt rats," said Luis De Cubas Jr., Lara's manager, referring to the three suspended judges. "The margin was so wide in favor of Lara winning this fight, I can't see how else these judges missed this so badly."

Ironically, Lara gained with the defeat, emerging as a victim with outstanding talent, able to hold his own against the elite level of his division, being promised new opportunities in televised shows. He did bounce back impressively scoring a first round TKO of Ronald Hearns, which placed him among the top five contenders in the division.

Lara continued his quest. He fought a hard draw with undefeated Vannes Martyrosian, scored an impressive TKO win over tough contender Alfredo Angulo and outpointed former world champion Austin Trout.

In 2014, Erislandy Lara dropped a split decision to Mexican mega star Canelo Alvarez at the MGM Cassino in Las Vegas. Lara dominated the early rounds while Alvarez controlled the final stage of the fight. Lara felt he was robbed but it was a close fight with some hard to score rounds that could have been judged either way.

Lara bounced back from defeat by defeating Ishe Smith for the WBA Super Welterweight title and in 2015 defended his crown twice closing out the year with a 22-2-2 record with 13 KO wins.

Lara proclaimed that he was "The American Dream." Indeed, things seemed to be going well for him, happily married with a newborn baby, residing in a fine home he purchased in Houston, a world champion loved by boxing fans.

Meanwhile, Rigondeaux turned pro in 2009 as a super bantam, moving fast in his climb; in his third fight he stopped Giovanni Andrade, a very experienced fighter with a 59-11 pro record. In his seventh fight he fought for one of the so called "interim" titles of the WBA against a very tough boxer puncher from Panama named Ricardo Cordoba who had 23 KO wins in a 37-2-2 record.

Cordoba went down in the fourth and the Cuban southpaw hit the deck in the sixth. From the seventh to the end of the twelfth round, Rigondeaux avoided being within striking distance of Cordoba, winning but drawing strong criticism from fans and the boxing press which bemoaned his running tactics.

Four months later, Rigondeaux stopped Willie Casey in Dublin in the first round, bringing up his professional record to eight wins –six of them by KO- and no losses. Another victory followed as he stopped Rico Ramos for the WBA Super Bantamweight championship, making Rigondeaux the thirteenth Cuban world champion.

After defeating Teon Kennedy and Robert Marroquin, Rigondeaux established himself by defeating Nonito Donaire, using a very technical peck and move strategy that was effective but criticized for its lack of aggressiveness. In his next bout against Joseph Agbeko the television viewer ratings were among the worst in the history of HBO boxing broadcasts. Rigo beat Agbeko but complaints that he was boring increased and promoters did not rush forward to offer attractive purses.

Rigondeaux was stripped of his title because of inactivity but his management team complained that promoters did not want to offer decent paydays and deals were not being consummated.

Even the most hardcore Rigondeaux fans voiced their disappointment after he closed out the year by beating Drian Francisco, a slugger from the Phillipines. Francisco was made to order for Rigondeaux for the brawling fighter took the bout on short notice, was much slower than the Cuban and his aggressive style opened him up to be hit with well aimed counterpunches.

The match went the full ten rounds. Francisco moved forward and was able to land three or four punches per round while Rigondeaux jabbed, held or backed up, only landing 72 punches in the whole contest, about seven per round. It was a slow, boring fight in which most felt that had Rigondeaux opened up with four or five punch combinations he would have easily stopped the brave Phillipino. Winning effortlessly, Rigondeaux's flawless boxing performance was as dull as a lame sparring session.

Besides his lack of gate appeal bad luck seemed to follow Rigo. In early 2016 a fight in Liverpool was called off after the boxer and his entourage failed to obtain visas in time to enter the United Kingdom.

Rigondeaux was 16-0 with 10 KO wins by the spring of 2016. The talented performer –now 35 years old- was still very fast, well conditioned and extremely gifted but as one sports writer stated: " Watching Rigondeaux fight anyone is like watching a race between a Ferrari and a Volkswagen and the Ferrari is content to win by a car length and not by a mile."

CHAPTER THIRTY-FIVE: MANY NEW WARRIORS

As Lara and Rigondeaux were busy developing their careers, more than fifty other Cuban defectors were also busy trading leather in rings around the World. Although most had been prominent elite amateurs not all went well in the pro ranks where some achieved greatness and other careers fizzled.

Over seventy Cubans fought professionally in the time span of 2010-2015, most in the United States, followed by Germany, Ireland, Bolivia, Mexico and even one in Cambodia.

THE HEAVYWEIGHTS

In Ireland, a muscular heavyweight named Mike Perez -with a stellar amateur career that saw him win the 2004 World Junior title- rolled nineteen straight wins by the summer of 2013. Matched in Madison Square Garden against also undefeated Mago Abdusalamov, Perez won his New York debut in impressive fashion, outpointing the Russian fighter who refused to fall in spite of being rocked numerous times by the Cuban's hooks and uppercuts.

As a result of the beating, Abdusalamov sustained a blood clot on his brain, being placed into a medically induced coma to give the swelling in his brain time to subside. While in coma, Abdusalamov suffered a stroke, almost dying. Two years later his recuperation has been slow and the former contender is able to speak some sentences and has recuperated some mental capacity but will be forever disabled.

Having almost killed Abdusalamov destroyed Perez. The heavily muscled Cuban – now a family man with three daughters residing in Cork, Ireland- became despondent and he was psychologically the same, losing some of his aggressiveness and becoming more tentative in his attacks. In his next four bouts he won one, lost two and drew one. In his last bout of 2015 he was stopped in 91 seconds by Alexander Povetkin. Perez ended the year with a 21-2-1 record with 13 KO wins.

Another Cuban heavyweight also fizzled. Yasmany Consuegra (17-3 with 14 KO) nicknamed *Tiburon* (Shark) was built up to a streak of seventeen victories then went from prospect to journeyman opponent when he was stopped three times in a row.

As 2015 drew to a close the Cubans best bet for a possible titleholder was embodied in Luis *King Kong* Ortiz. A six foot four 235 pounder, Ortiz had won a Panamerican Games gold medal and silver in the World Cup as well as a Cuban national amateur title, scoring 343 wins against 19 defeats.

An imporessive win over rated Bryan Jennings by seventh round TKO placed Ortiz high in the rankings, in line for a possible title shot. As 2015 ended Ortiz had a 24-0-0 record with 21 KO). His record also includes two no contests. The first occurred when his opponent fell out of the ring and was unable to continue while the second one was a first round knockout of Lateef Kayode changed to no contest when Ortiz failed a substance test.

CRUISERS AND LIGHT HEAVYWEIGHTS

In Germany, Yoan Pablo Hernandez (29-1 with 14 KO), became the first Cuban to win a cruiserweight title when he beat Steve Cunningham by technical decision due to a cut suffered from an accidental head clash. Hernandez defended his IBF title three times in three years and either retired or stayed inactive in 2015.

As 2015 ended the best Cuban prospect among the cruisers was Yunier Dorticos (20-0 with 19 KO). A veteran of 257 amateur bouts, Dorticos scored his first 17 wins by KO, breaking a Cuban record of 16 straight that had been established in the 1950's by Florentino Fernandez.

Umberto Savigne (12-3 with 9 KO) had a distinguished amateur pedigree, winning the World Cup, Panam Games, Caribbean and Central American games and multiple Cuban national titles. At the age of thirty six the likeable Savigne was fighting against the clock and losing. He beat Jeff Lacy and a worn out Richard Hall but retired after being stopped twice in a row.

Yordanis Despaigne (9-2 with 4 KO) an Olympic veteran started well and lost a couple being forced to retire due to a damaged retina.

The two best light heavyweight prospects at the end of 2015 were Sullivan Barrera and Yunieski Gonzalez.

Sullivan Barrera (17-1 with 12 KO) entered the ratings with KO wins of Kato Murat and former champion Jeff Lacy. As an amateur, the tough Cuban held wins over Chad Dawson and Beibut Shumenov. As a pro his only loss to date was on points against Andre Ward.

Yunieski Gonzalez (16-2 with 12 KO) lost his last two fights of 2015 but remained highly regarded in the division. Gonzalez lost a close, controversial decision to highly rated Jean Pascal in Las Vegas, a fight many believed he deserved the victory. The defeat was followed by a point loss to undefeated Ucrainian Yacheslav Shabranskyy. In both losing efforts, Gonzalez proved that he could be a viable contender in the future.

MIDDLEWEIGHTS AND WELTERWEIGHTS

Judel Johnson (17-3 with 9 KO) had an impressive amateur record. He won Olympic silver in 2004 and gold in the Panam Games, World Cup, Goodwill Games and Central American and Caribbean Games yet as a pro he never reached his full potential, losing his last two bouts in 2015.

A veteran of over 300 amateur fights, Inocente Fizz (19-0 with 13 KO) remains undefeated but has faced very soft opposition.

The best Cuban middleweight of this era was not born in Cuba. Peter Quillin was born in Michigan, the son of a Mariel boatlift Cuban refugee. After a brief amateur career he turned pro, calling himself Kid Chocolate in homage to the first Cuban world champion. A well spoken man, Quillin (32-1-1 with 23 KO) held the WBO middleweight title but ended 2015 by losing in a stunning one round knockout to the talented Danny Jacobs.

THE LOWER WEIGHTS: CHAMPIONS AND JOURNEYMEN

After early triumphs, some of the hot prospects ran into difficulties.

Junior welter Yordenis Ugas (15-3 with 7 KO) a former amateur world champion and Olympic bronze medallist in 2008, went into retirement after losing two in a row.

Featherweight Yoandry Salinas (21-2-2 with 14 KO) was an outstanding amateur who fought almost 300 bouts, winning gold in the 2007 Panam Games but fizzling at the main event level of the pros, only winning one of his last four bouts.

Featherweight Hairon Socarras (14-0-2 with 10 KO) was a product of the Florida Golden Gloves, becoming a very popular local star. His still undefeated career has been plagued with promotional problems for his management team includes close family members that have become difficult with various promotional entities. As a result, Socarras last fight of 2015 took place in Cancun, Mexico where he ended up with a hometown draw against a very mediocre club fighter named Marco Antonio Chable (6-13-3 with 4 KO).

Luis Franco (13-1-1 with 9 KO) a 2004 Olympian started out well managed by Cuban American promoter Richard Dobal. Franco stunned his management team by turning down a title fight claiming the purse money was not adequate. Instead, for less money, he fought in Argentina losing on points.

"To win a fight you have to throw punches," sportswriter Melchor Rodriguez stated, "and many of these fighters are used to the amateur mentality of scoring points and keeping a safe distance and that does not always work. In pro boxing you can't give away rounds, you can't take for granted that you are ahead on points and you must try to inflict damage convincingly so there's no doubt who wins…. Also, some of these fighters signed with people who had money and good intentions but did not know matchmaking or had the contacts to move them properly and the fighters themselves who had nothing in Cuba and were disciplined by the government have trouble adapting to the freedom and consumer goods of American society and some tend to slack off in training or act as prima donnas…"

"Some fighters insist on keeping the same trainers they had in Cuba, many of whom have also come over and that is a mistake. A good amateur trainer does not necessarily know what he is doing in the pros. The pros have more rounds, a fighter needs different conditioning, more aggressiveness, has to pace himself different, not only physically but also mentally…. Some of these amateur trainers talk like they are nuclear scientists spouting formulas about mass, weight and their relationships and they claim to have all sorts of college degrees but the fact is they are still amateur trainers and need to learn how to work with the pros."

Promoter Ramiro Ortiz agrees with Rodriguez when he states: "The difference between amateurs and pros is huge. You take a trainer like Orlando Cuellar who has worked with the pros like Glenn Johnson and you see the difference. Cuellar teaches a fighter to set up punches that hurt and do damage and some of the newcomers, although fine trainers for amateurs don't understand this and are content with trying to score points….and there are a lot of little details from the pros that the trainers do not know. I walked into a gym and saw two guys –both with scheduled fights- going at it without headgear which was ridiculous. An accidental cut can cause a cancellation. Another fighter complained his hand hurt and he could not hit the bag. I told him when he wrapped his hands to use a kitchen sponge for padding and he did not know what I was talking about but that's a trick that any pro trainer knows."

"The best Cuban trainers in the pros," Melchor Rodriguez stated, "are the ones that have been around a long time in the game in the USA. Orlando Cuellar started out as a kid in New York working corners and knows a lot about strategy, conditioning and corner work. Jorge Rubio had a great career as an amateur coach and has learned to work with pros over a period of several years. Roberto Quesada who started as a trainer in Cuba, has also patiently adapted to the pros and is today a first trainer who handles all of Tuto Zabala's fighters."

Promoter Bob Arum complained that Cuban exiles do not support the new arrivals, a statement that was widely commented on the Miami media.

"First of all," boxing writer Melchor Rodriguez stated, "Very few of these fighters have been built up locally. Since many of them were such great amateurs, promoters have been showcasing them all over the place without building a local following. Look at Gamboa, of his fights only three were in Florida. Odlanier Solis has fought mostly in Germany or Turkey. Of Rances Barthelemy's first sixteen fights only three have been in South Florida… When matched locally, sometimes they are not matched competitively and the sad fact is that many of these stars are unknown among Cubans in Miami. Oh, we might know so and so to be a gold medalist and know his name but the only ones that ever saw him fight are the exiles that arrived from Cuba in the last few years and they are too busy getting started in their new life in the USA and can't afford tickets to the fights. Besides, since in Cuba amateur shows are free, those that know a Despaigne or a Glendy Hernandez are not used to paying money to see them perform."

In spite of all setbacks, some continued to shine.

The very tough Richar Abril (19-3-1 with 8 KO) surprised the boxing world when he beat undefeated Sharif Bogere for the WBA lightweight crown in 2013 but only defended the crown once, being inactive in 2015.

Yan Barthelemy, the Olympic champion who had reached exile with Gamboa and Solis, had two brothers that reached the United States in 2009, both turning pro. As of the spring of 2016 featherweight Leduan is undefeated in nine bouts with five wins by knockout and Rances Barthelemy is the current IBF Lightweight champion.

Rances had won as a teenager the Cuban national junior championship. Upon arrival in the United States he tuned up his skills winning the Florida Golden Gloves championship. Turning pro as a super featherweight, Barthelemy had the advantage of being almost six feet tall and with 200 fights amateur experience.

"I tried to escape from Cuba about thirty some times," he said in an interview, "and they kept catching me, throwing me in jail and lecturing me but eventually we made it to the United States."

In an interview with television sports reporter Amber Dixon in Las Vegas, Rances and Leduan admitted that when they arrived in the United States it was as though they were in another planet. They were so culturally naïve that when given two large bottles of mouthwash one brother figured it to be a soft drink while the other splashed it on his face as cologne.

Rances caught on quick. Well matched by Cuban American promoter Richard Dobal and by Seminole Warriors Boxing Promotions of Florida, Rances raked up a string of wins over increasingly tougher opposition. In his 24 bout career he has won two titles. He won the IBF Super Featherweight title, defending it once before moving up to the lightweight division.

A win over tough Antonio De Marco set up a fight for the vacant IBF lightweight title against Denis Shafikov, a tough Russian who had only lost once in 38 bouts. Barthelemy won the fight by a comfortable margin in his new hometown of Las Vegas where he is now happily married and accompanied by both his brothers.

In spite of the setbacks and difficulties, the future of Cuban professional boxing still burns bright.

The Barthelemy brothers: Yan, Leduan and Rances.

Cuban American promoter Richard Dobal promoted and guided the careers of Luis Franco and Rances Barthelemy.

STATISTICS AND DATA ON CUBAN BOXING

CUBAN WORLD CHAMPIONS:

1. Kid Chocolate (135-10-6 with 51 KO) –Featherweight and Junior Lightweight Champion.

2. Kid Gavilan (108-30-5 with 28 KO) -Welterweight champion.

3. Benny Kid Paret (35-12-3 with 10 KO) -Welterweight champion.

4. Ultiminio Sugar Ramos (55-7-4 with 40 KO) -Featherweight champion.

5. Luis Manuel Rodriguez (107-13 with one NC and 49 KO) - Welterweight champion.

6. Jose Legra (133-11-4 with 50 KO) –WBC Featherweight champion.

7. Jose Napoles (81-7 with 54 KO) –WBC and WBA Welterweight champion.

8. Diosbelis Hurtado (43-3-1 with 26 KO –Still active) IBA and WBA Junior Welterweight champion.

9. Joel Casamayor (38-6-1 with 22 KO) –WBA Junior Lightweight champion and WBC Lightweight champion.

10. Juan Carlos Gomez (50-4 with 37 KO-Still active) WBC Cruiserweight champion.

11. Yuriorkis Gamboa (25-1 with 17 KO –Still active) IBF and WBA Featherweight champion.

12. Yoan Pablo Hernandez (29-1-0 with 14 KO-Still active) IBF Cruiserweight champion.

13. Guillermo Rigondeaux (16-0 with 10 KO-Still active) WBC Super Bantamweight Champion).

14. Peter Quillin (32-1-1 with 23 KO –Still active) WBO Middleweight champion. Cuban American born in Michigan, whose father arrived in the US in the Mariel boalift of 1980.

15. Richar Abril (19-3-1 with 8 KO –Still active) WBA Lightweight Champion.

16. Erislandy Lara (22-2-2 with 13 KO-Still Active) WBC Light Middleweight title.

17. Rances Barthelemy (24-0 with 13 KO- Still Active) IBF Super Featherweight and IBF Lightweight Champion.

Not included in this list are the so called "interim" world championships, created by alphabet soup organizations. Over 100 Cuban boxers have been world ranked. Cubans who have fought unsuccessfully for world titles include Black Bill, Kid Tunero, Isaac Logart, Orlando Zulueta, Jose Stable and others.

WORLD TITLE FIGHTS IN CUBA:

April 5, 1915: Heavyweight title: Jess Willard beat Jack Johnson in the 26th round of a scheduled 45 rounder at Oriental Park Racetrack in Havana.

April 10, 1932: Junior Lightweight title: Kid Chocolate defended his crown with a 15 round points win over Davey Abad in Havana.

February 28, 1951: Junior Lightweight title: Sandy Saddler stopped Diego Sosa in two rounds.

October 5, 1952: Welterweight title: Kid Gavilan won a 15 rounder from challenger Billy Graham at Stadium Ball Park in Havana.

CUBAN IN MOST WORLD CHAMPIONSHIP FIGHTS: Welterweight Jose *Mantequilla* Napoles participated in 18 world title bouts.

CUBAN FIGHTERS WITH OVER 100 PRO BOUTS

1. Angel Robinson Garcia........................238
2. Chino Alvarez 187
3. Black Bill. 168
4. Kid Chocolate......................................152
5. Jose Legra..148
6. Kid Tunero...146
7. Kid Gavilan..143
8. Diego Sosa...140
9. Relampago Saguero............................131
10. Orlando Zulueta..................................128
11. Pete Nebo. 126
12. Baby Manuel. 122
13. Luis Manuel Rodriguez........................121
14. Enrique Ponce de Leon........................115
15. Mario Chico Morales...........................113
16. Isaac Logart..111
17. Manuel Armenteros............................. 111
18. Cabey Lewis..106
19. Ciro Morasen......................................102
20. Billy Lima...101
21. Peter Sung..101
22. Alberto Leon.......................................101
23. Rene Cantero......................................100
24. Chico Varona...................................... 100

Nebo, billed in the US as part Seminole Indian was really Cuban born Key West resident Pedro Nebot. Cabey Lewis, never mentioned as a Cuban fighter has been listed as being born in Cuba. Other Cuban fighters with over 100 fights whose documented records are still incomplete under the century mark include: Sixto Morales, Lalo Dominguez, Louis Smith, Eliseo Quintana, Serafin Centeno, Kid Chivo, Battleship Martinez, Kid Ernestico, Ramon Castillo and Antonio Dominguez.

GREATEST CUBAN GLOBETROTTER: Angel Robinson Garcia was not only the greatest boxing traveler in Cuban pugilism, but was the second greatest traveler in all of boxing, only surpassed by Eddie Perkins. Garcia plied his trade in 18 countries.

MOST KNOCKDOWNS IN ONE FIGHT: Lalo Dominguez has the record for scoring 26 knockdowns over Jack Coullimber in a 1919 Havana fight.

MOST CONSECUTIVE KNOCKOUTS: Florentino Fernandez scored 16 straight knockouts in Havana rings between 1957 and 1959. Yunier Dorticos beat the long record by scoring 17 knockouts in the United States between 2009 and 2014.

LONGEST WINNING STREAK BY A CUBAN FIGHTER: Kid Chocolate had a streak of 55 wins and a draw before losing a decision to Jackie Kid Berg in 1930.

FIRST RING FATALITY: Joe Marroquin, a sailor in the Cuban military died in a 1919 bout in which he was knocked out in two rounds by welterweight Alex Publes.

FIRST CUBAN TO WIN A US CHAMPIONSHIP: Frankie Otero –The Cuban Bomber- won the NABF Junior Lightweight title by outpointing Kenny Weldon in Miami Beach in 1971. Otero defended his title twice.

FIRST CUBAN WOMAN BOXER: Lola Munoz was the first Cuban boxer –in the 1920's- having fought exhibitions with Cuban lightweight king Lalo Dominguez and with a topnotch Spanish fighter named Juan Carlos Casala. Female boxing in Cuba was almost nonexistent. In the fifties, a well known professional female wrestler named Silvia Torres –who was for a while married to boxer Lino Garcia- fought a few bouts in Cuba and Aruba and in her old age ran a gym where she trained and cornered pro boxers in Miami during the eighties and nineties.

FIRST CUBAN AMATEUR TO WIN AN OLYMPIC MEDAL: In Mexico in 1968, light middleweight Rolando Garbey won the silver medal in a losing performance against gold medalist Boris Lagutin. The first gold medal was won by Orlando Martinez in 1972. Cuba's boxers have produced 34 Olympic champions and scored over sixty Olympic medals from 1968-2011.

FIRST CUBANS TO FIGHT WORLD CHAMPIONS: On September 15, 1898, Cuban Eugene Garcia lost to future featherweight king Terry McGovern. On January 20, 1902, in a Chicago ring, Cuban lightweight Emilio Sanchez scored a six rounds point win over future title claimant champion Cyclone Thompson, thus becoming the first Cuban to defeat a world champion. There is also a claimed –but not verified- fight sometime around 1878, of an amateur draw between Cuban-American Ramon Guiteras and John L. Sullivan.

FIRST WORLD CHAMPION TO FIGHT ON CUBAN SOIL: On March 10, 1915, Ted Kid Lewis beat Frank Mack in a twenty rounder in Havana. Lewis was a future world champion. The first former world champion to fight in Cuba was Battling Nelson who a week after the Lewis-Mack fight headlined the first of three cards, which he won. The first current champion to fight in Cuba was Jack Johnson defending against Jess Willard in April, 1915.

Table of Contents

INTRODUCTION 9

PROLOGUE 11

CHAPTER ONE: IN THE BEGINNING 13

CHAPTER TWO: THE CHARMING JOHN BUDINICH 21

CHAPTER THREE: TITLE FIGHT IN HAVANA 37

CHAPTER FOUR: THE FIRST NATIONAL HEROES 45

CHAPTER FIVE: THE LEGENDARY BLACK BILL 50

CHAPTER SIX: THE CHOCOLATE KID 57

CHAPTER SEVEN: THE LEGEND OF THE CUBAN BARON 67

CHAPTER EIGHT: THE TWENTIES AND THIRTIES 76

THE MIDDLEWEIGHTS 77

THE WELTERWEIGHTS 78

THE LIGHTWEIGHTS 79

THE SMALLER GUNS 81

FIGHTERS FROM OTHER LANDS 82

CHAPTER NINE: THE LIFE AND TIMES OF AN OLD WARRIOR 85

CHAPTER TEN: GAVILAN, THE SPARROW HAWK 97

CHAPTER ELEVEN: THE 1940-1950 DECADES 105

THE MIDDLEWEIGHTS AND WELTERWEIGHTS 105

LIGHTWEIGHTS AND FEATHERWEIGHTS 107

THE FLYWEIGHTS 109

FIGHTERS FROM OTHER LANDS 110

CHAPTER TWELVE: THE GREAT HEAVYWEIGHT 112

CHAPTER THIRTEEN; THE END OF AN ERA 118

CHAPTER FOURTEEN: ANGEL ROBINSON 128

CHAPTER FIFTEEN: DEATH IN THE RING 136

CHAPTER SIXTEEN: PUPI WAS SPECIAL 140

CHAPTER SEVENTEEN: LUIS SARRIA 147

CHAPTER EIGHTEEN: A CHAMPION'S FUNERAL 155

CHAPTER NINETEEN: BANTAM JOHNNY SARDUY 161

CHAPTER TWENTY: SUGAR RAMOS 165

CHAPTER TWENTY-ONE: THE POCKET ALI 169

CHAPTER TWENTY-TWO: SMOOTH AS BUTTER 174

CHAPTER TWENTY-THREE: THE OX 182

CHAPTER TWENTY-FOUR: JOSE STABLE 191

CHAPTER TWENTY-FIVE: THE CUBAN BOMBER 195

CHAPTER TWENTY-SIX: THE BOATLIFT FIGHTERS 201

THE PROMOTERS 204

CHAPTER TWENTY-SEVEN: ELVIS YERO 206

CHAPTER TWENTY-EIGHT: A GREAT PROMOTER 212

CHAPTER TWENTY-NINE: THE BUILD UP 219

CHAPTER THIRTY: THE TALENTED HURTADO 223

CHAPTER THIRTY-ONE: THE BLACK PANTHER 226

CHAPTER THIRTY-TWO: TEAM FREEDOM 229

CHAPTER THIRTY-THREE: A GREAT ESCAPE 234

CHAPTER THIRTY-FOUR: LARA AND RIGONDEAUX 239

CHAPTER THIRTY-FIVE: MANY NEW WARRIORS 244

   THE HEAVYWEIGHTS 244

   CRUISERS AND LIGHT HEAVYWEIGHTS 245

   MIDDLEWEIGHTS AND WELTERWEIGHTS 246

   THE LOWER WEIGHTS: CHAMPIONS AND JOURNEYMEN 247

STATISTICS AND DATA ON CUBAN BOXING 252

   CUBAN WORLD CHAMPIONS 252

   WORLD TITLE FIGHTS IN CUBA 253

   CUBAN IN MOST WORLD CHAMPIONSHIP FIGHTS 254

   CUBAN FIGHTERS WITH OVER 100 PRO BOUTS 254

   GREATEST CUBAN GLOBETROTTER 255

   MOST KNOCKDOWNS IN ONE FIGHT 255

   MOST CONSECUTIVE KNOCKOUTS 255

   LONGEST WINNING STREAK BY A CUBAN FIGHTER 255

   FIRST RING FATALITY 255

   FIRST CUBAN TO WIN A US CHAMPIONSHIP 255

   FIRST CUBAN WOMAN BOXER 255

   FIRST CUBAN AMATEUR TO WIN AN OLYMPIC MEDAL 255

   FIRST CUBANS TO FIGHT WORLD CHAMPIONS 256

   FIRST WORLD CHAMPION TO FIGHT ON CUBAN SOIL 256

www.ingramcontent.com/pod-product-compliance
Lightning Source LLC
Chambersburg PA
CBHW080333170426
43194CB00014B/2555